The Transgressive
Iain Banks

The Transgressive Iain Banks

Essays on a Writer Beyond Borders

Edited by MARTYN COLEBROOK *and* KATHARINE COX

McFarland & Company, Inc., Publishers
Jefferson, North Carolina, and London

ALSO OF INTEREST

Critical Perspectives on Philip Pullman's His Dark Materials*: Essays on the Novels, the Film and the Stage Productions,* edited by Steven Barfield and Katharine Cox (McFarland, 2011)

LIBRARY OF CONGRESS CATALOGUING-IN-PUBLICATION DATA

The transgressive Iain Banks : essays on a writer beyond borders ; edited by Martyn Colebrook and Katharine Cox.
    p.   cm.
    Includes bibliographical references and index.

ISBN 978-0-7864-4225-6
softcover : acid free paper ∞

1. Banks, Iain, 1954– — Criticism and interpretation. I. Colebrook, Martyn, editor of compilation. II. Cox, Katharine, 1976– — editor of compilation.
PR6052.A485Z89 2013
823'.914—dc23   2013005168

BRITISH LIBRARY CATALOGUING DATA ARE AVAILABLE

© 2013 Martyn Colebrook and Katharine Cox. All rights reserved

No part of this book may be reproduced or transmitted in any form or by any means, electronic or mechanical, including photocopying or recording, or by any information storage and retrieval system, without permission in writing from the publisher.

Front cover images: Planet earth armageddon; Neist Point, Scotland; sky (iStockphoto/Thinkstock)

Manufactured in the United States of America

McFarland & Company, Inc., Publishers
   Box 611, Jefferson, North Carolina 28640
      www.mcfarlandpub.com

Katharine would like to dedicate this book
to her Auntie Liz who, despite thinking
Canal Dreams was likely to be a "mucky" book,
bought her the remaining Iain Banks'
novels she was missing

Table of Contents

Introduction
    Martyn Colebrook, Katharine Cox *and* David Haddock   1

I. Scottish Context

The Lessons of *Lanark*: Iain Banks, Alasdair Gray and the Scottish Political Novel
    David Pattie   9

Lanark and *The Bridge*: Narrating Scotland as Post-Industrial Space
    Martyn Colebrook   28

II. Geographies

"I have never been to Nasqueron": A Geographer Reads Banks
    James Kneale   45

Landscape and the Imagination: Banks' Representation of Argyll in *The Crow Road*
    Tim Middleton   63

Imperfect Doubles: The Recasting of Place, Object and Character in the Dream Narratives of *The Bridge*
    Bethan Jones   76

III. Genre

Textual Crossings: Transgressive Devices in Banks' Fiction
    Katharine Cox   87

"Still magic in the world": Banks and the Psychosomatic Supernatural
    Kirsty A. Macdonald   100

Teaching Banks: *The Wasp Factory* and *Frankenstein*
 EMILY GARSIDE *and* KATHARINE COX   112

IV. Gender, Games and Play

Contesting Gender in *The Wasp Factory*, *Whit* and *The Business*
 SARAH FALCUS   123

Games Playing Roles in Banks' Fiction
 WILL SLOCOMBE   136

Digital Souls and Virtual Afterlives in the Culture Series
 JOSEPH NORMAN   150

"Hippies with mega nukes": The Culture, Terror and the War Machine in *Consider Phlebas* and *The Player of Games*
 WILLIAM STEPHENSON   165

Afterword
 KATHARINE COX   179

Bibliography   181

About the Contributors   190

Index   193

Introduction

MARTYN COLEBROOK,
KATHARINE COX *and* DAVID HADDOCK

This collection focuses on the varied fictions of Iain (M.) Banks and the different domains of the imagination which he traverses and upon which he trespasses. As this collection demonstrates, Banks' fiction represents a continued fascination with the transgression of borders and limits, whether technical, cultural, corporeal, national or otherwise. In exploring these borders, the collection applies contemporary and innovative theory to the analysis of his fiction with the result that these original essays offer new and insightful ways to consider his writing. The essays, all explicitly concerned with border crossing, are divided into four parts. These explore the Scottish context, in which connections with Alasdair Gray and Scottish politics are discussed in detail; the geographies of his writing, which explores space and place in his work; genre, which investigates the transgressive nature of his writing; and finally, gender, games and play, in which narrative and metafictional strategies within Banks' novels, particularly through analysis of the Culture, are examined.

Banks has established himself as one of the most inventive, experimental and prolific writers of his generation and yet, despite the innovation of his ideas and narratives, critical acclaim has been slow to respond. Over the course of his career, Banks' work has been traditionally marginalized for a variety of reasons: these include the prominence of his early fiction (especially his debut novel), which has tended to overshadow his later work; his decision to write and maintain himself as a science fiction writer, which has drawn an uncertain response from literary critics; his geographical and political focus on "niche" Scottish concerns or, ironically, that his writing is too removed from such concerns.[1]

Banks publishes two different styles of novel: mainstream, commercial fictions that sometimes focus on transformations of thriller genres and works of science or speculative fiction which are usually set in his critical utopia, the Culture. These two outputs are published under different names, Iain Banks and Iain (M.) Banks, respectively. The naming of the author is explored throughout the collection, as the borders between the personae are often bridged and the differentiation between the two is overcome by the overlapping references, themes and motifs he uses between his work. Banks, then, is a novelist who has his own "double," an author for whom the idea of a split writing persona is as emphatic as the articulation and presentation of the "double" motif in his work.[2]

The strongest case for Banks' bridging of genres and his eclectic inhabitation of the double domains of the high and low/popular and literary is to be made through an examination of his more recognizably mainstream fiction and his science fiction writing, the overlaps being sufficiently evident for Thom Nairn to claim that "his work outside the science-fiction field [...] is rarely far from its edges" (Nairn 1993, 127). Duncan Petrie claims that Banks is a novelist who explores the "conventions and limits of genre" (Petrie 2004, 119) and his ability to operate comfortably in a multitude of different genres is also recognized by the reference to Banks as a "fiction factory" (Nairn 1993: 127; see also March 2002: 81) (a term which recognizes both his prolific and commercially successful output). This idea of a fiction factory positions Banks as the physical embodiment of Umberto Eco's concern (voiced about a text) that a writer become a machine for generating interpretations (Eco 1984). And perhaps there is something machine-like about Banks' routine ability to produce bestsellers by compartmentalizing his year, writing "roughly 3,000 words a day, eight hours a day, five days a week, till the book [is] finished" (Hughes 1999, n.p.). However, this is offset by his famously hedonistic lifestyle (which has been overhyped by both press and author alike). Banks is a writer who is often represented as having fun, whether that be indulging in his love of fast cars, classic whiskey (immortalized in his non-fiction work *Raw Spirit*), drugs (up to about 2006), or women (he's recently talked about his adulterous period).[3] However, he's also a very tricky novelist who is deliberately provocative; when discussing research for *The Business* (1999) and *Look to Windward* (2000), for example, he responded, "I do as little as possible" (Hunt 1999, n.p.). This metronomic ability to publish a book a year, usually alternating mainstream and science fiction titles (Wilson 1994), coupled with their popularity and Banks' own obvious and jokey enjoyment for what he's doing, has perhaps contributed to a smaller, non-unified and more critical reception than his work deserves.

This introduction offers an insight into Banks' pre-publication writing, as well as a brief biographical summary before briefly glossing the essays that follow.

Banks Before The Wasp Factory

Regarded as a shocking, visceral and disturbing entry into the world of contemporary British fiction, *The Wasp Factory* (1984) gained a notorious response, which was significant for its lack of unification. This mixed critical reaction included reviews ranging from astonishment to repulsion, from praise to derision. Among the detractors, Banks' writing was referred to as "juvenile" (Craig, P. qtd. Banks 1984, ii) and even "rubbish" or "a joke" (Gimson qtd. Banks 1984, i). Using these scathing reviews as a marketing tool (especially those that highlighted the violence and the unpleasantness of the reading experience), editions of the novel incorporated these warnings as totems (rather like Frank's sacrifice poles) to pass by before beginning the novel. As a result, the novel quickly acquired and has kept, some twenty-five years on, a cult status among its readers.

There is something uncanny about *The Wasp Factory*. It seems too comprehensive, too different and too fully-fledged for a first-time novelist, as exploring the pre-publication history of Banks demonstrates. The pre-publication and unpublished work of Banks is of major significance in the study of his early published work. His career, in particular, has experienced a bifurcation in what he has described as his Y-shaped split. His juvenilia is as follows, and in the later pieces includes work that he would return to and finally publish: *The Top of Poseidon* (also referred to as the novella length first draft of *The Hungarian Lift-Jet*), *The Hungarian Lift-Jet, The Tashkent Rambler, Use of Weapons* (1974), *Against a Dark Background, The State of the Art* (Culture novella), *The Player of Games, The Wasp Factory, Consider Phlebas, Walking on Glass, O, The Bridge*.

Like many writers, Iain Banks set his stall out to be a writer at an early age.[4] After writing a number of novel-length books[5] while at school and then at university (often in science fiction) he completed the first draft of his breakthrough work, *The Wasp Factory*, in 1980. Though he considered himself to be a science fiction writer, and with his self-imposed deadline of being published by thirty fast approaching, he decided to write something more "mainstream" that he could send to a wider range of publishers. This decision was not arrived at lightly, as an author so committed to science fiction there seems to be a part of him that considered it selling out (see Rundle 2010). Despite this new approach it took nearly three years and at least six publishers later before *The Wasp Factory* was finally accepted for publication. In all, Banks estimates that he wrote over a million words before getting published (Hunt 1999).

Early work, including his first full-length novel (running to 140,000 words and called *The Hungarian Lift-Jet*), was based on a premise that has since been taken up by writers such as Anthony Horowitz and Charlie Higson in their young adult adventure books:

> The secret service would have to employ a young, but very cunning and clever Scots boy, of whatever age I happened to be at the time. Hungary has invented this radical lift jet — a sort of hovering warplane — and the secret service had nicked it. It was just an excuse for vast amounts of mayhem. It all ended badly. Everybody died [Banks qtd. Leith 2003, n.p.].

His early works were handwritten and even at the time of writing Banks dismissed them as juvenile and decided not to type them up, instead moving onto a new work that he did type and send to a few publishers. *The Tashkent Rambler* lived up to its title by meandering to a length of 400,000 words. Written without a plan, he struggled to end the novel and has plotted his work ever since. Banks' first rejection slip was for this work,[6] and is pinned to the notice board of his study in North Queensferry, his home town where he moved back to after *The Wasp Factory* was published.

His next phase was a science fiction one, and saw the development of his utopian civilization, the Culture, starting in the mid seventies. This creation has been the backbone of his alter-ego's career as Iain M. Banks, spawning a series of 10 novels, a novella and a handful of short stories. The author has stressed the politics of his science fiction and his decision to write space opera when cyberpunk was in vogue as a means to explore the "moral high ground in space opera, and [...] reclaim it for the Left!" (Banks qtd. Rundle 2010). This project, begun in *Consider Phlebas* (1987), was reaction to the right wing science fiction from the United States and also the generally depressing British science fiction.

The Player of Games was nearly accepted for publication and Banks notes that if this had actually happened before he had written *The Wasp Factory* then it is possible that he would have just been a science fiction writer.[7] Even if he had wanted to write non science fiction he imagines that he would have been ghettoized like many before him. The first draft of this was written in 1979, after the short story "The State of the Art" which then expanded into a 30,000 word novella. This Culture story saw a ship from the utopian civilization encounter Earth in 1977, and struggle to decide whether to intervene with the planet. It was published on its own in the United States in 1988, and then in the U.K. in 1991 in a collection with other Banks' short stories.

Another of his early science fiction works that was conceived earlier was *Use of Weapons*, which eventually saw publication in 1990 after extensive reworking. The published novel is dedicated to Ken MacLeod with the phrase "I blame Ken MacLeod for the whole thing" (Banks 1992, iii). Ken is another science fiction writer from Glasgow that Iain was at school with, and the two discussed their respective plot ideas with each other. MacLeod had read the work around the time that it was first written, and later asked to read it again. The original was rather tangled though and MacLeod suggested various structural modifications, one of which was put the climax at the end rather than halfway through the book. Thus was born the parallel stories, one going forward in time and one heading backwards.

Scottish Context

As a politically adroit thinker and a writer who is passionate about his country it seems appropriate to locate Banks as a Scottish writer; a process begun by critics such as Craig (1999), March (2002), and Petrie (2004). Though his position as a science fiction writer has sometimes problematized this categorization and obscured his national sensibilities. The opening section of this collection investigates the Scottish context surrounding Banks, but we have chosen not to limit our analysis of Banks within a trajectory of contemporary Scottish fiction. This decision not to rigidly define his oeuvre within the specifics of a literary geography is determined by Banks himself who has claimed:

> I don't really know enough about Scottish literature, so I'm very dubious about saying "Yes, I'm part of this tradition." I'm certainly part of the English *language* tradition. I've been a lot more influenced by *Catch 22, Fear and Loathing in Las Vegas* and *The Tin Drum*, and almost anything by Kafka, than by anything in Scottish literature apart from the single influence of *Lanark* [Robertson 1989–1990, 27].

In his essay, David Pattie positions Banks alongside his compatriot Alasdair Gray, whose postmodern, unreliably narrated novels heralded a united, political dimension to Scottish writing which Banks has inherited and expanded upon. His respect for *Lanark* and for Gray's other writing is routinely alluded to by Banks in interview. The importance of this writer to Banks is explored by Martyn Colebrook, who reads both Gray and Banks as exploring Scotland as a post-industrial space, one that is defined by the construction of a "critical utopia."

Geographies

The writing of space and place is critical for Banks who as a writer of both mainstream and science fiction promotes us to rethink our spatial imagination. In his work on space and place in Banks' *The Algebraist* (2004), James Kneale explores the relationship between geography (literally — "writing the earth") and literature. His discussion of contemporary approaches to geography complement recent concerns in literary theory and so demonstrate that this multidisciplinary approach can yield new avenues of analysis on both "sides." In comparison, Tim Middleton explores the physical landscape of Argyllshire to debunk Banks' assertion that he does minimal research. Using *The Crow Road* as a central text, Middleton uses photographic and linguistic examples to resituate this work and to promote a new critical response to the novel. Bethan Jones, in her close reading of *The Bridge*, compares the real (Forth Bridge), which features so prominently in Banks' history, with the various fictional and metafictional bridges of the novel. In doing so, she recognizes the many doubling within the novel which might well be extended beyond this work and even to the author himself.

Genre

"The hybridity in Banks' work reflects the ways in which he successfully moves between genres and is able to blend different strategies while retaining his popular appeal and the loyalty of his readership" (Nairn n.d.). In this respect, texts such as *The Wasp Factory* (1984), *Walking on Glass* (1985) and *The Bridge* (1986) expect the reader to accept such disruption as a natural consequence of play and experiment.

Banks fully exploits his position as author of both mainstream and science fiction work to further unsettle the boundaries between these. The essays in this section explore the construct of the author as well as his authorial positioning within different genre. In her essay, Katharine Cox reads Banks through the lens of Michel Foucault's "A Preface to Transgression" and argues that Banks is foremost a writer of transgression whose work moves playfully over and across a variety of boundaries. Focusing on *The Wasp Factory* (1984), *The Crow Road* (1992) and *Whit* (1995), Kirsty A. Macdonald considers fantasy and the fantastic as qualities in Banks' writing and in particular how this might be theorized in relation to his label as being a writer of science fiction. She argues that these terms are nuanced in his writing and that they are related to, but not subordinate to, his science fiction writing. Emily Garside and Katharine Cox's essay explores the instance of teaching Banks in higher education. They explore how the use of *The Wasp Factory* can open up other avenues of enquiry within a student class, and help to make connections with Mary Wollstonecraft Shelley's *Frankenstein*, in particular.

Gender, Games and Play

Characteristically the humor, the in-jokes and the commonly held opinion that he is being part-provocateur, part-prankster, has led to Banks' reputation as a novelist who gleefully and shamelessly plays games with critics, with genre and with many other aspects of the writing process. In concluding the collection, the final section on games and play examines narrative and metafictional strategies and transgressions within Banks' novels, particularly "the Culture." Sarah Falcus considers gender in the three novels *The Wasp Factory*, *Whit* (1995) and *The Business*. In doing so, she explores the under theorized novel *Whit* and finds a problematic depiction of femininity in each which categorizes Banks' writing of women. Banks' games playing is explicit in all of his fictions as well as his interviews; Will Slocombe theorizes this games playing, arguing that is not whether we take part but *how* we do so that is pivotal in Banks' appreciation of gaming. In doing so, Slocombe's analysis offers a coherent way of considering both Banks' mainstream and science fiction outputs. Joseph Norman's essay examines the theological implications of Banks' *Surface Detail* (2010) represented by the neural lace and the question of a soul. He traces this concern back through Banks' science fiction writing and argues for the distinctiveness of Banks' vision. Deleuze and Guattari's prophetic writing about the war machine offers William Stephenson an insight into Banks' writing of war and politics. Though both *Consider Phlebas* (1987) and *The Player of Games* (1988) predate the events of 9/11, Stephenson demonstrates that their depictions of war undermine the dichotomy of East-West and instead offer a far more complex political landscape, more akin to contemporary political machinations.

Coda

This collection addresses the growing interest in Banks' maturing status whereby his fictions, both mainstream and science fiction, are drawing increased critical attention. Banks' writing, part of the Scottish Highers syllabus for English (*The Crow Road* 1992, *Complicity* 1993), is now regularly being studied and taught at university level and by extension at postgraduate level.[8] This collection provides a timely critical intervention into the reception of Banks' writing, to highlight new critical directions in his writing and to establish his position and reputation as one of the foremost writers of his generation.

Notes

1. See Cristie Leigh March (2002, 81) for a gloss on these critical responses.
2. For a more detailed discussion of this see Foundation Special Edition (1999) on Iain and Iain M. Banks as well as Colebrook (2010) and Bethan Jones' essay in this collection.

3. See Wilson (1994), Leith (2003) or Banks' website (http://www.iain-banks.net/).

4. Asked at school at the age of 11 to draw what he wanted to be when he grew up, he drew an actor on a stage but in the corner wrote "and writer" (see Leigh 2003). Telling this story at events when asked about when he started to think about writing, he claims to still have the drawing.

5. He describes his writing of this time as being full of sex and violence, neither of which he had much experience of at the time, saying, "I had just gone from being much influenced by Captain W. E. Johns and Biggles to having just read absolutely everything by Alistair MacLean I could lay my hands on" (Wilson 1994, n.p.).

6. It came from Jonathon Cape and is dated 27 January 1974. At public appearances Banks also frequently quotes from another rejection this book received, which began, "Due to the paper shortage..." (Hunt 1999).

7. Banks' thoughts about his writing status as a mainstream or science fiction writer are well documented in his interviews. In brief, he considers himself "as a science fiction writer who was deigning to dabble in mainstream" but who revels in "being able to write in two different genres, one of which I've exploited ruthlessly" (Banks qtd. Rundle 2010, n.p.).

8. Given the Scottish government's recent announcement regarding the Scottish qualifications, "Exams to include Scottish texts" (2012), Banks' importance as a Scottish writer seems set to continue. See Tim Middleton's essay in this collection for ways in which Banks can be viewed as a Scottish writer of place.

WORKS CITED

Colebrook, Martyn. 2010. "Journeys Into Lands of Silence: *The Wasp Factory* and Mental Disorder." In *Demons of the Body and Mind: Essays on Disability and Literature*. Ruth Anolik, ed. Jefferson, NC: McFarland.

Craig, Cairns. 1999. *The Modern Scottish Novel: Narrative and the National Imagination*. Edinburgh: Edinburgh University Press.

Eco, Umberto. 1984. "The Role of the Reader: A Postscript to *The Name of the Rose*." Trans. William Weaver. New York: Harcourt Brace Jovanovich.

Hughes, Colin. 1999. "Doing the Business." *The Guardian*. Saturday, 7 August 1999. http://www.guardian.co.uk/books/1999/aug/07/books.guardianreview11/print.

Hunt, Stephen. 1999. "Chart-topping authors, Iain Banks & Ken McLeod interviewed." *SF Crowsnest*. http://www.sfcrowsnest.com/articles/features/1999/Chart-topping-authors-Iain-Banks-Ken-McLeod-interviewed-5784.php.

Leith, William. 2003. "A Writer's Life: Iain Banks." *The Telegraph*. 3 November 2003. http://www.telegraph.co.uk/culture/3605692/A-writers-life-Iain-Banks.html.

March, Christie Leigh. 2002. *Rewriting Scotland: Welsh, McLean, Warner, Banks, Galloway, and Kennedy*. Manchester: Manchester University Press.

Nairn, Thom. 1993. "Iain Banks and the Fiction Factory." Gavin Wallace and Randall Stevenson, eds. *The Scottish Novel Since the Seventies*. Edinburgh: Edinburgh University Press, 127–135.

_____. n.d. "Reading Double, Writing Double: The Fiction of Iain (M.) Banks." www.arts.gla.ac.uk.

Petrie, Duncan. 2004. *Contemporary Scottish Fictions: Film, Television and the Novel*. Edinburgh: Edinburgh University Press.

Rundle, James. 2010. "Interview: Iain M. Banks." *SciFiNow*. http://www.scifinow.co.uk/news/interview-iain-m-banks/.

The Scottish Government. 25 January 2012. "Exams to include Scottish texts." http://www.scotland.gov.uk/News/Releases/2012/01/exams25012012.

Wilson, Andrew. 1994. "Iain Banks Interview." *Textualities*. http://textualities.net/andrew-wilson/iain-banks-interview/.

I. Scottish Context

The Lessons of *Lanark*
Iain Banks, Alasdair Gray and the Scottish Political Novel
David Pattie

Lanark *and the 1980s*

By common consent[1] the 1980s was a significant decade for Scottish literature, as it was for Scottish culture generally. To a great extent, the decade was simply the point at which work which had been developing steadily during the '60s and '70s attained critical mass. However, and fortunately for those who came to prominence during the 1980s, this coincided with a political sea change, which had a profound and lasting impact on Scotland and on the rest of Britain. As Randall Stevenson put it,

> The origin of the Scottish Literary revival at the end of the twentieth century has often been seen as compensating for the failure of the Referendum bill in 1979, and for the imposition on a predominantly socialist country of nearly twenty years of unelected Tory government. Critical determinations to consolidate an independent Scottish literary tradition can be seen to derive from the same source [Stevenson 2004, 224–5].

It is fair to say that the publication of Alasdair Gray's debut novel *Lanark* in 1981 was the first and most visible sign of this revival. *Lanark* is a key text in the recent history of Scottish literature. Begun when Gray was a teenager in the early 1950s, and composed in fits and starts in the intervening decades, the novel tells the story of Duncan Thaw, a semi-autobiographical version of Gray, whose life and art are stunted both by the society that surrounds him, and by his response to it. After Thaw's death, a version of him is reborn in Lanark, an innocent abroad in a brutally surreal version of Western Scotland.

The novel had acquired semi-legendary status even before its publication; when it finally appeared, it was greeted by other Scottish novelists as something of a liberation. Irvine Welsh called it "the closest thing Scotland's ever produced to Ulysses" (qtd. Glass 2008, 167), while Janice Galloway, writing in the introduction to the 2001 edition of *Lanark*, was even more fulsome:

> I'd always assumed that what my education had told me was true: that my country was a toty wee place with no political clout, a joke heritage, dour people, and writers who were all male and all dead. Not so, the book said: on a number of levels, not so [qtd. Glass 2008, 167].

Alan Warner, in 2000, remembered "the deep shock and amazement [at] Alasdair Gray's mighty *Lanark*," because "I believed there was nobody alive in Scotland writing a novel" (qtd. March 2002, 8).

Warner's youthful judgment was not exactly fair, but it is understandable. During the 1970s, Scottish literature flew, as it had done for much of the twentieth century, below the Britain's cultural radar. Though individual writers, such as the poets Edwin Morgan, Liz Lochhead and Norman MacCaig, the novelists William MacIlvanney and Robin Jenkins, the playwrights Bill Brydon and Tom McGrath, produced significant work, what was lacking, arguably, was a cultural narrative that linked the work of Scottish writers to the state of their country. This is what *Lanark* provided; and it did so, as Cairns Craig argued in an influential study of Scottish literature, partly because it treated Scottish culture as an absence. In a much quoted passage from the novel, Duncan Thaw describes Glasgow as "a music hall song and a few bad novels. That's all we've given to the world. That's all we've given to ourselves" (Gray 1981, 243). For Craig, this is a sure sign that

> Thaw is the inheritor of Scottish culture under erasure; the culture which has actually existed in Glasgow, the paintings of the Glasgow boys and the Glasgow girls, the work of designers and architects like Rennie Mackintosh, the novels of Catherine Carswell and George Friel, the theatre of James Bridie, have all disappeared in an all-encompassing cultural amnesia [Craig 1999, 33].

It was not that Scotland was being gradually subsumed into the British state. British governments since the end of the Second World War had been careful to maintain specifically Scottish state formations, and the Scottish National Party, after a number of significant by-election results in the late 1960s, had become a significant force in the country's political life. For some cultural commentators at the time, though, this was far from enough. In a very influential study *The Break-Up of Britain* (1981), based on a series of essays published incrementally throughout the 1960s and '70s, Tom Nairn argued that Scottish national sentiment was pathological in character; specifically, a hysterical over-reaction to the country's perceived powerlessness. The symptoms of this hysteria, such as sentimentality, ostentatious, tartan-shrouded nationalism, and the like, were exactly what was to be expected from a country with no secure sense of itself.

For a number of reasons, in the 1980s, the cultural amnesia Craig describes dispersed, and dispersed rapidly. Firstly, the 1970s had ended with two significant political events: the failure of the devolution referendum and the election of the Conservative Party under Margaret Thatcher. The referendum, set up by a Labour government in deep political and economic difficulties, failed because of a technicality (the total voting in favor of devolution did not reach the requisite percentage of the total electorate). In addition, the election of the Conservatives brought into government an administration dedicated to the rolling back of the Welfare State, a part of the post-war settlement particularly popular in Scotland.[2] During the 1980s, in reaction to a wider political environment that seemed to be running against Scotland's best interests, Scots expended a lot of cultural energy in rediscovering a sense of themselves — and with it, a sense of their difference from a British culture that no longer seemed to include them. *Lanark*, a product of the Scotland of the '50s, '60s and '70s, emerged into a political and cultural climate which was suddenly receptive to a key part of its message; that Scotland was unrepresented. As Douglas Gifford put it, in a gloss on Craig's argument,

> Scottish writers imagine themselves alone because they work within a national culture which has little time for the study of its traditions, and which fails to transmit the information regarding its past achievements [Gifford 2004, 34].

It was Gray's good fortune to publish a substantial work on this very theme, at the time when the study of Scotland's traditions, the transmission of past achievements, and the celebration of current developments, made sound political and cultural sense.

Gray's first novel, then, was taken up in a climate that seemed to favor the overt expression of Scottish cultural difference. This desire to mark off Scotland as different, as operating in accordance with a set of rules which identified it as a separate entity, was rather problematic; it left much about the nature of Scottish life, and the relation of Scotland to the wider network of power in the United Kingdom and elsewhere unaccounted for. Though it could be said that Gray's novel identifies and analyzes those networks in the novel's phantasmagorical third and fourth books, where Lanark wanders uncomprehendingly through power structures of increasingly bewildering complexity. These structures go by a number of names (the Institute, the Creature, and so on), but at base the process of exploitation, consumption and elimination is the same. The insight that comes to Duncan Thaw in the midst of a breakdown that "[m]en are pies that bake and eat themselves" (Gray 1981, 188) becomes a guiding principle for the organization of Lanark's world.

The impact of Lanark was not lost on Iain Banks as he has called the novel "one of the best pieces of Scottish literature since the second world war and possibly this century" (qtd. March 2002, 7). On a more personal note, Banks acknowledges his debt to the earlier novel as "*Lanark* had a huge effect on *The Bridge*. I'm quite happy to acknowledge that debt" (qtd. Wilson 1994, n.p.). Given the nature of Banks' writing, it is easy to see why: Gray switches genres, both between and within novels, as Banks does, his work displays considerable narrative complexity (see *Poor Things* 1992), embeds two competing life histories in an overarching narrative that is itself contested and so does Banks. Even in apparently conventional novels, such as *The Crow Road* (1992), *Dead Air* (2002), *The Steep Approach to Garbadale* (2007), the narrative is constructed as a palimpsest of events, taken out of temporal sequence. Moreover, Banks centralizes the key theme of Gray's work in his writing, which is the positioning of the individual in relation to overarching structures of power. As Liam MacIlvanney has pointed out:

> Throughout his fiction, the truth at which Gray worries is the old one — of exploitation, class brutality, man's inhumanity to man [....] This is the truth which seeks out Gray's protagonists, and shatters their complacency [MacIlvanney 2002, 197–8].

However, the relation of Gray's protagonists to power is rather more complex than this; they are warped by the structures they inhabit, even if they do not realize it. This chimes closely with the world inhabited by Banks' protagonists, and it also accords with the wider, national picture: with the condition of Scotland itself.

Power and Scotland: The Factory and the Trap

In 1984 the publication of *The Wasp Factory*, Banks' first novel, rather neatly coincided with the publication of *1982 Janine*, Gray's second novel. Anyone reading the initial reviews of both books might have been struck by a curious similarity in the critical responses. Both express a level of discomfort at the novels' contents, expressed in critical language that was frequently rather intemperate. On *The Wasp Factory*, *The Irish Times* commented,

> It is a sick, sick world when the confidence and investment of an astute firm of publishers is justified by a work of unparalleled depravity [qtd. Craig 2002, 8].

Peter Levi, speaking on BBC Radio 4's *Bookmark,* was equally as scathing about *1982 Janine*:

> I recommend nobody to read this book [....] It is sexually oppressive, the sentences are far too long and it is boring [...] hogwash. Radioactive hogwash. [Gray 1984, endpages].

The shocking debut of a previously unknown writer provides the critic with an easily recognizable narrative, one which *The Wasp Factory*'s initial detractors followed: this was a publicity stunt, designed to draw attention to someone previously unheard of. On the other hand, *1982 Janine* was the second novel from an author whose work had been universally admired. As noted above, in a relatively short time Gray had established himself at the forefront of a burgeoning renaissance in Scottish literature, and his second full-length novel seemed to place that growing reputation in some jeopardy.[3]

It is true, of course, that both novels had their admirers and that the number of admirers outweighed their detractors, and that both novelists were unabashed by the criticism they received. However, the comparisons between the two novels extend beyond the year of their initial publication, and the controversy that attended it; it could be said that both tell the same story. A powerless central character erects a framework of rituals which provide both momentary respite (the thrill of violence, the release of orgasm) and a sense of power and control over the world. The framework that they erect is oppressive, confining and unsustainable; external and internal forces (a brother returning, the playing out of a primal conflict with the father, intrusive and troubling memories, and the promptings of conscience) unsettle and finally destroy it; and at the end of each novel, the central characters face a new, uncertain world with trepidation and muted hope.

This story, a tale of the individual's witting or unwitting entrapment in all enveloping structures of power is a common one in Scottish fiction. This narrative is told in the shifting economic structure of small town life, which brings down John Gourlay in George Douglas Brown's *The House with the Green Shutters* (1901); the Norse invasions in Neil Gunn's *Sun Circle* (1933); or the Highland clearances in *Butcher's Broom* (1977). Equally, it is seen in the passing of the old life of the Mearns in Lewis Grassic Gibbon's *Sunset Song* (1932), in MacIlvanney's *Docherty* (1975), and its updated counterpart, *The Big Man* (1985), which detail the slow destruction of working class communities in the Ayrshire coalfields. In James Kelman's *A Disaffection* (1989), Patrick Doyle is uneasily aware that he is training his pupils for exploitation when they join the working world. For example, it is the story told in Muriel Spark's *The Prime of Miss Jean Brodie* (1961), where Jean Brodie, keen to emphasize her individuality in the midst of the stifling convention of Marcia Blaine's Academy, manages nothing more than the creation of a warped version of the dubious political philosophy she admires. The structures that she creates, the ur-fascist cadre of regimented individualists that she tries to fashion from the student body, are the structures that ultimately destroy her.

The protagonists of these and other novels (characters deformed to fit the power structures that surround them, or destroyed if they cannot be bent into shape) would, for some critical commentators, be nothing more than the fictional reflection of Scotland's political situation. Tom Nairn, surveying the state of the country twenty-five years after the publication of *The Break-Up of Britain,* commented despairingly:

> If there is one thing that the Scots in particular do know all about, it is self-colonisation [....] The sententious moralism of the marginalised; disregard of democratic deficit for economic opportunity; cultural over-compensation and romantic chest-beating to efface or embellish powerlessness; over-effusive loyalty to a distant cause and metropolis, welcomed and yet somehow never welcome enough — all those tropes of a supposedly post-national world are, alas, tired old family skeletons in Edinburgh and Glasgow [Nairn 2004, 29].

In *1982 Janine,* Jock McLeish puts it rather more pithily:

> The truth is that we are a nation of arselickers, though we disguise it with surfaces: a surface of generous, openhanded manliness, a surface of dour, practical integrity, a surface of futile maudlin defiance [Gray 1984, 65].

In other words, Scottish identity is nothing more than a performance, designed to hide our real, warped natures from others and from ourselves. The state that McLeish describes is the state in which Frank Cauldhame lives. Frank/Frances is ruled by the quasi-religious rituals of masculine power that have compensated for his/her supposed emasculation are exposed as meaningless, because they are based on a misunderstanding of the forces that have controlled her his/life:

> I was proud; eunuch but unique; a fierce and noble presence in my lands, a crippled warrior, fallen prince [....]
> Now I find I was the fool all along [Banks 1984, 183].

Both Jock and Frank live in what could be described as a condition of impotent exceptionalism. Isolated and manipulated, they construct identities that are not grounded in a secure sense of community, or a secure relationship to a wider, civic society. Jock is happy to think of himself as mysterious: a cipher, impenetrable to those around him, while Frank reacts to most of the people outside of his family with wariness or outright fear. In this, they mirror the condition of the country in which they live, as described by David McCrone in 1992. McCrone, writing in the wake of the Scottish cultural revival of the 1980s, takes issue with a pervasive Scottish myth, one caught neatly in the traditional toast, "here's tae us, wha's like us, damn few and they're a' deid." He exposes the myth of a real Scottish identity that exists, somehow untainted by the larger power structures that surround it.

> The obsession with a unified Scottish national culture has its parallel in the assertion that, in order to explain Scotland's political divergence from England, its industrial and occupational structures must be different from those south of the border. When this turns out not to be the case, we worry about the fact that it is not, in case it denies Scotland's right to exist [qtd. Punter 1999, 194].

As McCrone noted, this is a peculiarly self-defeating position. Believing in one's exceptionalism might very well provide a sense of self-worth, it might compensate for one's subordinate status, but it is a trap, leading only to the consideration of "The trivial and the epiphenomenal, which will be found only in the past or in the museum" (Punter 1999, 194).

There are signs in both novels that the protagonists are aware of the constraints that their chosen rituals place upon them; indeed, it is a crucial part of the redemptive conclusion of both narratives that they place themselves in the position of the creatures they have manipulated. Jock has spent the first part of the book sadistically enjoying a favorite fantasy, in which women are manipulated sexually by an international cartel. At the end of the novel, after working his way through his past (in a chapter called, significantly, "FROM THE CAGE TO THE TRAP: ... or, Scotland 1952–82" [Gray 1984, contents page]) he ends the novel identifying himself directly with the exploited women he previously fantasized about. At the end of *The Wasp Factory*, Frank implicitly places himself and us in the midst of the mechanism. He no longer stands apart from its operations, but realizes that he is as caught up in the workings of an arbitrary justice as any of the wasps that he has released into the factory:

> Each of us, in our own personal Factory, may believe we have stumbled down one corridor, and that our fate is sealed and certain (dream or nightmare, humdrum or bizarre, good or bad), but a word or a glance, a slip — anything can change that, alter it entirely, and our marble hall becomes a gutter, or our rat-maze a golden path [Banks 1984, 183–4].

In other words, there is at the end of both novels the strong suggestion that an impasse has been overcome, and that this new type of experience, one which operates on the basis of a clearer understanding of the protagonist's place in the world, is about to begin.

These are, then, paradigmatically Scottish stories, and they are also representative of Banks' and Gray's work as a whole. David Punter noticed much the same dynamic in Banks' *Feersum Endjinn* and Gray's short story, "The Cause of Some Recent Changes," collected in *Unlikely Stories, Mostly*, whereby Banks'

> *Feersum Endjinn* clearly has a planetary significance. It also, I would argue, has a Scottish one, as does the steam engine which drives the world in Gray's "The Cause of Some Recent Changes." If, upon entering the apparent "escape tunnel," what one finds, "on another scene," to quote Freud, is a hidden source of power, then the choices become stark: complicity with that machine or exile from its effects [Punter 1999, 118].

One could broaden this out: finding oneself enmeshed in hidden power structures is a characteristic trope in Banks' novels. In the science fiction novels, Horza is a game player, and a pawn in a larger game (*The Player of Games* 1988); the humans in *Excession* (1996) are subsidiary to the main plot, which is played out over their heads by the Minds; Quilan, in *Look to Windward* (2000), is manipulated both by his own superiors and by the Culture; Faasin Taak (*The Algebraist* 2004) and Ferbin (*Matter* 2008) both refuse the kind of complicity Punter describes, but at great personal cost. The bridge in *The Bridge* (1986) becomes, over the course of the novel, a complex and resonant image of entrapment; Hiasko (*Canal Dreams* 1989), Whit (*Whit* 1995), and Kate (*The Business* 1999) all come to understand, question and contest the power structures that surround them. The same dynamic is found is Gray's work. Lanark, as noted above, stumbles through an increasingly labyrinthine and surreal version of acquisitive, aggressive Capitalism; Kelvin Walker (*The Fall of Kelvin Walker* 1985) and Mungo McGrotty (*McGrotty and Ludmilla* 1990) fight their way up the British establishment; Bella Baxter/McCandless (*Poor Things* 1992) undergoes a painful education in the true nature of colonialism and gender relations in the Victorian era; John Tunnock (*Old Men in Love* 2007) tries to construct a comprehensive accounting of the cost of the unequal organization of the world, but is blind to the fact that he himself is being manipulated.

However, it is not the case that Gray and Banks simply rehash an old Scottish tale. Impotent exceptionalism, as a trope, might be sufficient to explain a significant strand of Scottish literature, from *The House with The Green Shutters* to Alan Warner's *The Sopranos* (1998). It could be said that in Banks and Gray's work that it is merely one manifestation of a wider problem. The construction of a narrative which gives the character that assembles it a sense of difference and power is one response to a more general dilemma that their work explores. It has been noted that gaming is a dominant metaphor in Banks' fiction.[4] As Craig put it,

> The conflict between being a player and being played upon, and the difficulty of discovering the rules of the game in which one is playing, are the insistent themes of Banks' fiction [Craig 2005, 233].

One could also say that it is an embedded metaphor in Gray's work, which is the world his characters encounter turns on a version of this distinction — whether it is between the consumed and the consumer in *Lanark*, the screwer and the screwed in *1982 Janine*, or the maker and the made in *Poor Things*. This is not a simple opposition, though. There is more to the relation of characters than the choice between complicity and exile that Punter describes above. There are instances in both their writings where the game is played to the benefit of all contestants, and where the choice between complicity and exile is successfully made. There are other instances, where the rules of the game prove too intractable; and times when it is impossible to resolve the relationship between characters in a way which reconciles the painful contradictions of their lives. In all cases, the power structures that form the rules of the game skew its operation; player and played are by definition in a relationship of fundamental inequality. Believing oneself exceptional is one solution to this problem; however, as both Banks and Gray demonstrate, there are others.

Power and the Self: Connections, Shellworlds and Complicity

In 1994, Banks provided his science fiction fans with a short introductory guide to the Culture. As part of the guide, Banks set out the underlying ethos for his fictional galactic society.

> Philosophically, the Culture accepts, generally, that questions such as "What is the meaning of life?" are themselves meaningless. The question implies — indeed an answer to it would demand — a moral framework beyond the only moral framework we can comprehend without resorting to superstition (and thus abandoning the moral framework informing — and symbiotic with — language itself) [Banks 1994, n.p.].

This statement will come as no surprise to any of Banks' readers. It is clearly espoused by the representatives of the Culture that we encounter in book after book. For example, in *The Player of Games* the final dialogue between Gurgeh and Nicosar is an exercise in culturally determined misapprehension. The argument between them cannot be won, because neither of them can accept the rules that govern the conversation of the other. Gurgeh, to his credit, comes to realize and accept this:

> What could he say to this apex? Were they to argue metaphysics, here, now, with the imperfect tool of language, when they'd spent the last ten days devising the most perfect image of their competing philosophies they were capable of expressing, probably in any form? [Banks 1988, 282].

Gurgeh and Nicosar cannot communicate because the orientation of their respective worldviews is fundamentally different. Nicosar sees a world in which each action is part of a higher, all-encompassing structure, and Gurgeh sees a world where each action takes its meaning from its immediate context.

The same opposition, between what might be termed a vertical worldview and a horizontal one, is for Gray an integral part of the Scottish psyche, at least when it comes to the practice of religion:

> It is as if we had a small god in our brain who may sometimes sound like John Knox or a local schoolteacher but has nothing to do with landlords, kings and such gentry. The demands of this little god are sometimes so severe that whenever he has been supported by clergymen of his own kind he has destroyed the happiness of whole communities, delighted in smashing church organs and sculptures, and revelled in the burning of poor old women; but Scots with radical new ideas who get their deity to co-operate with them have acted with courage and independence — the opposition or indifference of clergy, kings, bosses and nations has seemed trivial compared with their staunch self-approval [Gray 1992, 28].

Once again, this opposition plays itself out in Gray's fiction. In *Lanark*, Lanark meets Nastler (a rather deflating self-portrait of Gray himself), who informs Lanark that his life is entirely predetermined. Lanark, understandably, baulks at this, and is pleased to note that Nastler does not know about the existence of a son, born to Lanark and Rima after they return to Unthank. *Poor Things* can be thought of as a struggle between a pathetic narrator attempting to exercise god-like control over the narrative, and a central character who, in close co-operation with her god (the appropriately named surgeon, Godwin Baxter), tries to gain control of the narrative of her life. In *1982 Janine*, god appears, but as a colleague and helpmate:

> I see you, God, in my mind's eye. You are a naked old man stooping down from the middle of the sun, your beard and hair stream sideways like the tail of a comet, you are based on a print which became popular a few years ago. In the print you probe the space below you with forceps or callipers, but in my mind's eye your hand reaches down to me with the palm open [Gray 1984, 334].

This is not the stern, protestant god of Knox and Calvin. This is the god whose influence and help will, Jock hopes, allow him to act with the "courage and independence" Gray describes above.

For both Gray and Banks, the opposition of these two worldviews carries with it an ethical and political dimension. The hierarchical arrangement of power structures is fundamentally immoral, because it relies on a process of clear social separation. A society organized along horizontal lines of communication is, almost by definition, a just society. It might confirm Nicosar's sense of himself, to see the game that organizes his society as a brutally Darwinian exercise, while Gurgeh, on the other hand, sees it as an evolving language through which, for the first time, he, Nicosar, and their respective cultures can communicate. For Craig, such an argument is rooted deeply in Scottish philosophy. He draws a sharp distinction between a postmodernity predicated on Lyotard's declaration that grand narratives are decaying,[5] and a postmodernity which seeks to advance beyond the atomization of society into "isolated agents." Craig roots this definition in the work of the Scots philosopher John Macmurray:

> Any "self"—that is to say, any agent—is an existing being, a person.... The idea of an isolated agent is self-contradictory. Any agent is necessarily in relation to the Other. Apart from this essential relation he does not exist. But, further, the Other in this constitutive relation must itself be personal. Persons, therefore, are constituted by their mutual relation to one another [Macmurray 1961, 23–4].[6]

For Craig, this is a concept that can be traced through the work of a number of Scottish authors; and in particular, in those authors whose work has routinely been described as postmodern:

> Indeed, uncovering the "You and I" in the isolated individual of modernity has been the driving force of precisely those Scottish writers who are most often associated with the stylistic gestures of postmodernism, from Muriel Spark and Alasdair Gray to A.L. Kennedy, Janice Galloway and Iain Banks [Craig 2004, 273].

There is much to agree with in this argument. As noted above, both Jock and Frank's narratives follow the trajectory outlined by Macmurray. It also usefully captures the trajectory followed by other protagonists. Prentice McHoan (his name a sure indication that he has much to learn) begins *The Crow Road* (1992) in angry, self-imposed isolation from his father and his family. He ends the narrative centrally placed, literally the "pivot," in his grandmother's terms, around which the rest of his family turns. No matter which version of her story is followed, Bella Baxter in *Poor Things* moves from socially determined isolation to a useful engagement with her community. The title of the booklet she publishes, *A Loving Economy—A Mother's Recipe for the End of All National and Class Warfare* (Gray 1992, 307), clearly indicates that, for her, a just society is predicated on the realization that its members are "constituted by their mutual relation to one another."

Both Banks and Gray are uneasily aware that, in the world as it currently exists, such connections are made difficult. The underlying political philosophy of the past thirty years, the encroaching privatization of all aspects of daily life, the elevation of competition to an all-encompassing good, and the apparent victory of a particularly virulent form of free-market capitalism, has been precisely about the idea of the self as isolated agent. Both authors, then, are in a rather difficult position. The political ideology they espouse is the dominant ideology in Scottish politics,[7] but it is an ideology which seems to have little purchase in London. Both authors have been vocal in their opposition to the dominant political trends of the time. Gray has produced a number of pamphlets arguing for Scottish self-governance, and Banks, famously, cut up his passport in protest at the British and American governments' invasion of Iraq. Both have made it quite clear in interview that there is much about the direction of the America/British foreign policy that disturbs them. Gray has often spoken of his debt to the post war Welfare State, and so he is particularly angered by the misappropriation of these organizations:

> Nations, cities, schools, marketing companies, hospitals, police forces have been made by people for the good of people.... But when we see them working to increase dirt, poverty, pain and death, then they have obviously gone wrong [Gray in Axelrod 1995, n.p.].

In interview, Banks has identified the Culture as his utopia, but he is clear that although the Culture is humanoid, it is not necessarily human:

> The Culture isn't us. I thought long and hard about this long before the books were published and decided, that the Culture wasn't going to be us in the future [....] It's a very pessimistic thing to say that we do seem to be wedded to war and destruction and torture and racism and sexism — all the horrible things, all the xenophobic things — we seem to have a xenophobic gene sequence [Banks 2009, n.p.].

Macmurray's argument might suggest that we simply need to reorient ourselves, and to accept that the self as isolated agent can and should be replaced by the self formed in relation to the Other. However, the relationship might not be that simple. Gray suggests that organizations set up to facilitate the connection between self and Other can as easily be turned into instruments of oppression. For Banks, the connection between individual subjects might be harmful, because it allows access to our worst selves. Craig might argue that in Scottish postmodern fiction as a whole the quest for a connection that is based on "You and I" predominates, but in Banks and Gray's fiction, there are moments when this trajectory is impeded; moments when the "You and I" which defines the subject in community cannot be achieved because the structures that force individuals apart are simply too strong, or where the relation between characters is fundamentally destructive, even when the relation between self and Other is as Macmurray describes.

In "Near the Driver" (a short story collected in *Ten Tales Tall and True* 1993) Gray spins a bitter fable about the failure to achieve community out of what was, at the time of the story's composition, a relatively new and controversial innovation: the privatization of the U.K.'s rail network. A group of passengers find themselves locked into a collision course with another train; the driver, however, seems entirely unconcerned by the impending crash. He is not in control of the train, as the driver's cabin is fully automated, and is being operated centrally from a control centre in Stoke on Trent. Just before the crash, the driver is summoned to the guard's van. He "explains he is forced to leave them because someone must survive the wreck to report it at the official enquiry" (Gray 1993, 150). The passengers are unable to resist: they cannot agree on a course of action, and as the other train nears they are strapped firmly to their seats. In other words, the train is organized to keep its passengers powerless, isolated and passive. At the beginning of the story, it is described in terms which make it sound like a prison or a tomb:

> And walking along the platform she [one of the passengers — a retired schoolteacher] sees the carriages have very small square windows with rounded corners. [She ...] remembers when carriages were divided into compartments like the insides of stage coaches, each with a door in the middle of either side, a door whose window could be raised or lowered by fitting holes in a thick leather strap onto shining brass studs [....] She stops and examines a door of a carriage near the front of the modern train. It has neither window nor handle, just a square plastic button in the middle with PRESS engraved on it. She presses. The door snaps open like a blind. She steps through and the door snaps shut behind her [Gray 1993, 128–9].

There is more to the description of the way that trains used to be than simple nostalgia. The older train was fitted for human use; it invited interaction (large windows to look out of, doors that could be easily opened, windows that could be raised or lowered). In contrast, the new train is designed as an exercise in social control. It is an image of the kind of malformed state organization that Gray talks about in the interview quoted above, one that exists only (as it turns out) to keep its clients locked in place, even if the result of that confinement is death.

There are many other examples of such confining organizations in Gray's work. In "Five Letters from an Eastern Empire" (1977), the poet, Tohu, thinks that he has broken through the confines imposed on him by a tyrannical state, to create a poem which speaks directly to others. After his death, the poem is used to support the very state he wanted to destroy. In "The End of the Axletree" (1983) the inhabitants of a sealed, ever-growing tower are destroyed when they attempt to force their way through an impermeable barrier between the earth and the heavens. In *Poor Things*, Bella Baxter's attempts to create the loving economy outlined in her pamphlet are resisted and destroyed, because they do not fit in to the prevailing social ethos. Finally, in *Old Men in Love*, Henry Prince founds a religious order whose tenets lead, with inexorable logic, to exploitation and rape.

To borrow a useful metaphor from Banks' science fiction novel, *Matter* (2008), what Gray is describing in each one of these texts is the operation of a Shellworld. In *Matter*, Shellworlds are massive, artificial satellites, hollowed out, and capable of supporting a number of civilizations, on a number of levels, from the planet's surface to its core. They are dangerous, for two reasons. Firstly, because travel between the different levels is tightly controlled, it is always possible for smaller civilizations that inhabit the Shellworld to be manipulated by their more powerful neighbors. This is a resonant image of an inherently destructive hierarchy. The split societies within each Shellworld operate blindly within a system that might, at any point, come to an apocalyptic end. Although the societies in Shellworlds operate blindly, because they can be manipulated their struggles and conflicts can be made to mirror and advance the struggles and conflicts played out literally over their heads. Even if the smaller society opposes the values of the greater society within which it is embedded, and the values of the greater society are very hard to overturn. In *Matter*, such an attempt leads to the death of most of the novels' main protagonists. In the examples from Gray's fiction, characters either operate comfortably within the enclosing strictures of their respective Shellworlds, or find the barriers that surround them impossible to breach.

For both Banks and Gray it is not a simple matter to replace one form of social organization (the hierarchical, which promotes and supports the self as isolated agent), with another (the communal, which promotes and supports the self in relation to the Other). The structures supporting the hierarchical organization of society are very strong indeed, and they will actively resist attempts to dismantle them. The Bridge in *The Bridge* seems to go on forever, while the Business in *The Business* seems to cover the whole world. Even when, as in *Whit*, an organization is transformed, it is transformed into a model of community which is explicitly opposed to the wider, exploitative society that surrounds it. Hierarchical structures might frequently prove too strong to be successfully contested, and there are also no guarantees that the relation between self and Other will be as beneficial, as Macmurray and Craig would wish, if it is bound up with the exercise of, or the desire for, oppression. In Gray's *A History Maker* (1994) human development seems to have come to an end. Everything this future society requires is provided by power plants, women effectively rule, and men occupy themselves by waging war competitively, in televised battles. A young soldier, Wat Dryhope, tiring of the unchanging world in which he lives, is violently seduced by a woman, Meg Mountbenger, who promises him a return to a world governed by warfare and exploitation: "[w]e will recreate the system which overpowered [Communism], the competitive exploitation of human resources" (Gray 1994, 118). Although the plot to infect and destroy the power plants finally fails, the power plants are destroyed, and human society adapts, rediscovering agrarian technology and sustaining a basically peaceable lifestyle. Wat and Meg, however, remain locked in a mutually destructive *folie a deux*, which ends only with their deaths. In a manner that Macmurray would recognize, Wat is constituted through his relationship with Meg, but that relationship is a profoundly negative version of the existentially healthy discovery of the "You and I" that Craig describes.

In Banks, too, the relation between self and Other can be a source of violence and pain. In *Look to Windward,* the Chelgrian soldier Quilan allows himself to be used in a complex plot to destroy a Culture Orbital. Although we never learn the full details, the attack has been organized by his race, in collaboration with other unnamed allies, in retaliation for a war that the Culture helped to promote. Although the war was supposed ultimately to be beneficial to the Chelgrian race, it is, by the time that the novel opens, regarded as a failed attempt at cultural intervention, and is profoundly regretted by the Culture. Quilan agrees to go on the mission (which will end with his death) because his lover was one of the war's many casualties. He nearly succeeds except that, at the moment when he is about to carry out his task, he is stopped by the Hub Mind, which is itself mourning the loss of its twin. The two meet at the novel's end, when they see their experience mirrored in the Other, and yet the encounter only leads to their double suicide. As the Mind points out, there can be no reconciliation, when the isolated agent meets his double, they confirm their mutuality only in death:

> — Are you ready, Quilan? Will you be my twin in this?
> [Quilan] took [the avatar's] other hand
> — If you will be my mate [Banks 2000, 384].

It is in *Complicity* (1993) that the "You and I" relation is at its most troubling. As Craig notes in a guide to the novel, *Complicity* plays on the idea of the double.[8] Cameron Colley's left-leaning gonzo journalism is put into murderous practice by Andy, his life-long friend. As Craig notes, their complex relationship is shaped as a series of echoes of two primal scenes: Colley, pulling his friend from the ice when they were children, and Colley and Andy's killing of a child molester. These echoes are of a past which has not been assimilated by either of them, and a past which is still troublingly present:

> When Andy phones to alert the police to the murder of William, he announces it as being a "present" left for Colley: each death is an exorcism of a past which remains always present between them [Craig 2002, 58].

Colley, too, finds it impossible to close their relationship. He might give the police Andy's name, but when given him the choice at the novel's end, he allows his friend enough time to escape. The novel is overtly concerned with the effects of Thatcherite ideology on British and Scottish society. In the novel, the all-pervasive influence of the free market has infected all the main characters; even those like Colley, who espouse a form of radical socialism.[9] Andy, too, is driven to take revenge on the representatives of a rampant capitalism that has in the past directly benefitted him. Both are caught exactly between the twin poles described by Punter (1999): complicity with the machine of the market, and attempted political exile from its effects. This oscillation between intimacy and distance is also mirrored in the sections of the novel that describe Andy's murders. Strikingly, they are written in the second person, a device which both masks the murderer (by taking the protagonist out of the familiar narrative frame of the first or third person) and strongly suggests complicity with him (because the word "you" implies the existence of an unnamed "I," closely tied to the progression of events). Tellingly, by the end of the novel, Colley's narrative shifts into the second person, forcing the reader into the same uneasy relation to a by now thoroughly compromised man.

Conclusion: The Lessons of Lanark

Post devolution, Scotland has had appreciably more control over its own affairs. For some critical commentators, Craig among them, the new political dispensation would naturally lead to a change in the nature of the country's literary culture:

> [As] the devolutionary period turned into the inter-devolutionary period, and then finally into the post-devolutionary period with the opening of the Scottish parliament in 1999, the radical assertion of authorial control evidenced in works such as *1982 Janine* or *The Trick Is to Keep Breathing* disappeared, along with the amnesiac and dislocated individuals whom they had encased [Craig 2006, 138].

Power has come home, or at least a measure of it. This new power brings to an end the old story of alienated Scots, living an amnesiac life, literally overruled by those more powerful than them. Although Scotland is partly self-determining (and, as I write, is ruled locally by the SNP), it is still nested within a wider political structure that is governed by a different ideology. Post devolution, Scotland's political trajectory still differs from, and is stifled by, supranational political and economic tides that it is simply too weak to resist.

Just before his execution at the end of *A Song of Stone* (1997), Abel Morgan finds himself musing despairingly about the forces that are destroying him.

> The way things happen, just how they operate, includes [...] an encompassing lack of ceremony and respect against which we shore all our pious holdings and most cherished institutions and which we may rail against and oppose for as long as we live, but which [...] sweeps us in the end aside with less effort than metaphor can convey [Banks 1997, 278–9].

How to understand "the way things happen"[10] and how to model the relationship between the player and the played, the powerful and the powerless? It is here that Gray's fiction, and that of Banks, who is in this respect Gray's heir in Scottish literature, is at its most useful and powerful. They craft precisely observed fables of power, and of the complex networks of misplaced exceptionalism, resistance, incorporation, and complicity that always arise, when individuals, groups and societies are enmeshed in structures over which they have little control.

Notes

1. See, for example, Craig (1999), March (2002), and Stevenson (2004).
2. See Mitchell (1996).
3. Burgess, for example, said the novel displayed Gray's talent "deployed to a somewhat juvenile end" (Gray 1984, endpages).
4. See Will Slocombe's essay in this volume.
5. An argument which cannot be usefully applied to writers like Banks and Gray, whose continued commitment to one of those grand narratives (socialism) is clearly demonstrated in their work.
6. This essay follows Macmurray's use of the capitalized "O" for "Other."
7. Even the Scottish Nationalist Party is distinctly left-leaning and the Conservative Party has not been a significant force in Scottish politics for well over twenty years.
8. A staple of Scottish literature, from James Hogg's *The Private Memoirs and Confessions of a Justified Sinner* (1824) onward.
9. As Craig points out, Colley both critiques the free market and avidly consumes its products (2002).
10. Because things never simply happen: Abel's death, the death of his half-sister, and the destruction of their home are the by-products of a wider conflict.

WORKS CITED

Axelrod, Mark. 1995. *The Review of Contemporary Fiction.* Summer 1995. Available: http://www.alasdairgray.co.uk/info.htm.
Banks, Iain. 1984. *The Wasp Factory.* London: Abacus.
_____. 1986. *The Bridge.* London: Abacus.
_____. 1988. *The Player of Games.* London: Orbit.
_____. 1992. *The Crow Road.* London: Abacus.
_____. 1993. *Complicity.* London: Abacus.
_____. 1994. "A Few Notes on the Culture." http://www.vavatch.co.uk/books/banks/cult note.htm.
_____. 1995. *Whit.* London: Abacus.
_____. 1997. *A Song of Stone.* London: Abacus.
_____. 1999. *The Business.* London: Abacus.
_____. 2000. *Look to Windward.* London: Orbit.
_____. 2008. *Matter.* London: Orbit.
_____. 2009. "Author Iain M. Banks: 'Humanity's future is blister-free calluses!'" CNN. http://edition.cnn.com/2008/TECH/space/05/15/iain.banks/.
Craig, Cairns. 1999. *The Modern Scottish Novel: Narrative and the National Imagination.* Edinburgh: Edinburgh University Press.
_____. 2002. *Complicity: A Reader's Guide.* London: Continuum.
_____. 2004. "Beyond Reason — Hume, Seth, Macmurray and Scotland's Postmodernity." In *Scotland in Theory: Reflections on Culture and Literature.* Eleanor Bell and Gavin Miller, eds. Amsterdam: Rodopi, 249–273.
_____. 2005. "Player of Games: Iain (M) Banks, Jean Francois Lyotard and Sublime terror." In *The Contemporary British Novel.* James Acheson and Sarah C.E. Ross, eds. Edinburgh: Edinburgh University Press, 229–238.
_____. 2006. "Devolving the Scottish Novel." In *A Concise Guide to Contemporary British Fiction.* James F. English, ed. Oxford: Blackwell, 121–140.
Devine, T.M., and R.J. Finlay, eds. 1996. *Scotland in the Twentieth Century.* Edinburgh: Edinburgh University Press.
Gifford, Douglas. 2004. "Re-mapping Renaissance in Modern Scottish Literature." In *Beyond Scotland: New Contexts for Twentieth Century Scottish Literature.* Gerard Carruthers, David Goldie and Alastair Renfrew, eds. Amsterdam: Rodopi.
Glass, Rodge. 2008. *Alasdair Gray: A Secretary's Biography.* London: Bloomsbury.
Gray, Alasdair. 1981. *Lanark.* Edinburgh: Canongate.
_____. 1983. *Unlikely Stories, Mostly.* London: Jonathan Cape.
_____. 1984. *1982 Janine.* London: Jonathan Cape.
_____. 1992. *Poor Things.* London: Bloomsbury.
_____. 1992. *Why Scots Should Rule Scotland.* Edinburgh: Canongate.
_____. 1993. *Ten Tales Tall and True.* London: Bloomsbury.
_____. 1994. *A History Maker.* Edinburgh: Canongate.
MacIlvanney, Liam. 2002. "The politics of narrative in the post-war Scottish novel." In *On Modern British Fiction.* Zachary Leader, ed. Oxford: Oxford University Press, 181–208.
Macmurray, John. 1961. *Persons in Relation.* London: Faber and Faber.
March, Cristie. 2002. *Rewriting Scotland.* Manchester: Manchester University Press.
Mitchell, James. "Scotland in the Union 1945–95." In *Scotland in the 20th Century.* T.M. Devine and R.J. Finlay, eds. Edinburgh: Edinburgh University Press.
Nairn, Tom. 2004. "Break-Up: Twenty-Five Years On." In *Scotland in Theory: Reflections on Culture and Literature.* Eleanor Bell and Gavin Miller, eds. Amsterdam: Rodopi.

Punter, David. 1999. "Heart Lands: Contemporary Scottish Gothic." *Gothic Studies*, vol. 1, no. 1, May 1999, 101–118.
Stevenson, Randall. 2004. "A Postmodern Scotland." In *Beyond Scotland: New Contexts for Twentieth Century Scottish Literature*. Gerard Carruthers, David Goldie and Alastair Renfrew, eds. Amsterdam: Rodopi, 209–228.

Lanark and *The Bridge*
Narrating Scotland as Post-Industrial Space
Martyn Colebrook

This essay begins by foregrounding the links between *Lanark* and *The Bridge* and the critical debates regarding "critical utopia" and "narrating Scotland as post-industrial space" before moving into a close reading of both texts. There are two principal reasons for the comparison of *Lanark* and *The Bridge*. Banks has acknowledged that

> certainly of all the books I have written, *The Bridge* is the one that was most influenced by any other single work, definitely *Lanark*—I don't think *The Bridge* would be the work it is at all if it wasn't for *Lanark* [Banks qtd. Robertson 1989, 26–27].

Not only is Gray's novel a predecessor to Banks' text, it has acquired a monumental status. Anthony Burgess states that "[i]t was time Scotland produced a shattering work of fiction in the modern idiom and this is it" (qtd. Gray 1991, x) and Brian Aldiss comments on the "surreal imagination" of Gray who dreamt up "[a] saga of a city where reality is about as reliable as a Salvador Dali watch" (Aldiss qtd. Gray 1991, x). Considering this, *Lanark* can claim status as the catalyst for developments in contemporary Scottish fiction and the departure from straight realism into fantasy and critique that these developments created.

Thematic and Genre Similarities

The Bridge is a tri-partite narrative, beginning with Alex Lennox, a wealthy and ambitious Scotsman whose business interests have succeeded in the thriving economics of Thatcherism. The tension between the politics of the past and present, the struggle and the success, along with the inevitable contradictions that it identifies in respective characters is a consistent theme of Banks' novels. Alex suffers a car accident and while comatose in hospital is replaced in the narrative by John Orr, an (initially) opulent resident of the utopian society known as the Bridge, whose experiences in and out of this society are recorded to form the second strand within the novel. This triple narrative progresses from Alex's days as a student through to the moment when he regains consciousness in the hospital, and is interspersed with episodes from John Orr's life on the Bridge. Combined with this bipartite structure is the intriguingly ambivalent narrative of a wandering barbarian, voiced in a pseudo–Burnsean Scots vernacular that is thuggish and stereotypical but hinting at much greater narrative complexity. Each section of *The Bridge* raises many textual questions of primary and secondary fantastic worlds but provide few definite answers.

On the other hand, Lanark is "a modern vision of Hell" which "tells the interwoven tales of Lanark and Duncan Thaw in the disintegrating cities of Unthank and Glasgow" (Craig 1991, 88). Self-consciously metafictional, saturated with analogues and intertexts, the "text" is structured around four books which are ordered out of sequence and an index of annotated plagiarisms, perhaps forming a history of other people's (failed?) escape attempts. Duncan Thaw is a working-class schoolchild seeking to attend Art School while his counterpart, Lanark, finds himself in Unthank, a city stranded in almost permanent darkness, where creative indolence and the pursuit of leisure are supported by a state welfare system. The pronunciation of Lanark corresponds with Banks' choice of Lennox as a protagonist, while Thaw's rhyming quality with Orr is noted.[1]

The speculative/dystopian nature of Banks' work is reflected by his juxtaposition of different social arrangements such as the highly stratified hierarchy of the Bridge against the militaristic, orderless barbarism occurring in the surrounding rural environment. By contrast, Gray uses a natural landscape in *Lanark* to give a firm geographical context to a city that in economic, political and cultural terms is "subsumed, consumed, and then destroyed by fire and flood. This destruction seems to signify the *death* of the modern industrial city, very like Glasgow, as it fails to find the means to sustain itself" (Smethurst 2000, 139). The clash between the urban and the natural landscape is also reflected in Banks' structuring of *The Bridge* and its different narrative layers, moving between Edinburgh and the Bridge itself.

In a further parallel with *The Bridge*, Gray's novel was marketed in the U.S. as a work of science fiction:

In the USA, the novel was due to be published 6 months or so after the original UK issue, to use whatever promotion had been garnered. As it happened, management changes at Harpers and Row meant that they were issued at the same time, it was marketed as a straight science-fiction novel in the States and disappeared without trace [Lanark Internet Source, n.p.].

This decision and reduction of the marketing space made available in the U.S. further emphasizes the problem of classifying *Lanark* in terms of genre. At one point in the novel the faux authorial figure of Nastler asserts, "*I am not writing* science fiction" (Gray 1991, 497–498), but, as Randall Stevenson points out, "it is really in this recent context of combined science-fiction and postmodernist forms that *Lanark* belongs" (Stevenson 1991, 57).[2]

Canongate published *Lanark* in 1981 in the spirit of incendiary authors delivering charges to the depths of Literary London. This was a novel, according to Gavin Wallace, that "detonated a cultural time-bomb which had been ticking away patiently for years" (Wallace 1992, 4). With its publication, there sparked the new contours of thematic, narratological and ideological concerns that have come to pervade the resurgence in politicized Scottish literature. Recent analyzes of Gray's work have suggested it is both an exploration of and a fantastical removal from the systems of political, economic or emotional entrapment that choose to encapsulate and consume the individual. Any compensation in this text is linked to those who will challenge such structures. Lanark tells his son:

> Of course you changed nothing. This world is only improved by people who do the ordinary jobs and refuse to be bullied. Nobody can persuade owners to share with makers, when makers won't shift for themselves [Gray 1991, 504].

The challenging of such existing structures links with the critical utopia, where the problematizing of oppressive social and economic relationships and subsequent efforts to transgress these create tension.

Contesting Genre

Gray's novel straddles the boundaries of mainstream and "escapist fiction" and it is the use of this term instead of "science fiction" which hints at one of the main themes in *Lanark* and *The Bridge*; namely, the desire to escape from realities into the freedom of fantastic worlds. Cairns Craig argues that the reader is taken "through a fantasy world that is a journey that is part sciencefiction, part medieval romance [...] turning *Lanark* into a compendium of the modern mind — but through many different kinds of society, so that the novel is also a compendium of human histories, and of the societies that humanity has envisaged as the end to which it aspires" (Craig 1991, 93). The suggestion that *Lanark* is a "compendium of the modern mind" connects with Beat Witschi's concept of "psychological interiors," as though the text now becomes a manifestation of internal knowledge and information, observations about the human condition and the conditions in which humanity exists and interacts while ultimately seeking to achieve these states of living.

The resistance to, or subversion of, the conventions of genre are apparent in the work of both novelists. This subversive stance towards the expectations of the reader is highlighted in the way that *Lanark* as an object comes to represent, at one level, avant-garde experimentalism and at another, the manufacturing process that creates the novel:

> A book is not simply a text, it is an object and in this case a substantial object. Its making is not just the genius of the author but of the production processes which connects typesetters in Tennessee with publishers in Edinburgh, readers around the English-speaking world and an author in Glasgow [....] That *Lanark* should emphasise its physical place within the system of production in its way points towards the nature of the culture from which it came and the major theme around which it is set [Smethurst 2000, 91].

The use of fantasy and speculative fiction characteristics allows the authors to bypass and move away from the typically "working class" representations of the city that are to be found in the work of novelists such as James Kelman or Jeff Torrington.[3] The creative space that is Scotland has inspired a range of novelists whose positions could be seen as hostile and oppositional to the dominant literary forms. Writing contemporaneously with Torrington and Gray is the hardline invective of James Kelman whose desire for realism creates a volatile melange of traditional Scots' language and demotic vernacular. This is a complex and provocative combination that further assaults the reader when Kelman "allows that language to fuse together with his own narrative voice so that the distinction between the language of narration and the language of dialogue is dissolved" (Craig 1991, 102). Kelman has managed to find a highly personal and innovative method of solving a problem that has plagued Scottish writers: the distinction between English as a medium for narration and Scots as the form of dialogue. As demonstrated by the character of Sammy Samuels in Kelman's momentous *How Late It Was, How Late* (1994), the freeing of the narrative voice from written English is a moment of lingual solidarity because the narrative occupies a world commensurate with that of its characters.

Post-Industrial Space Into Critical Utopia

Paul Smethurst observes that "[a]lthough the tradition of Scottish urban writing was realistic, it left a dark and heavy legacy for post–Industrial Glasgow" (Smethurst 2000, 125) and by transforming the post-industrial into the postmodern, Gray presents "the power of multinational corporations in postmodernity, as they homogenise and command economic space which then subsumes other spaces: social, political and cultural" (Smethurst 2000, 115). Beat Witschi reveals the ancient Gaelic name for Glasgow, *Gles Chu*, meant "Dear Green Place," and Scottish urban writing has traditionally depicted the corruption of "this dear green place" by the forces of industrialization (Witschi 1991). One suspects that this break by Gray may, (pertinent to Scottish literature), have prompted the migration of other authors into using more fantastic forms and narrative methods such as the examples we have already considered. Moving away from realism, Smethurst suggests that "the imaginative re-creation of Glasgow begins with earlier literary representations of the city through a harsh, gritty realism concentrating on the inescapable and unrelenting hardship of life for the working classes" (Smethurst 2000, 116) but the movement away from such a harsh representation allows for more elaborate, critical and, one may argue, sophisticated opportunities for critique, which are to be found in the "critical utopia," as identified in the work of Tom Moylan. The "critical utopia" is marked by

> the awareness of the limitations of the utopian tradition, so that the texts reject Utopia as blueprint while presenting it as dream. Furthermore the novels dwell on the conflicts between the originary world and the utopian society opposed to it so that the process of social change is more directly articulated. Finally, the novels' focus on the continuing presence of difference and imperfection with utopian society itself and thus render more recognizable and dynamic alternatives [Moylan 1986, 10–11].

The presentation of the utopia as a dream concurs directly with the structure of *The Bridge*, while the meditations on conflicts between separate worlds links the work of Gray and Banks. In his essay, "Culture Theory: Iain M. Banks' 'Culture' as Utopia," Simon Guerrier identifies the inhabitants of the Culture as a "leisured middle-class" (Guerrier 1999, 30) which would be an appropriate marker for the lives that John Orr and Lanark make. However, as Tom Moylan argues, the critical utopia regards utopia as "ambiguous" with "faults, inconsistencies, problems and even denials of the utopian impulse" (Moylan 1986, 12). Indeed he suggests and Guerrier agrees that "the social alternatives offered in the texts are dialogues rather than monologues" (Guerrier 1999, 36). To this effect, "critical utopias keep the utopian impulse alive by challenging it and deconstructing it within [their] very pages" (Guerrier 1999, 36).

The idealistic society in which John Orr attempts to progress and thrive is certainly not all that it seems. Writing on more classical varieties of utopia, Martin Gerber suggests that life in the future haunts the utopian's mind in many different ways. It affords the subject-matter for various kinds of speculation on human destiny, but it also gives rise to a new kind of grammatical statement. In a utopia the narrator first jumps forward into the future in order to be able to look back at the present [Gerber 1973, 81].

The idea of speculation and a possible grammar of utopia raises interesting questions about the status and significance of genre throughout Banks' oeuvre. The idea of a grammar anticipates such a discussion by asserting correctly that genres (or forms) such as the utopia have existing characteristics and conventions by which their classical models are identified and, importantly, by which their contemporary transformations can also be considered. In this context, there are evident temporal shifts in the narrative of *The Bridge* and the deliberate overlaps between scenes make it apparent that rather than the future haunting the present, it is an alternative world which is running concurrently with his own, derived from the psyche of Alex Lennox. In this respect, Guerrier and Moylan's respective analyzes seem to diagnose the acute problems inherent in trying to classify Banks' fiction and thus the genres in which he operates, namely his ability to use elements of different genres but insufficient amounts to allow a conclusive and comprehensive analysis that comfortably locates his work. Highlighting his particular penchant for the speculative and, according to Ian Bell, the influence of the European literary tradition in his work, there is a clear indication that Banks' technique could feasibly be what Gerber notes as "the technique of fantastic realism" (Gerber 1973, 87).

From Utopia Into the Postmodern

According to David Armstrong in his unpublished thesis, *Gestures Towards a Better Place: Approaches to Contemporary British Fiction*, Banks is implementing his own literary allusions with the third narrative in *The Bridge*, featuring the barbarian and the familiar, a sequence that Armstrong interprets as rendering "the culturally elevated form of epic poem into the ramblings of ordinary description" (Armstrong 1999, 70). This connects with Martin Horskotte who suggests that

> the period of postmodernism questions the traditional value judgements of literary critics and stimulates their discussion concerning the integration of "lower" forms of literature into the canon. Postmodern texts make use of genre conventions to fuse several genres and to level the differences between them. This "closing of the gap" between disparate genres and the juxtaposition of "low" and "high" forms of literature shows a change that also concerns the fantastic. In

many postmodern novels, the conventions of the fantastic are used in conjunction with genres like the historical novel or with postmodern literary techniques [Horstkotte 2004, 10].

Despite Banks' apparent determination to operate firmly between realism and fantasy, he employs Scots dialect and phonetics for the purposes of establishing a sense of place to the narrative by using the pseudo-comic figure of the barbarian.

When *The Bridge* and *Lanark* are compared further, there are distinct structural similarities: both novels have multiple narrators and overlapping narratives and there is strong thematic convergence through the representation of the cities and post-industrial spaces. The protagonists' personality traits demonstrate mutual feelings of social alienation from the society around them and at the conclusion of each novel there are moments of self-discovery or revelation. Both texts trespass on the boundaries between mainstream and speculative fiction and both transgress the conventional narrative forms employed by realist novels. In the case of Alasdair Gray he places each "book" in a non-sequential or non-chronological order, meaning both authors signal an immediate intent to subvert the familiar paradigms of time and to transgress the usual flow of a linear text. Each narrative deals with a society that offers support for its inhabitants through an advanced social welfare system. Similarly each novel has two male protagonists whose respected narratives are interwoven throughout; Duncan Thaw and Lanark in Gray's novel, and Alex Lennox and John Orr in Banks' novel.

Commenting on the structure of *Lanark*, Craig suggests that "Duncan can only see history as like the Glasgow in which he is trapped [as] an infinitely diseased worm without head or tail, beginning or end" (Craig 1991, 95). This absence of separation and duality, the identification of a body without head or tail echoes the status of the Bridge itself with the connections to land at either end often alluded to but only revealed towards the conclusion of narrative. Later, Craig pronounces that

> Thaw and Lanark divide between them the possibilities only so that they live in a nightmare world in which every escape route that they take leads straight into the maw of another monstrous head on the hydra of a system in which one is either the exploiter or the exploited, in which one is almost inevitably, both at the same time [Craig 1991, 94].

This persistent duality, the living in a "nightmare world" links *Lanark* and *The Bridge* as texts aiming to represent Scotland before and after, retaining the dark industrial novel but venturing forth into a more fantastical style in order to challenge the imaginations of the reader.

In Paul Smethurst's terms *Lanark* and *The Bridge* depict the post-industrial city as a "postmodern chronotope," as identified in his study, *The Postmodern Chronotope* (2000), which addresses spatial and temporal readings of contemporary fiction. Smethurst claims that "a chronotope is a time-space in which the conscious mind frames and organizes the real, but it can also be the time-space where it disorganises and re-presents the real" (Smethurst 2000, 5) and that it functions as "an attempt to organise and articulate the main features of the shift in time-space relations that gives rise to postmodern ways of seeing" (Smethurst 2000, 6). With this in mind, both Gray and Banks are appropriating their respective geographical locales in order to assert a re-imagination of these fantastic spaces yet they are adopting different techniques to achieve this, methods of representation which are expressed through a striking variety of play using different forms of narrative and different genres. Whereas Gray borrows from Blake and Dante the idea of connecting the "hell" of contemporary life with other religious and imagined spaces that might not only transcend, but also help transform them (Smethurst 2000). Banks offers his own connections between contemporary life and the imagination using the world of the Bridge as the product of a comatose mind, that of Alex Lennox as he recovers from a car accident that occurs at the beginning of the novel. In the case of both texts, "the urban spaces of Scotland are transformed and extended into an extravagant literary 'park': a representational space in which the inhabitants of [Scotland] might take their imaginations for a walk" (Smethurst 2000, 116).

Post-Industrial Landscape of the Bridge

The feeling of a "representational space" and departure into this "imagination" is reflected on the first page when Alex's narration begins moments after his car crash, drawing the reader into a disorienting internal stream of consciousness:

> Trapped. Crushed. Weight coming from all directions, entangled in the wreckage (you have to become one with the machine). Please no fire, no fire. Shit. This hurts. Bloody bridge; own fault (yes, bloody bridge, right colour; see the bridge, see the man drive the car, see the man not see the other car, see the big CRASH, see the bone-broken man bleed; blood colour of the bridge. Oh well own fault. Idiot). Please no fire. Blood red. Red blood. See the man bleed, see the car leak; radiator red, blood red, blood like red oil. Pump still working — shit, I said *shit* this hurts — pump still working but the fluid leaking out all over the fucking place [Banks 1990, 11].

The idea of "leakage" features as a narrative convention, with material leaking from the convergent narratives. "Entangled in the wreckage" may refer not just to the car accident, but also the wreckage of the text and the Bridge itself as both appear to disintegrate at different points in the novel. The formal conventions of grammar and language are omitted from this passage of text and later they move into Scottish vernacular; the Bridge is attacked by forces from outside and similarly the different narratives seem to collapse under the weight of textual pressures. Alex observes, "You have to become one with the machine," which recurs in different forms throughout *The Bridge*. The machine represents a multitude of relationships within the text: his dependency on the hospital equipment as he exists in the comfort and the totality of the Bridge and its spectral omnipresence that haunts the inhabitants as well as his economic support from the Capitalist machine that ensure his middle-class lifestyle before the car crash. Alex's alter ego, John Orr, endures numerous difficulties when he tries to escape the confines of the Bridge, suggesting that the positioning of the Bridge makes it the novel's centrality.

Shortly after the beginning of *The Bridge*, Banks playfully imitates the plagiarisms used by Gray to emphasize both the self-conscious referentiality of the narrative and his own knowing ludic fictional practice. As Alex Lennox's car crashes, he verges on immersion in a coma, the environment around him merging into a cinematic sequence:

> It's stopped. The scene whitens, holes appear in it; a film burning through (fire!), trapped in the gate (jaguar in the gate?); stopped, the scene melts, the seen scene disintegrates (see the seen scene disintegrate); nothing stands too close to enquiry. White screen left.
> Pain. Circle of pain on chest. Like a brand, a circular impression (am I a figure on a stamp, postmarked? A piece of parchment embossed with "From the library of ,,,,,,,,,," (Please complete):
> (a) God, Esq
> (b) Nature (Mrs)
> (c) C. Darwin & Sons
> (d) K. Marx plc
> (e) all of the above.) [Banks 1990, 12].

Playing with sources has a considerable resonance in Scottish literature where there is "a questionable disposition to separate a narrative from a wider national context: a work from a 'corpus' [...] intimately connected with the preservation and correct transmission of a manuscript" (Wright 2007, 74). The circle is significant, not just because of its relationship to the title of the manuscript that inspired *The Bridge* (entitled *O*), but also for the circular nature of the narrative. This begins with Alex's monologue just after the car accident and culminates 277 pages later with his waking up from the coma with Andrea Cramond, his long-term lover from university, by his beside.

The suggestion of a film burning through itself and a scene disintegrating immediately highlights an awareness of the multiplicity of media that Banks perceives as being at his disposal. Repeated punning on the "seen/scene" demonstrates an open engagement with the novelistic antecedents of this text: the metafictional novel that willingly displays its own part in the creative process. Identifying the "stamp" on the "piece of parchment" and its location in a relevant "library" highlights the composition of *The Bridge* as being similar to a palimpsest, fragmentary in its structures as a coherent narrative and brazen in its intertexts and references. This is also an index of references that indicates potential sources for Banks' writing and political pronouncements, comparable with the way Gray establishes with his own index of plagiarisms as part of the respective epilogue in *Lanark*.

The "piece of parchment" is also suggestive of Orr's later dreams, which frequently take the form of fragmented scenes from mythology and literature and are usually framed in environments that are specific to a particular style of architecture or geographical feature that is drawn from the influences of Alex's geological work.

The circle itself also echoes the narrative logic Banks employs and is a return to his previous novel, *Walking on Glass* (1985), which employed the same technique but with much less success. That "nothing stands too close to enquiry" suggests a distancing process between observer and object, a view of the outside when there is a partition between the seer and seen, a deliberate decision on the part of the author to ensure the reader can see the symbols and metaphors but may not be entirely certain as to how they can be understood, interpreted or used in their understanding of the text. The language imitates the opening of *Walking on Glass* which also uses a theatrical/revelatory tone to reveal the narrative structure, foundations and overarching technique that Banks will use throughout the novel.

As well as being a patient, John Orr is also a wealthy member of the higher social strata on the Bridge. In the early stages of his narrative, Orr reveals that his allowance is principally spent "things which amuse me or which I find beautiful; I visit galleries, I go to the theatre, concerts, the cinema; I read" (Banks 1990, 35). Such pursuits are those of an individual who is sufficiently free from the obligations of work to patronize the artistic and cultural facilities offered by a moneyed society. Further parallels can be made with the character of Lanark who, when asked how he occupies himself, states, "I walk and visit libraries and cinemas. When short of money I go to the security place. But most of the time I watch the sky from the balcony" (Gray 1991, 5).

The contrasts in fortune for each character are important when examining the John Orr's role within the society of the Bridge. Orr's long-term project involves attempting to discover historical documents that will offer information about the Bridge and avoiding the hypnosis that Dr. Joyce offers him in order to cure his amnesia. However, early in the novel, the welcoming and cultural freedom of the Bridge is swiftly revoked. Orr's determination to reach the lost library results in his demotion to U7, "where the ordinary workers live" (Banks 1990, 134), a decision that is authorized by Dr. Joyce. Following this, Orr discovers that he is excluded from his regular haunts and institutions and forced to wear the uniform usually given to the workers who occupy the lower orders in the bridge.

Both Banks and Gray's choice of a protagonist with artistic ambitions is significant because of the potential to realize this expression of the post-industrial landscape and express it through the medium of their work. In the case of John Orr, he posits himself as a historian and as Sludden announces in *Lanark*, it is their function which poses the greatest threat to the Utopian or dystopian State: "[a]n artist doesn't tell people things, he expresses himself. If the self is unusual, his work shocks or excites people. Anyway, it forces his personality on them" (Gray 1991, 6). With regard to *The Bridge*, this is a vital contribution to John Orr being demoted because his status as a historian gives him the opportunity to offer a revision of the accepted and standard history ascribed to the Bridge, the narrative employed by the dominant order to prevent its occupants questioning the different practices and strata which are currently used to pacify the citizens.

The dystopian aspect of the Bridge's social construction is demonstrated during a conversation between John Orr and his friend, Engineer Brooke. An unauthorized fly-past occurs, involving aircraft that do not have a connection with the Bridge or its authorities and this starts a debate about the acceptability of these actions. Brooke claims that it is not his decision to "approve or disapprove" (Banks 1990, 48) but when Orr enquires as to whether there are any laws against it, Brooke responds, "There are no laws to *permit* it, Orr, that's the point. Good grief man, you can't have people going off and doing things just because they think something up. You have to have a ... a framework" (Banks 1990, 48). Such emphasis on structure and framework not only reflects the way that the rigid structure of the bridge is embodied in its social values, and the methods of control that ensure the populace do not have the opportunity to think or act independently. The Bridge represents a totalitarian society that that will take care of its occupants' needs but does so by removing their capacity for question or dissent. This is essentially an endorsement for "freedom from responsibility" politics that manifests itself as a state-controlled society where one finds it difficult to generate opposition because a recorded statement of laws does not exist. Therefore, if ideas do not exist in law then they cannot exist in the minds of the populace.

Smethurst observes that "[i]n literature, the modern 'hero' in the city is depicted as a shadowy figure, lonely and alienated, and failing to bond with others in a seemingly unknowable mass of individuals" (Smethurst 2000, 133) and this correlates with the status of Thaw, Lanark and Orr in their respective societies. Orr's demotion and comparable estrangement from the societal values shared by his colleagues emphasizes this sense of alienation while Lanark and Thaw are driven respectively to suicide and escape in order to overcome their disillusionment with the society in which they have become trapped. Furthermore, Smethurst argues that

> the demise of community in this once great industrial city is presented partly as social realism, or at least that sub-genre of social realism in which the working class artist fails both to climb out of his class and to stay in it. He [Thaw] fails to bond in his community, becomes alienated both as an individual and an artist, and finally commits suicide [Smethurst 2000, 122].

Thus "as Modernity created the alienated individual soul, figured here in the failing artist/writer, postmodernity creates a whole alienated place" (Smethurst 2000, 119). Such persistent tensions between the protagonist and the utopian state function as the imperative which creates the "critical" aspect, the potential for individual revolution and transgression.

The image of a whole place in alienation recurs in *The Bridge* through the depiction of Alex's home in Edinburgh, the "industrial heartland," "already failing, silting up with cheap fat, starved of energy, clogging and clotting and thickening and threatened" (Banks 1990, 101). He remembers the lofts "tall, misshapen, made of corrugated iron painted black" (Banks 1990, 101). The use of "clogging, thickening, threatened and clotting" suggests an artery at the point of implosion, a lifeline or channel destroyed by the consumption of low-grade food and which, like the body it supports, is declining into a bloated, lethargic obesity. This environment has bred and prepared Alex for his future prosperity, a locale and people that later he will admit to becoming ashamed of. However, his neglect to return works as a representation of the educated and aspiring middle-class who abandoned their roots and migrated South in order to improve, while their relatives were systematically cut adrift, trapped in the North. For Alex, Edinburgh is a "village within the city in its not-yet-quaint decrepitude, a stark volcanic remnant" (Banks 1990, 103). There is a resonance of memory, history, stark geographical evolution, the use of "real" emphasizes this desire for authenticity, while "crags" and "corrugations" have a particularly harsh tone. This city in transition, reinforced by the "not-yet-quaint decrepitude" of Edinburgh, suggests that the pervasive nostalgia and memory associated with historical commemorations of industrial dominance is still absent from this temporary home. Making the connection with the politicization of the Gothic through its response to industrialization, Catherine Spooner argues that "[t]he past chokes the present, prevents progress" (Spooner 2006, 18) and in this respect the decaying body of industrial heartland suggests a symbol of the future that Banks sees as the industrial age becomes more reliant upon technology in place of human labor.

This can be supported further when considering the characterization of the Bridge, which is portrayed as "sloping sides rise, russet-red and ribbed from the granite-plinthed feet in the sea" (Banks 1990, 154), containing a hospital complex formed "like an energetically growing tumour" (Banks 1990, 154) and shops that are sited "like brittle hernias popping out between immense collections of muscles" (Banks 1990, 154). Banks portrayal of the Bridge renders it as an illness-ridden body, paralleling the links with Alex's body lying comatose in the hospital and the metaphor of the body politic. The Bridge would appear to represent the physical structure of a human body, with John Orr's initial social milieu symbolizing the mind with its rarefied existence and artistic sensibilities.

Further evidence of the post-industrial can be seen between the land that exists at both ends of the Bridge, known as the City and the Kingdom. These two titles highlight the Bridge as a link between a Capitalist, labor-intensive sphere and the fantasy-inspiring, leisure-oriented society. In this respect, the Bridge exists in a functional capacity and so offers an appropriate link between the two states, as demonstrated by the marked contrast with Orr's aestheticism that is found when he ventures below his own level. The indulgence in debauchery and licentious behavior that he partakes of suggests that the dichotomy between different layers of the bridge represents a symbol of his psyche, with two different levels of pleasure fighting for dominance.

Similarly to the decaying body in post-industrial decline, the monstrous Hell envisaged by Gray is the postmodern city's relationship to the illogic of late Capitalism, "industrial Glasgow becomes a monster" (Smethurst 2000, 120), a Leviathan whose rapacious appetite is the market itself. The multinational corporations who seek to consume Glasgow or Unthank see it as being a substantial energy grab, "a conspiracy which owns and manipulates everything for profit" (Smethurst 2000, 120) and when multinational corporations subsume the unproductive space of Glasgow, "Unthank, the fantastic vision of post-industrial Glasgow set in the near future, is eventually swallowed *en bloc* by a multinational economic and political conspiracy: Gray's Leviathan" (Smethurst 2000, 120). In opposition to this highly mechanized, controlled and Capitalist society is the Intercalendrical Zone, the name itself highlighting the rejection of conventional considerations of time and chronology, its status of being between calendars and thus in the space where such formal structures cannot extend to. As Lanark enters here, he experiences a sense of relief, a sense of escape from "the material of time ... respect for the decimal hour" (Gray 1991, 416) and he is no longer trapped within rigid and controlling boundaries.

This sense of relief permeates the narrative when Lennox makes the decision to move out of the coma at the conclusion of *The Bridge*. Similarly, he releases a burden but he is moving back into a world where the constraints exist. One suspects at this point, Banks' selection of a different conclusion may be suggesting that this moment of relief in *Lanark* is not so much optimism as temporary sanctuary from the realities Gray later comes to portray: the apocalyptic end and rebirth of Unthank, and the political and Capitalistic machinations which lead to Unthank's demise. Banks' conclusion presents a far less idealistic resolution to the reimagination of Scotland, offering less a cynical assessment but a more socially responsible conclusion by ensuring Alex/Orr rejects the status of his terminal condition, a life without commitment or accountability and makes his way back from the coma into the world from which he seemingly departed. Unthank could be read as a terminal afterlife for Thaw as the Bridge so nearly is for Alex Lennox; so that *The Bridge* is a kind of extension of, or reading of, the debate raised by *Lanark*.

Conclusion

Smethurst argues that "[t]he object of all of this literary and geographical play is to create a rich contemporary identity for Glasgow that incorporates the past, but does not attempt to recapture or dwell on it" (Smethurst 2000, 116) and the reimagination by Banks raises questions about whether it functions as progression or critique. With these two opposing functions it becomes more apparent that whereas *The Bridge* is a critical utopia, *Lanark* is "a heterotopia": "a city constructed of oddly connected, aberrant, chaotic and outlandish chronotopes" (Smethurst 2000, 117). Martin Gerber suggests that

> in modern utopias, the need for organization has become stronger than ever before [....] Therefore a modern utopia cannot be a state in which man would feel naturally happy as he might in an arcadian one. He is hemmed in on every side. The utopian economic organization may be perfect, but the individual may not be satisfied with his political status. If he is tempted to revolt, the whole utopian structure is in danger. The most admirably constructed utopia fails to convince if we are not led to believe that the danger of revolt is excluded [Gerber 1973, 68].

The distinction between arcadia and utopia is important here. Defining "arcadia" as "any real or imaginary place offering peace and simplicity" (Schwarz

1996, 657) contrasts usefully with the utopian ideal. Although both "places" are cultural products designed to reflect the desires and wishes of their inhabitants, the difference between the two is vital. The arcadia represents an Elysium for its inhabitants, free from conflict, oppression, deprivation or other social problems whereas the modern utopia suggests a society in which persistent restrictions affect the conditions in which the individual is placed.

The status of the utopia as a "no place" indicates how attempts by its inhabitants to represent it in different artistic media pose a threat to the subsequent stability and control of the ruling orders and it is significant that when Duncan Thaw begins repeatedly to capture Glasgow's tenements and streets in pictorial form, Lanark escapes from Unthank and find himself located in the Institute, a sinister, encapsulating building where heat and light are generated from the bodies of the terminally ill patients. The shift from dark to light may suggest progression but this is tempered by the literally body-intensive Capital system used to power the Institute, where the inmates and patients are used to generate energy and heat. As one protagonist begins to achieve their artistic output, the other character escapes his own "hell" but finds the sanctuary to be equally problematic.

Gray places responsibility on the society from which the individual is produced whereas Banks adopts a contrasting position by emphasizing the role of the individual in changing the society around them, or at least making an attempt to extricate themselves from this society. Craig argues that the existing conditions do not offer reasons for the problems, they just offer their existence without any hope for solution, whereas the conclusion to *The Bridge* offers a far more optimistic vision, the protagonist rejecting the opportunity to remain absolved of responsibility and choosing to return to life, the problematic aspect of this being that although Banks uses Lennox as a potential vehicle for social change or adjustment, the reader is never informed of the outcome of this until *Complicity* (1993), where the Lennox re-appears as the protagonist.

The distinction between the conclusions which Gray and Banks draw and the success of both novelists in their representation of the post-industrial is emphasized by their contrasting positions as members of this production process: Banks has achieved populist, commercial success through publication and marketability whereas Gray's text emerged from the minor, eccentric Canongate press, but for both writers there is a talent for politicization, putting hard edges onto our postmodern soft cities. This is just one of the persistent debates about the relationship between Banks and his contemporaries: how much "value" or "significance" is attached to a text which addresses important concerns such as the post-industrial (which are often considered to be the territory for more "literary" authors) *and* achieves substantial critical success in the process.

Notes

1. Orr also representing a pun on the word "or"/"ore" which would correspond with the blurring of the identities and the geological puns that are embedded within *The Bridge*.
2. The same combination of science fiction and postmodernist form has come to characterise Banks' oeuvre too.
3. The latter's *Swing Hammer Swing* (1992) being greeted with acclaim for its fierce portrayal of the Gorbals area of Glasgow.

Works Cited

Armstrong, David. 1999. *Gestures Towards a Better Place: Approaches to Contemporary British Fiction*. Unpublished doctoral dissertation, De Montforte University.
Banks, Iain. 1985. *Walking on Glass*. London: Abacus.
_____. 1990 [1986]. *The Bridge*. London: Abacus.
_____. 1993. *Complicity*. London: Abacus.
Burgess, Anthony. 1984. *Ninety-nine Novels: The Best in English Since 1939*. London: Alison and Busby.
Craig, Cairns. 1991. "Going Down to Hell Is Easy: *Lanark*, Realism and the Limits of the Imagination." In *The Arts of Alasdair Gray*. Robert Crawford and Thom Nairn, eds. Edinburgh: Edinburgh University Press, 90–107.
_____. 1993. "Resisting Arrest: James Kelman." In *The Scottish Novel since the Seventies: New Visions, Old Dreams*. Gavin Wallace and Randall Stevenson, eds. Edinburgh: Edinburgh University Press, 99–114.
Galloway, Janice. 2002. "Introduction: Something to Say." In Alasdair Gray, 1985 [2002], *Lanark: A Life in Four Books*. Edinburgh: Canongate, ix-xvi.
Gerber, Richard. 1973 [1955]. *Utopian Fantasy*. London: Routledge and Kegan Paul.
Gray, Alasdair. 1981 [1985]. *Lanark: A Life in Four Books*. Edinburgh: Canongate.
_____. 2002 [1981]. *Lanark: A Life in Four Books*. Edinburgh: Canongate.
Guerrier, Simon. 1999. "Culture Theory: Iain M. Banks' 'Culture as Utopia.'" *Foundation: The International Review of Science Fiction*, vol. 28, no. 76, 28–38.
Horstkotte, Martin. 2004. *The Postmodern Fantastic in Contemporary British Fiction*. Dusseldorf: Wissenschaftlicher Verlag Trier.
Kelman, James. 1994. *How Late It Was, How Late*. London: Secker & Warburg.
Lanark Internet Source. N.d. *Lanark: A Life in 4 Books*. http://www.lanark1982.co.uk/lanark.html. Accessed 14 February 2012.
"Lanark 1982: An unofficial Alasdair Gray Site." 2006. http://www.lanark1982.co.uk/home.html.
Moylan, Tom. 1986. *Demand the Impossible — Science Fiction and the Utopian Imagination*. London: Methuen.
Robertson, James. December 1989/January 1990. "Bridging Styles: A conversation with Iain Banks." *Radical Scotland* (42), 26–27.
Schwarz, Catherine, ed. 1993. *The Chambers Dictionary*. Edinburgh: Chambers.
Smethurst, Paul. 2000. *The Postmodern Chronotope: Reading Space and Time in Contemporary Fiction*. Atlanta: Editions Rodopi.
Spooner, Catherine. 2006. *Contemporary Gothic*. London: Reaktion.
Stevenson, Randall. 1991. "Alasdair Gray and the Postmodern." In *The Arts of Alasdair Gray*. Robert Crawford and Thom Nairn, eds. Edinburgh: Edinburgh University Press, 48–63.

Torrington, Jeff. 1992. *Swing Hammer Swing*. London: Secker and Warburg.
Wallace, Gavin. 1993. "Introduction." In *The Scottish Novel Since the Seventies: New Visions, Old Dreams*. Gavin Wallace and Randall Stevenson, eds. Edinburgh: Edinburgh University Press, 1–7.
Witschi, Beat. 1991. *Scottish Studies: Glasgow Urban Writing and Postmodernism*. Frankfurt: Peter Lang.
Wright, Angela. 2007. "Scottish Gothic." *The Routledge Companion to the Gothic*. Catherine Spooner and Emma McEvoy, eds. Abingdon: Routledge, 73–82.

II. GEOGRAPHIES

"I have never been to Nasqueron"
A Geographer Reads Banks
JAMES KNEALE

Iain Banks' Geographical Imagination

I wish to begin by confessing two things. The first — that I have never been to the gas giant Nasqueron — I will explain in a moment. The second is that I am a geographer, which inevitably affects the way that I approach literature. This essay sets out to explore what it means to read "as a geographer," with an eye to space, place, landscape and so on. This can be done in two ways. On the one hand I want to suggest that thinking about space can develop new critical insights into Iain Banks' fiction; on the other hand, thinking about literature can also help us theorize the representation and experience of space in useful ways. This essay is therefore an opportunity to consider some of the ways in which we might approach Banks as a writer with a particular "geographical imagination."

In his classic *Sociological Imagination* Charles Wright Mills argued that when we think of the relationship between our own biographies and wider histories of social change we develop a "sociological imagination" (1959). We put ourselves and others in a wider context ("the family" or "class") while simultaneously grounding those abstract sociological elements in the messy details of real lives and social relations. Similarly it is possible to talk of a geographical imagination, the way that people locate themselves in space, see landscapes, or deal with different scales from the global to the local. This essay explores the geographical imagination that seems to inform Iain Banks' writing, a geographical imagination that seems subtle, sophisticated and critical.

The remainder of this essay is divided into five sections. The first explores the relationship between space and literature, rejecting approaches that take the "setting" of a text as its focus, and moving on in the second section to consider recent attempts to re-theorize the nature of space in geography. The third suggests that considering space in terms of networks and narratives allows for a more sophisticated understanding of Banks' work, as well as helping us to draw upon Banks' fiction to think about space. The fourth thinks about the way that Banks goes about "worldbuilding," fabricating (science) fictional places that we know do not exist, or which cannot be visited, and the fifth takes a more detailed exploration of one of his most interesting recent science fiction novels, *The Algebraist* (2004). This novel is discussed throughout the essay, but while I spend more time on this novel than any other, I will also be drawing on a wide selection of Banks' Culture and non–Culture science fiction novels, as well as his "mainstream" texts.[1] *The Algebraist* is a richly suggestive novel for a geographer to read, because Nasqueron (the gas-giant that is one of its key concerns) presents us with an interesting example of science fiction worldbuilding.

Space and Literature

When we think of the relationship between space and literature, we are normally putting the former in the service of the latter, using space as a critical tool with which to analyze literature. This is usually done with reference to real places or an author's experience of real places (or both). The idea of "setting" is enormously influential here, informing much of the critical writing on representations of space and place, as well as driving literary tourism. Writing about Thomas Hardy's Wessex, James Joyce's Dublin or Virginia Woolf's London seems to require studying the maps, walking the ground, and generally getting to know the territory. Archival and biographical research fills out the historical dimension, tracing the presence of authors in landscapes they have represented.

Despite the appeal of this work, recent research on textual space has developed a critical alternative, drawing on recent re-theorizations of space by geographers. Sheila Hones, for example, argues that the idea of setting rests on three erroneous assumptions. Firstly, that is possible to make a simple distinction between real and fictional places, as if they do not shape each other in profound ways, and as if only one of them is "textual." Secondly, that a real geography is "a collection of named places that are internally coherent and totally knowable" (Hones 2005, 1), when in fact many geographers now argue that spaces are multiple, constantly changing, shaped in relation to other places and by internal contradictions. And finally, that the real world possesses a "definitive and self-evident geography which is more authoritative than the geography of the text" so that an apparently concrete world is used to anchor the complexities of a text that is always open to other readings (Hones 2005, 1). Seen from this perspective, "setting" only allows the simplest of stories to be told about the relationship between literature and space. It resembles Franco Moretti's strategy of locating fictional events on maps, taking the latter as neutral and objective records (1998); as David Harvey notes, "Moretti's cartographic banalities" reduce spatiality to a meaningless cipher (Harvey 2001, 86, fn10). Instead, Harvey suggests, we must recognize the *construction of space* as well as of fiction, and the dialectical relationship between the two: "Balzac actively constructs a map of the city's terrain.... He is his own cartographer" (Harvey 2001, 66).

Representations of place can never "capture" either real places *or* our subjective experiences of them (Brosseau, 1994). Perhaps for this reason, John Barrell's important essay on the geographies of Hardy's Wessex begins with the words "I have never been to Dorset":

> I make that confession, not to disqualify myself from writing this essay, but to indicate at the outset the sort of essay it will not be. It will not be concerned with the identification of place in the Wessex novels with their possible originals in Dorset and the neighbouring counties [Barrell 1982, 347].

Barrell's analysis considers the different ways in which space and place are represented in these novels, and the place of these representations within their narratives; he does *not* compare "representation" and "reality." The resulting essay is thought-provoking, but this argument is even more interesting when the referent is not a real place, like "Dorset," but a place that does not or cannot exist.

So in the spirit of Barrell's confession, I must admit that I have never been to Nasqueron, the gas-giant planet which is central to Banks' *The Algebraist*. David Samuelson notes that "all writers of fiction hypothesize virtual interactions of invented entities. Like science and engineering, however, SF makes plausible models of beings, places and times nobody has yet encountered" (Samuelson 1993, 192). Science fiction is "fiction squared," then, because it represents things that are themselves explicitly fictitious (Suvin 1979, 117). Banks' essay "A few notes on the Culture" begins with the words "Firstly, and most importantly: the Culture doesn't really exist. It's only a story. It only exists in my mind and the minds of the people who've read about it" (Banks 1994a, n.p.). Consequently a textual place like Nasqueron cannot be regarded as a copy — distorted or faithful — of some real-world equivalent. So what can we make of a geographical description like the following?

> They were floating in a small eddy around a gentle ammonia upwell the diameter of a small planet, about two hundred klicks down from the cloud tops [Banks 2004, 200].

Though this sentence starts off looking like straightforward description, by the time the reader has finished with it questions of scale, a lack of fixed references, and immersion in a strange and hostile environment have all contributed to a feeling of "cognitive estrangement." Of course even the most fantastical setting must contain elements that are familiar to author and reader — we might read Nasqueron as a cousin of Jupiter, for example — but visiting a real gas-giant is just as impossible as visiting a fictional one, or at least it is at the moment of writing. All Banks and his readers have to go on, as I will explain later, are representations of Jupiter, and these are just other texts.

If it is not easy to imagine these more fantastic settings, perhaps we might draw on Banks' biography to analyze his fictional places? We might start with Banks' home in Fife, for example, taking Edinburgh Castle and Old Town, or the Forth Railway Bridge, as the possible inspiration for all the enormous and labyrinthine buildings, engineering structures and vehicles in his science fiction: the giant's castle-city of *Feersum Enjinn* (1994b) or the vast ships of *Consider Phlebas* (1987) and *Use of Weapons* (1990). We know that the Bridge lends its geography to *The Bridge* (1986), though this is more than a "setting," as Lucie Armitt has demonstrated in her reading of this "architectural narrative" (1996, 103–111). However it is not *necessary* to know Banks' biography when reading his fictions; to suggest otherwise would mean that there is only one way to read a text — the expert's way.

More importantly, however, this analytical strategy must confront the problem that the events of Banks' life, and his experiences of place, are not simple facts that can be faithfully transcribed. We cannot treat one text (a novel) as open to interpretation, while treating another (his biography) as simple truth. Banks might not even be the most reliable narrator of his *own* life, in fact. I do not agree with Chris Brown's suggestion that Banks has not received much critical attention because of "the self-consciousness of [his] work, which makes it a less suitable subject for speculation" (Brown 2001, fn15, 631). Banks *does* seem to have clear intentions for his fictions, but he is also extraordinarily playful with them. We might note, for example, that Bascule, one of the protagonists of *Feersum Enjinn*, shares his name with another kind of bridge (ones with sections that can be raised, like London's Tower Bridge), and see this as another sign of Banks' interest in engineering; but does it mean anything in the context of the novel, or is it just an interesting name?

Spaces (real and fictional) are texts; multiple, contradictory, and mutable. So are their authors. We cannot ground our interpretation of fictional spaces by appealing to the real world or to any other conveniently fixed standpoints. We can, however, think differently about space.

Rethinking Space

Geographers are increasingly critical of the idea that space is a neutral or natural backdrop, a setting or container, something simply "there." In *For Space* the geographer Doreen Massey suggests three alternative propositions about the nature of space (2005).[2] Firstly, *space is relational*—it is not anything in itself but derives its apparently natural characteristics from its relations with other places, people and things. Secondly, and as a consequence of this, space is *multiple and heterogeneous*. Places contain different elements and possibilities, can be experienced in many different ways, and are contested by clashing forms of social difference. Finally, space is *in process*, not closed and fixed. The agonistic relations between and within places ensure that their futures are always open. This is a significant critique of the prevailing assumption that change can only come with time and history, something Massey is determined to challenge.

Banks' geographical imagination seems to encompass these ideas. In *The Crow Road* (1992), the town of Gallanach is described in some detail and clearly serves as a distinctive textual place (perhaps even a "setting"). Yet it is not a *singular* one. Ashley takes Prentice to the old docks to show him something he has always thought of as "a wee lump of ground," but which is, she tells him, "the Ballast-Mound, the World-Hill" (Banks 1992, 74). The mound is formed of the ballast that ships took from the starting-points of their journeys; Ashley's grandfather told her "there's aw ra world unner yon turp a grass" and as a kid she used to think "I was sitting on rocks that had once been a bit of China or Brazil, or Australia or America..." While Banks may only be interested in the way this prompts Prentice to think of his Uncle Rory, "our family connection to the rest of the globe" (Banks 1992, 75), it also encourages the geographer-reader to consider the way in which even the most ordinary landscapes are formed by their connections with some places and their contrast with others. Banks' description also suggests that the ballast mounds of distant ports contain earth from Gallanach (though some of this earth might itself be from somewhere else). The ballast mounds are hybrid places, materializing relations between a network of specific places, and, in so doing, Gallanach is a relational space.

Gallanach is also multiple, heterogeneous and changing. Along with its relations to the outside world it has also been shaped by antagonisms within the town, partly to do with class (a key element of the novel's plot). Banks' fictions do seem to associate change with life, if not progress. During a discussion of the afterlife in *Look to Windward* (2000) a party-goer suggests that nothing can happen in heaven because "if something happens, in fact if something *can* happen, then it doesn't represent eternity. Our lives are about development, mutation and the possibility of change; that is almost a definition of what life is: change" (Banks 2000, 203). Similarly, in *Feersum Enjinn* Mr. Zoliparias tells Bascule, one of the narrators, that the Fastness is an admission of defeat, a waiting for death, because it is a retreat into stasis: Bascule records this in his unique vernacular as "2 liv is 2 moov" (Banks 1994b, 21). It is possible to read the movements of Bascule and the other protagonists of *Feersum Enjinn* as attempts to shake the Fastness, with its rigid hierarchies and stalemated war, into a new kind of life that will be able to face up to the Encroachment (in fact the solution to this problem also involves producing a new kind of mobility). Their movements through different spaces transform these key characters; mobility can lead to metamorphosis.

We are used to associating change with time and history, a succession of different states, one after another, but as Massey suggests change can also be associated with geography, with movement through a succession of different spaces. And while we are used to associating movement with freedom, we should be wary of this. Marc Angenot described Jules Verne as "the last happy utopianist" because his novels emphasized the unfettered movement of travelers taken to be central to a liberal culture, underpinned by the free circulation of capital (Angenot 1979). This reminds us that this association of movement with freedom has particular consequences: "If freedom is the transcendence of power [then] such isolation spells death" (Bennett 2001, 20). Still, while the changes brought by movement are not always positive, "to live is to move."

Armed with these and other ideas, geographers have begun to talk about re-animating space, starting to acknowledge the liveliness and teeming multiplicity of complex sites like cities, as well as the movements of people, ideas and objects within and through spaces. Banks' geographical imagination also seems to be interested in showing us that change is not simply associated with time and history, but also with space, or rather with *space-time*.

Networks and Narrative Spaces

I am not the only critic to consider Banks' geographical imagination. Both Istvan Csicsery-Ronay (2002) and Roger Luckhurst (2005) have suggested that Banks' science fiction seems to reflect changing experiences of space in an era of globalization, just as Fredric Jameson argued that William Gibson's cyberspace allowed for the cognitive mapping of postmodern spaces (Jameson 1991). Luckhurst argues that globalization, like Banks' "New Space Opera," involves rapid shifts between utterly different places and times and a dizzying cutting between and collapsing of scales: "Banks invokes the SF sublime, that 'sense of wonder'" associated with space opera, through "technological and cosmological scales [that] dwarf any sense of individual agency" (Luckhurst 2005, 224).[3]

To some extent I think that Banks does offer us a new critical geographical imagination; but the sense of globalization as an era of "time-space compression," limitless and all-powerful flows and the collapse of national and other boundaries needs careful qualification. Some things flow faster and more smoothly than others (finance moves quicker than refugees), nothing flows everywhere (try finding a McDonald's in large swathes of Sub-Saharan Africa, for example), some people are less mobile and some places more isolated than they were a century ago. We need to recognize that the world is made up of complex networks of things, standing still or moving at different speeds, connecting some places and absent from others, and that there are different forms of distance in any relationship between two places; we can be spatially close but socially distant, like neighbors who do not share a common language. Space is not, and will never be, an uninterrupted or undifferentiated volume, in other words, despite what we are told by the champions of "globalisation."

Banks' *The Algebraist* allows us to explore the alternative by presenting the idea of a relativistic galaxy in some depth. A network of wormholes allows near-instantaneous travel to many (but not all) systems within the galaxy. However, the Ulubis system where much of the novel is set, was cut off by the destruction of its wormhole portal over seven thousand years before the novel begins:

> From being no more remote than any other system at the end of a single wormhole — and so orders of magnitude less remote than the many hundreds of thousands of Faring systems still to be connected or reconnected — [the constituent parts of the Ulubis system] were fully as remote and exposed as they'd always seemed from any casual glance at a galactic star chart [Banks 2004, 88].

Ulubis is about to be re-connected to the network but this requires dragging a portal to it at less than the speed of light, which will take several centuries. When Ulubis is threatened with attack it must be rescued by a fleet of warships also traveling at sublight speeds, and therefore a long way away. However the plot concerns the rumored existence of a massive network of previously hidden portals, which would mean "the bringing together of almost everybody everywhere" and "the near-instant revitalising [...] of the entire galactic community" (Banks 2004, 113). Banks' galaxy is in effect a *network space*, made up of connections, but also gaps where links are absent. The plot depends upon — and is in fact set in motion by — this unevenness.

Just as significantly, the various species that inhabit this galaxy are divided into the Quick and the Slow, depending on how they live and perceive the world. The Dwellers who make Nasqueron and other gas-giants their home are a Slow species and have a different attitude to "time and space and scale"; by slowing down their perceptions they can transform a journey of ten thousand years into an experience that takes only hours (Banks 2004, 111). The different temporalities of Quick and Slow species mean that they travel at different speeds, have different goals, and inhabit different spaces. "It was a truism that there was not just one galaxy, there were many"; "all these different galaxies existed alongside every other one, each interpenetrating the rest, surrounding *[sic]* by and surrounding the others, yet hardly affecting or being affected by them" (Banks 2004, 239, 240). These different species usually only meet at wormhole portals, "where people of varying species-types were forced to meet and to some extent mingle" (Banks 2004, 240), though "even this seemingly profound tying-together made very little difference to the ultimate disconnectedness of the many different life-strands," with species staying near suitable habitats. A Dweller notes that the Starveling Cult seems only interested in attacking environments suitable for human species and is therefore uninterested in gas-giants, for example (Banks 2004, 392).

The second way of thinking about space concerns the geographies produced by Banks' narratives. Banks is a superb plotter, well known for his intricate narratives and surprising twists. His non-science fiction[4] often concerns the revelation of family secrets through clearly gothic tropes: uncanny homes and families, dangerous desires, tragic plots, and revelations in hidden letters. This reworking of the gothic also informs his science fiction, perhaps as a consequence of the encounter between cultures of very different kinds. Robert Mighall reminds us that there was a distinctive geography to the gothic, one shaped by the contrast between northern, modern Protestantism and what was represented as an archaic, reactionary past located in the Catholic Mediterranean (Mighall 1999). In much the same way, Banks' Culture stories dramatize the conflict between the Culture and hierarchical, divided societies: the Idirans in *Consider Phlebas,* the Affront in *Excession* (1996) or the Empire of Azad in *The Player of Games* (1988). The Mercatoria in *The Algebraist* is similarly described as having "baroque, intentionally labyrinthine power structures," though there is no society like the Culture to compare them to, beyond the Dwellers (Banks 2004, 48).

While these conflicts allow Banks to explore notions of empire and intervention (Brown, 2001), they also suggest that enlightenment of some sort might come out of engaging with murkiness, complexity and backwardness. And as Jameson suggests of another space opera in his discussion of science fiction as a spatial genre, "[w]hat is dialectical about the shock of contact between feudal regression and scientific and technological manipulation is that [...] neither type of space is valorized and both are ideologically and emotionally flawed" (Jameson 2005, 309). This might not seem to apply to the apparently perfect Culture, which does not seem to be flawed in these ways. However if it *is* a utopian society, then I agree with Jameson that that "the best Utopias are those that fail the most comprehensively" (Jameson 2005, xiii). Recent re-appraisals of utopia tend to suggest that it is a *process*, an ongoing critique of the present, not an end in itself. The sometimes-bungled interventions of Special Circumstances might therefore present Banks' protagonists with opportunities to renew their evolving utopia. *Inversions* (1998) takes the issue of Culture intervention in other societies as its organizing theme, with its two main characters taking different sides of Special Circumstances' dilemma — whether to intervene or simply observe in a civilization's development — as well as different roles within a particular society. The fact that they end up acknowledging and even adopting each other's position seems to suggest that this dialectic is a fruitful one.

Interestingly this gothic tension is often produced by a journey, one of the simplest ways of representing space in narrative form (Bakhtin 1981). It is worth returning to the movements described in *Feersum Enjinn* here. These journeys create what Lennard Davis describes as "thick" textual spaces:

> Space in novels, particularly realistic novels, must be more than simply a backdrop. That is, paradoxically, novelistic spaces must have dimensions and depth; they must have byways and back alleys; there must be open rooms and hidden places; dining rooms and locked drawers; there must be a thickness and interiority to the mental constructions that constitute the novel's space. It is almost impossible to imagine the novel as a form divorced from a complex rendering of space [Davis 1987, 53].

This is one reason why the gothic is strongly associated with enclosure and interiority; secrets must be hidden within thick literary spaces. In *Feersum Enjinn* one of the key characters, Count Sessine, is dead and exists only as a disembodied digitized consciousness. He descends into the cyberspatial underworld — the cryptosphere or Crypt — to retrieve the hidden knowledge that will explain his death (and much more). Further metaphors of encryption and the monstrous manifestation of hidden truths make this gothic element even more explicit, and Bascule, another searcher, has more than a hidden letter in a locked drawer to look for: "Weave lookt in books & films & files & feeshes & discs & chips & byos & hollers & fomes & cores & evry form ov storidge noan 2 humaniti" (Banks 1994b, 23). These searches, and the revelations they uncover, are represented through journeys down, in, up and through "thick" textual spaces.

Banks also has some fun with this in *The Algebraist*, which also concerns a search and a journey; the narrative produces its own textual geography. The object of this search is a piece of information that will allow access to the hidden portals, an equation that must be applied to a set of coordinates in space. It is effectively the key for a coded map — a treasure map like the one that drives the narrative of Robert Louis Stevenson's *Treasure Island* (1883). The searcher, Fassin Taak, is ruefully aware of his place in this story: "He could be carried unconscious [...] like a fey maiden under the influence of a sleeping draught in some Gothic romance, but he wasn't allowed to know the secret behind it all" (Banks 2004, 383).

Textual space can be thought of as something both networked and narrated. It is clearly possible to read Banks in these ways, to see how he explores ways of representing space. However we should also investigate the ways in which he engages in the practice of creating science-fictional places, or "worldbuilding."

Worldbuilding

Science fiction authors must engage in some form of worldbuilding because they are dealing with places that do not have a one-to-one referent in reality. Like other worldbuilders, Banks must balance the fantastic possibilities of his new worlds with their adherence to scientific principles. In "A Few Notes on the Culture" he discusses the construction of Orbitals, the Culture's artificial habitats in the shape of rings ten million kilometers in circumference:

> Of course, the materials used in the construction of [Orbitals] are far beyond anything we can realistically imagine now, and it is quite possible that the physical constraints imposed by the strength of atomic bonds ensure that such structures will prove impossible to construct [Banks 1994a, n.p.].

Author Gregory Benford observes that "rendering the alien, making the reader experience it, is the crucial contribution of SF" (qtd. Malmgren 1991, 15). What Benford calls "effing the ineffable"— making the strange understandable — means transforming the impossible into the plausible, largely by reference to what we know about the universe and by ensuring narrative coherence. Generally speaking much sf is built on this tension between the fantastic and a scientific or rational explanation.[5] David Samuelson suggests that "in SF ... scientific accuracy is also limited by the competing demand for fantasy. Even hard SF requires an element of the unknown, into which writers cast a net fashioned of reigning theory" (Samuelson 1993, 193). However there are more fantastic forms of science fiction. Carl Malmgren suggests that "the author may proceed either by extrapolation, creating a fictional novum by logical projection or extension from existing actualities, or by speculation, making a quantum leap of the imagination toward an other state of affairs" (Malmgren 1991, 17). Banks' science fiction contains both extrapolative and speculative elements, and I want to take these in turn, considering two forms of worldbuilding.

Banks' science fiction often describes fictional spaces as expressions of different forms of social organization. In *Against a Dark Background* (1993a) the planet Golter is home to a largely unfettered capitalist society and as a result its states and territories are complex and changeable: "physical maps tended to resemble something plucked from the wreckage after an explosion in a paint factory" (Banks 1993a, 46). Banks explains that "within the chaos of Golter's furiously complicated economic ecology, finance — along with its relevant material manifestations — tended to concentrate and crystallize almost instantaneously around any region where the conditions for profit-making were even one shade more promising than elsewhere" (Banks 1993a, 69). Essentially Banks is exaggerating something already visible in our own world, what the geographer David Harvey called the "urbanisation of capital": the uneven and unequal development caused by cycles of urban boom and bust (Harvey 1982, 1985). The search for profit that makes Golter such a chaotic, shifting world is therefore an exaggerated or extrapolated version of Earth capitalism, something like Gibson's Night City, "a deranged experiment in social Darwinism, designed by a bored researcher who kept one thumb permanently on the fast-forward button" (Gibson 1984, 14), or even the city- and empire-building simulation games of Banks' *Complicity* (1993b).

The sense of familiarity we feel when we read about Banks' invented worlds is not that surprising, as authors and readers we must draw upon ideas of our own world when producing and making sense of these representations. However Stanislaw Lem's critique of "geocentrism" in *Solaris* should remind us of the limits of these science fictional representations.

> We don't want to conquer the cosmos, we simply want to extend the boundaries of the Earth to the frontiers of the cosmos. For us, such and such a planet is as arid as the Sahara, another as frozen as the North Pole, yet another as lush as the Amazon basin.... We are only seeking Man. We have no need of other worlds. We need mirrors [Lem 1987, 72].

Going further than Lem, M. John Harrison describes worldbuilding as "the colonization of the fantastic, the literalization of the improbable, the amazing made ordinary" (Harrison 2003, 436; and see also Kneale, 2009).

While these other worlds might only be "mirrors," they do allow us to reflect upon the way in which space is represented and upon our own assumptions about places. The Empire of Azad in *The Player of Games* is explored through the game that both reflects and constructs it; this game is extensively described but still almost impossible to imagine. It tells us as much about the Culture as it does about the Azad. And of course it also works to defamiliarize our societies, as fantastic sites often do: Azad is "this world re-placed and dis-located" (Jackson 1981, 19). In the Culture, Orbitals are taken for granted as the most natural — and certainly the most efficient — living habitats (Banks 2004a), to the point that a character in *Look to Windward* explains their reluctance to live on a planet in this way: "I think I'd find them a bit small and weird" (Banks 2000, 207). The most extreme form of this dislocation is of course "The State of the Art," detailing Special Circumstances' visit to Earth in 1977, where we explore the Culture through explicit comparison with the societies of Earth and are invited to identify with the former (Banks 1991).

Most speculative science fiction attempts to represent the truly alien, and Banks can certainly claim to have evoked a sense of wonder with his depictions of strange places and entities. Echronedal, the Fire Planet from *The Player of Games*, is a good example, with its never-ending fire sweeping around a band of land around the planet's equator. Gas-giants and their inhabitants have also featured heavily in Banks' recent science fiction, and the peculiar world of *Matter* also deserves a mention here (2008). Yet there are always dangers in attempting to "eff the ineffable," as Samuelson demonstrates:

> The greatest weakness in Hal Clement's classic of world-creation, *Mission of Gravity*, is the characterization of its aliens. They look like centipedes with lobster claws, act and think like Renaissance sailors, and talk largely like '50s engineers, at least as they are represented in American SF [Samuelson 1993, 205].

In this way "SF rigorously and systematically 'naturalizes' or 'domesticates' its displacements and discontinuities" (Malmgren 1991, 6). It does seem much harder to represent the Other than it does to create alien places. While their actions are clearly horrible, the Affront of *Excession* are instantly recognizable as boorish louts. Similarly, despite their unimaginable ages and Slow thoughts, the most alien thing about the Dwellers is that they hunt their own young (and even this seems to be an intentionally taboo-breaking way of making them seem strange).

Even the most formidable of Banks' aliens are likeable enough: Horza throws his lot in with the Idirans in *Consider Phlebas*; Shobohaum Za, the

Culture envoy to Azad in *The Player of Games*, even seems to show some sympathy for the Empire; and Genar-Hofoen takes it furthest by "going native" and actually becoming an Affronter in *Excession*. Of course this suggests that these kinds of encounters change those who participate in them, even when the Culture seems to assimilate its enemies. "The barbarians invade, and are taken over.... The empire survives, the barbarians survive, but the empire is no more and the barbarians are nowhere to be found. The Culture had become the Empire, the Empire the barbarians," as Banks puts it in *The Player of Games* (Banks 1988, 276). Places and entities are never singular or hermetically sealed; even utopias need something to define themselves against.

Perhaps the two most successful representations of otherness in Banks' work are the entity that is the *Excession*, and the Sublimed species from the Culture novels. In the former case the Epilogue's "report," apparently produced by the Excession itself in breathless, barely-punctuated prose, with sections that cannot be translated, presents us with something almost incomprehensible. Even this slides back into familiarity, though, with the realization that the Excession is something like a Contact emissary from somewhere else; it proposes that the entities it has taken back with it be studied further because the "micro-environment" is not ready for further "communication or association," placed as it is on the "advanced/chaotic spectrum section" on some comparative civilization chart (Banks 1996, 435). This reminds us of the anthropological work of Contact and Special Circumstances; in a way this is another "State of the Art" moment, this time with the Culture and the other "Involved" species in the position of gently-patronized contactees.

The Sublimed (civilizations that have voluntarily given up material existence in favor of some kind of transcendental existence) are genuinely strange in *Consider Phlebas* and *Look to Windward*. In the former novel the Dra'Azon are effectively offstage, with only a short communication to give some sense of their nature; their message ("THERE IS DEATH HERE") sets up the tense final third of the novel (Banks 1987, 292–5). In fact the entity looking after Schar's World seems to be whatever the observer wants to think it is. The rather hippie-ish Dorolow thinks it is a god, the skeptical Special Circumstances agent Balveda says it is something like an expert system, and the Changers dismiss it as "Mr. Adequate" (Banks 1987, 103); even the fugitive Mind hopes that "the Dra'Azon being would recognize *a fellow Mind* in trouble and help" (181, my emphasis). This seems to suggest that in this novel the Sublimed are something of a mystery. In *Look to Windward* the Sublimed are still engaged with the material universe and are able to intervene from something like an afterlife.

Banks also closely approaches the fantastic in his descriptions of the planet Nasqueron in *The Algebraist*. In the next section I spend some time exploring the ways in which Banks represents this startling world.

An Aerography of The Algebraist

When Lem concluded that our representations of other planets prove only that "we need Earths," he meant that our images of other science fiction places are simply new versions, "mirrors," of our own planet. While we have become used to representations of Mars as a desert planet resembling the American West, or Venus as a swampy jungle like those of Earth's past (Morton 2002; Aldiss 1968), it is hard to make Jupiter into anything like Earth. Gas-giants are nothing like Earth, and offer a much more promising site for imaginative science fiction worldbuilding (not least because they seem to be a common planet type). The gas-giant planet Nasqueron which is so central to *The Algebraist* is compared to Jupiter several times, and the book's cover bears a modified version of an image originally taken by the Cassini-Huygens spacecraft on its flight past Jupiter in 2001. However Banks is still able to conjure something sublime from this fictional place, as well as reminding us that there are some quite unbelievable places within our own system's "backyard." In fact "aerography"—writing about the atmosphere—consequently seems a better fit than "geography" when describing this gas-giant.[6]

The nature and scale of Nasqueron leaves the reader struggling to imagine it, to locate themselves:

> Where the Dwellers lived, where everything happened, there was no solid surface, and no features at all which lasted more than a few thousand years save for the bands of gas forever charging past each other.... In a gas giant, everything either evolved, revolved or just plain came and went, and the whole human mindset of surfaces, territory, land, sea and air was thrown into confusion.... Add the effects of a vastly powerful magnetic field, swathes of intense radiation and the sheer scale of the environment ... and the human brain was left with a lot to cope with [Banks 2004, 202].

As a result, "knowing where you were in Nasqueron or any gas-giant was important, but still less than half the story" (Banks 2004, 201). This profoundly alien place undoes our geographical certainties of solid ground, strictly delimited areas, and easy navigation. The atmosphere, "a mad, swirling dance of gases" (Banks 2004, 81), is everything: gas giants have temporary "weather districts" and "gas regions," and the shape of the city of Hauskip even resembles Nasqueron's interlocking storms and gas zones (Banks 2004, 402, 207).

Scale plays an important part in this disorientation. Dwellers think of their planets in the way that humans think of planetary systems; their gas giants possess more moons than most stars have planets, and their energy and atmospheric processes are largely generated by the planet, rather than the star. Nasqueron is described as "a planet you could drop a thousand glantines or Sepektes or Earths into and never notice the difference; a not so little system of its own within Ulubis system, a vast world that was almost as unlike home for any human as it was possible to imagine" (Banks 2004, 81–2). Even when the traveler does get their bearings, the environment itself is almost impossibly strange:

> They flew out into a wide bubble of relative slight-clarity, then into a squall of water snow. They dived deeper, through a band of pressure and temperature where water rain fell, pattering hard against the skins of their whirling double discs, then on down, down into even wide-light darkness, down to the warm hydrogen slush [Banks 2004, 162].

Of course Fassin cannot experience Nasqueron directly but through his gascraft, as a cyborg of sorts. Even so, it is no wonder that humans like him occasionally experience the subjective condition called "Swim": "when your head kind of seems to swim because you suddenly think, 'Hey, I'm a human being but I'm twenty thousand light years from home and we're all living in the midst of mad-shit aliens and super-weapons and the whole fucking bizarre insane swirl of galactic history and politics!'" (Banks 2004, 135). However, as a historian or anthropologist of Nasqueron's Dwellers, Fassin spends so long there that he starts to think of it as home, almost going "gas-giant native"; when he sees the Earthlike planet Mavirouelo it seems alien to him (Banks 2004, 380). This is presumably the effect that science fiction authors hope to engender in their readers, the "swim" of estrangement from the familiar.

Making our world seem strange is also the aim of a genuinely critical geography. A critical geographical imagination must allow itself to "swim" occasionally, realizing that what we take for granted is not natural and timeless. In this and other ways Banks' fictions encourage us to see that worldbuilding need not always be conservative. And unlike some other science fiction, this estrangement is not achieved through the technological sublime (Bukatman, 1993, 1999).

Conclusion

Jameson suggests that "SF seems particularly well-suited — or should I say vulnerable? — to paraphrase," so that it is read as the expression of something else, just as realist novels are "rewritten" by critics and other readers as manifestations of psychological or historical situations. He goes on to note that this "tends to call into question the very genre itself, whose specific conventions become so much external decoration" (Jameson 2005, 296). Jameson's answer to this was to characterize science fiction as a distinctively "spatial genre," with different spatial conventions (like the distinction between inside and outside) emerging at particular historical moments. He points out that "there are no 'natural' responses to or evaluations of space ... it is not nature, but culture and history, which determine the reading of the inside/outside dialectic at any given moment" (Jameson 2005, 310). This ambiguous but thought-provoking essay concludes with the suggestion that "the collective adventure [of science fiction narratives] becomes less that of a character (individual or collective) than that of a planet, a climate, a weather and a system of landscapes — in short, a map" (Jameson 2005, 313).

In the spirit of Jameson's essay, I am keen to read Banks' fictions as part of this spatial genre. It is clearly possible to read them in this way, though it is also possible to read other fictions for space, place and landscape. I am not suggesting that they are "really" or simply expressions of different forms of spatial experience, though. To read them as geography textbooks or gazetteers would be to treat the conventions of science fiction as mere "external decoration." However we might read Banks' work in two main ways, spatially speaking: to see how his geographical imagination helps us to think again about the taken-for-granted categories of space, place, and landscape, and to allow this reading to provide new ways of exploring these fictions. Textual spaces like Nasqueron are described as part of a networked and uneven space, and are narrated in terms of particular kinds of sites, presented in specific ways. They are not "settings," as this term is usually understood. As science fictional spaces they also draw our attention to their own artifice; this "world-building" takes different forms but must always address the tension that exists in sf between the fantastic and the realistic. As a result while Nasqueron is a carefully detailed textual place, conforming — on the whole, and as far as I am aware — to what we think is possible about gas giants, Banks also presents us with a disorienting and unsettling aerography, seeming to push at the limits of representation.

So while I will never be able to claim that I have been to Nasqueron, the attempt to take it seriously as a textual space might actually be of use to geographers and others wondering how it is we come to experience and represent places of all kinds.

Notes

1. Not that it easy to distinguish between his science fiction and "mainstream" novels, despite the presence or absence of the "M."

2. See Kneale (2009) for a more detailed discussion of this in relation to science fiction.
3. Banks is, of course, also happy to send himself up in this regard, describing the Vavatch Orbital in *Consider Phlebas* as almost unsurpassed in "what the Culture would call *gawp value*"—or maybe "the technological sublime" (Banks 1987, 111; author's emphasis).
4. Most obviously *The Wasp Factory* (1984), but also *The Crow Road*, *The Steep Approach to Garbadale* (2007) and his final novel *The Quarry* (2013).
5. See Mark Bould (2003) for a provocative argument concerning the roots of science fiction in the fantastic.
6. The word "aerography" is normally used to refer to the production of weather charts, but here it is analogous to geography, "writing about the earth."

Works Cited

Aldiss, Brian. 1968. *Farewell Fantastic Venus: A History of the Planet Venus in Fact and Fiction*. London: Macdonald.
Angenot, Marc. 1979. "Jules Verne: The Last Happy Utopianist." In *Science Fiction: A Critical Guide*. P. Parrinder, ed. New York: Longman, 18–33.
Armitt, Lucie. 1996. *Theorising the Fantastic*. London: Arnold.
Bakhtin, Mikhail Mikhailovich. 1981. "Forms of Time and of the Chronotope in the Novel." In *The Dialogic Imagination: Four Essays*. V. Liapunov and K. Brostrom, trans. Austin: University of Texas Press, 84–258.
Banks, Iain. 1984. *The Wasp Factory*. London: Abacus.
_____. 1986. *The Bridge*. Basingstoke: Macmillan.
_____. 1992. *The Crow Road*. London: Scribners.
_____. 1993b. *Complicity*. London: Little, Brown.
_____. 2007. *The Steep Approach to Garbadale*. London: Little, Brown.
Banks, Iain M. 1987. *Consider Phlebas*. London: Orbit.
_____. 1988. *Player of Games*. London: Orbit.
_____. 1990. *Use of Weapons*. London: Orbit.
_____. 1991. "The State of the Art." In *The State of the Art*. London: Orbit, 99–216.
_____. 1993a. *Against a Dark Background*. London: Orbit.
_____. 1994a. "A Few Notes on the Culture." http://www.futurehi.net/phlebas/text/cultnote.html. Accessed 13 July 2006.
_____. 1994b. *Feersum Enjinn*. London: Orbit.
_____. 1996. *Excession*. London: Orbit.
_____. 1998. *Inversions*. London: Orbit.
_____. 2000. *Look to Windward*. London: Orbit.
_____. 2004. *The Algebraist*. London: Orbit.
_____. 2008. *Matter*. London: Orbit.
Barrell, John. 1982. "Geographies of Hardy's Wessex." *Journal of Historical Geography* 8, 347–61.
Bennett, Jane. 2001. *The Enchantment of Modern Life: Attachments, Crossings, and Ethics*. Princeton: Princteon University Press.
Bould, M. 2003. "What Kind of Monster Are You? Situating the Boom." *Science Fiction Studies* 91: 394–416.
Brosseau, Marc. 1994. "Geography's Literature." *Progress in Human Geography* 18, 333–53.
Brown, Chris. 2001. "Special Circumstances: Intervention by a Liberal Utopia." *Millennium: Journal of International Studies*, vol. 30, no. 3, 625–633.
Bukatman, Scott. 1993. *Terminal Identity: The Virtual Subject in Postmodern Science Fiction*. Durham: Duke University Press.
_____. 1999. "The Artificial Infinite: On Special Effects and the Sublime." In *Alien Zone II: The Spaces of Science Fiction Cinema*. A. Kuhn, ed. London: Verso, 249–275.

Csicsery-Ronay, Istvan. 2002. "Dis-imagined Communities: The Future of Nations in Science Fiction." *Edging Into the Future: Science Fiction and Contemporary Cultural Transformation.* Veronica Hollinger and Joan Gordon, eds. University Park: University of Pennsylvania Press, 217–237.
Davis, Lennard. 1987. *Resisting Novels: Ideology and Fiction.* New York: Methuen.
Gibson, William. 1984. *Neuromancer.* London: HarperCollins.
Harrison, M. John. 2003. *Things That Never Happen.* San Francisco: Nightshade.
Harvey, David. 1982. *The Limits to Capital.* Oxford: Blackwell.
_____. 1985. *The Urbanization of Capital.* Oxford: Blackwell.
_____. 2001. "The Cartographic Imagination: Balzac in Paris." In *Cosmopolitan Geographies: New Locations in Literature and Culture.* V. Dharwadker, ed. New York: Routledge, 63–87.
Hones, Sheila. 2005. "Spectral Geography and Fictional Setting." Paper presented at the Royal Geographical Society/Institute of British Geographers Annual Conference, London.
Jackson, Rosemary. 1981. *Fantasy: The Literature of Subversion.* London: Routledge.
Jameson, Fredric. 1991. *Postmodernism, or the Cultural Logic of Late Capitalism.* London: Verso.
_____. 2005. *Archaeologies of the Future: The Desire Called Utopia and Other Science Fictions.* London: Verso.
Kneale, James. 2009. "Space." *The Routledge Companion to Science Fiction.* Mark Bould, Andrew Butler, Adam Roberts and Sherryl Vint, eds. London: Routledge, 423–432.
Lem, Stanislaw. 1987. *Solaris.* J. Kilmartin and S. Cox, trans. London: Harcourt, Brace, Jovanovich.
Luckhurst, Roger. 2005. *Science Fiction: Cultural History of Literature series.* Cambridge: Polity Press.
Malmgren, Carl D. 1991. *Worlds Apart: Narratology of Science Fiction.* Bloomington: Indiana University Press.
_____. 1993. "Self and Other in SF: Alien Encounters." *Science Fiction Studies* 20, 15–33.
Massey, Doreen. 2005. *For Space.* London: Sage.
Mighall, Richard. 1999. *A Geography of Victorian Gothic Fiction: Mapping History's Nightmares.* Oxford: Oxford University Press.
Mills, Charles Wright. 1959. *The Sociological Imagination.* Oxford: Oxford University Press.
Moretti, Franco. 1998. *Atlas of the European Novel 1800–1900.* London: Verso.
Morton, Oliver. 2002. *Mapping Mars: Science, Imagination and the Birth of a World.* London: Fourth Estate.
Samuelson, David. 1993. "Modes of Extrapolation: The Formulas of Hard Science Fiction." *Science Fiction Studies* 20.2 (July): 191–232.
Stevenson, Robert Louis. 1883. *Treasure Island.* London: Cassell.
Suvin, Darko. 1979. *Metamorphoses of Science Fiction: On the Poetics and History of a Literary Genre.* New Haven: Yale University Press.

Landscape and the Imagination
Banks' Representation of Argyll in The Crow Road
Tim Middleton

Iain Banks has not been conventionally regarded as a writer whose concerns with Scottish culture involve an imaginative engagement with Scottish landscapes and locations. Although it is clear that in works as diverse as *The Bridge* (1986), *Complicity* (1993) and *Whit* (1995) he draws upon a first-hand knowledge of Scottish locations, criticism has, in the main, treated these as mere backdrops to the action. In this essay I will examine this critical tradition in the light work in the field of cultural geography and suggest that the received wisdom is in need of revision. By way of an admittedly rather too easy test case I will outline some of the ways in which real locations from the region of Argyll feature in his 1992 novel *The Crow Road*.

The Crow Road

The novel offers a number of interwoven narratives, most notably Prentice McHoan's attempts to piece together the story of his long-lost (actually dead) uncle Rory's life from the scrappy evidence of Rory's work in progress, "The Crow Road." Prentice tells his own story while the remainder of the novel offers a third person narrative detailing the story of the McHoans, the Urvills and the Watts. Through the two narratives the book links the story of these families with the history of the imaginary Scottish West Coast town of Gallanach and the wider culture and history of Scotland and Europe from 1948 to the fall of the Berlin Wall in 1989. The novel has its share of Banksian black humor, most notably its opening chapter in which Prentice's grandmother's pacemaker explodes during her cremation, but its great strength is the very realistic portrayal of Prentice and his family. The novel is particular interested in sibling rivalry and also in the father and son relationship. By playing off the childhood experiences of Prentice with those of his father Kenneth, Banks helps the reader enter into the family's history in a very full fashion. *The Crow Road* is not just a family saga, but also a contemporary *bildungsroman* about the maturation of Prentice McHoan and a murder mystery about what happened to his uncle Rory: this mixing of genres generates a text of great richness.

As I read it, the book should be viewed as a characteristic product of Scottish Literature in the later twentieth century. It is supremely confident of its ability to explore the relationship between past and present in what seem to me specifically Scottish terms. Whilst *The Bridge* or *Complicity* focus on characters whose Scottishness is always already subsumed by or in conflict with a dominant Englishness, *The Crow Road* explores a subjectivity which is rooted in a specifically evoked Scottish community (albeit an idealised semi-rural and predominantly middle-class community). The novel can therefore readily be seen as part of that wider trend in Scottish culture in the 1980s and 1990s which Cairns Craig has described as the "struggle to reconstruct a mythic identity that is particular to Scotland"—a struggle that seeks to distinguish characteristic Scottish structure of feeling that, for Craig, can serve as a basis for a redemptive cultural opposition that seeks to fend off "the banality of a universal economism that would make us indistinguishable from everyone who lives in a modern industrial state" (Craig 1996, 220).[1]

Work from the field of cultural geography can both lend weight to and extend the argument developed by Craig by facilitating an examination of the function of landscape and locality in the literary representation of Scottish identity. Cultural geography offers the literary critic a critical apparatus that helps them tease out the ways in which places and spaces are shaped and can themselves come to shape the beliefs and values of those who inhabit them. As Peter Jackson has argued,

> Cultural geography ... focuses on the way cultures are produced and reproduced through actual social practices that take place in historically contingent and geographically specific contexts [Jackson 1989, 20].[2]

Places are filled with meanings and a cultural geography approach to literary studies is concerned to ensure that the relationship between place and the meanings which can be made within a given locale are not lost sight of. By focusing upon the competing and changing meanings of places for different individuals, cultural geography inevitably focuses upon the contingent nature of identity.

Far from being an irrelevance or mere "backdrop" the places in which the micro-episodes of our lives occur are actually part and parcel of the structure of feeling of a particular locale and as such central to any reading of the constructions of identity associated with a given locale. Places are overlain with meaning since they are incorporated into and/or produced by a human world which codes and classifies in terms of the hierarchies of discourse (and therefore of power) from a given culture. A place is thus encountered and experienced as always already constructed through the practices of signification which are employed to read it: in reading a place we make use of a repertoire of ways of seeing or, more accurately, discourses which help us decode but are also means of encoding an experience or place according to a particular set of beliefs. These ways of seeing may have nothing to do with the culture we are examining and can, in fact, distort our analysis.

Whilst Banks' novel focuses upon a few families in a rather obscure part of Argyll his work's insistence upon the importance of the individual and the local over and above the global and the national is part and parcel what helps Prentice develop a sharper sense of who he is, and who Rory was, and why where they come from becomes the starting point for a resistance to a whole range of dominant discourses, which seek to shape contemporary individuals solely as consuming subjects. In *The Crow Road* we see Prentice grappling with "the new spatial disorientation in postmodern society, where the inability of subjects to map [space …] is a manifestation of a larger and more serious problem of their inability to position themselves individually and collectively within the new decentred communication networks of capitalism" (Best and Kellner 1991, n.p.). One of the novel's strengths is its evocation of place and of the affinities and factions that arise in a given locale; the creation of the imagined small town some miles south is marvelously done. Banks takes a real landscape with particular historical significance for Scottish identity and builds upon it — often with ironic ends.

Banks and Landscape

Although Scottish locations are used in *The Wasp Factory* (1984), *The Bridge* (1986), *Espedair Street* (1987), *The Crow Road*, *Complicity* (1993), *Whit* (1995), briefly in *The Business* (1999) before returning to Scotland in *The Steep Approach to Garbadale* (2007) and *Stonemouth* (2012), Banks' use of the Scottish landscape has tended to be ignored in the majority of critical accounts. For example, David Daiches' *New Companion to Scottish Culture* (1993), in its one reference to Banks, suggests that Scottish subjects do not "loom large" in his work (Daiches 1993, 192). More recently Anna Patterson's study of *Scotland's Landscapes* (2002) argued that Banks is "a fantasist through and through and one of the least 'place sensitive' writers in Scotland" (Patterson 2002, 28). Lucie Armitt has been one of the few critics to see a different use of landscape in *The Crow Road* where "Scottish topography [is revealed ...] as the source of ancient powers that pre-date questions of nation state or human struggle." But this suggestive insight is left undeveloped since Armitt's insightful account focuses upon "the territory of Prentice's psyche," seeing the book as Prentice's struggle in "learning not just how to think, but also how to 'see'" (Armitt 2002, n.p.).

In this essay I will look at some of the real locations that I believe Banks used in his novel and offer some reflections on why knowing more about the landscape and history of Argyll can enrich a reading. In the summer of 2006 I led a field trip to the region of Argyll in which the novel is set. We wanted to document the landscape and hoped to create a multi-media resource which situates the novel in its geographical context that will be accessible via the web or through GPS enabled mobiles/PDAs and so allow visitors to the region to explore for themselves the ways in which Banks takes a particular location and reworks it in his fiction.[3]

At this point I ought to acknowledge that I'm well aware of Banks stated distaste for research but would counter that he is equally known for his passion for driving, gadgets, climbing over things and generally messing about in the pursuit of a good time. He is also on record for his love of Scottish landscapes and it seemed to me that visiting the region in which the book was set and going to the actual location referenced in the text, would give me some clues as to the process of his inspiration and might illuminate the novel.

Rewriting Argyll

Today the landscape of Argyll is one dominated by forests, bog, sea and rugged hills. The few roads meander along loch shores or follow well-worn routes across hills and the population is relatively sparse, collected in small town reliant upon forestry, farming and tourism. Studying the OS map of the region one is struck by the evidence of an apparently far more extensive earlier population: the burial mounds, standing stones, cup and ring marked rocks, remains of loch based crannogs (lake dwellings) and small fortified farmsteads (duns) all speak of a more peopled landscape than the one which we see today.

In this essay I will examine three locations — the imagined town of Gallanach; Fergus Urvill's castle and the significance for the novel of its proximity to the Dark Age fort of Dunadd.

Gallanach

In *Raw Spirit* Banks reminds us that he'd played fast and loose with geography in creating the town of Gallanach:

> I wanted to locate the fictional town of Gallanach near Crinan [...] I needed the place to have a deep water port with easy access to the Atlantic and I didn't want to edit out the Corryvrecken [whirlpool] so I blithely cut [the island of] Jura in two. You get to do that sort of thing when you are a writer [Banks 2004, 69].

Gallanach is a version of the port of Oban, moved south to occupy a position opposite the small village of Crinan; Banks' town "spreads round the deep waters of inner Loch Crinan like some slow but determined beach of architecture somehow landed from the sea" (Banks 1993, 53).

This description of the town is from the point of view of Gaineamh Castle, home to the Urvills, separated from the town by a couple of miles of parkland and woods. In reality Fergus Urvill's castle is separated from Inner Loch Crinan by the bog land of the Moine Mhor National Nature Reserve and the real Gallanach is a small uninhabited bay.

Fig. 1. Gallanach looking south towards Crinan.

The novel contains some quite precise descriptions of the town's features but these are easily seen as "borrowed" from Oban:

> Ash & I stood on a low little mound overlooking what had been the Slate Mine Wharf, at the north-west limit of Gallanach where the Kilmartin Burn flows out of the hills, meanders without conviction, then widens to form part of Gallanach bay before finally decanting into the deeper waters of Inner Loch Crinan. Here was where the docks had been, when the settlement had exported first coal, then slate then sand and glass, before the railway had arrived and a subtle Victorian form of gentrification had set in the shape of the railway pier, the Steam Packet Hotel and the clutch of sea-facing villas (only the fishing fleet had remained constant, sporadically crowded amongst its inner harbour in the stony lap of the old town, swelling, dying, burgeoning again, then falling away once more, shrinking like the holes in its nets) [Banks 1993, 72].

The Ballast Mound is a symbol of the past: a legacy of Scotland's connectedness with the earth. By the end of the novel it has been removed to make way for a marina development, part of the new economy of Scotland in which leisure and tourism are of more significance than shipping. Gallanach then, is a register of the shifting economic fortunes of this region, and its decline is part of what impels characters like Ashley away from the region. Banks is very careful to trace the ways in which class is linked to mobility, the Watts may live in social housing but via Lachy and Ashley seem geographically more mobile than either the McHoans or the Urvills, and Rory's wanderings have a far less happy outcome than Lachy's and Ashley's. Whilst the Urvills are rooted in the region and the older McHoans similarly entrenched, Prentice seems to feel the pull of region and the wider world. Banks gives Gallanach a reality by giving its descriptions an eidetic dimension: it is a place where memories jostle and shape a character's understanding. This makes his fiction unlike that of someone like Alan Warner whose west coast set fictions are peopled with young characters for whom their immediate location has little or no meaning. In *Morvern Callar* (1995) Oban is only ever referred to as "the port," as a shorthand way of registering the characters' alienation from their locale. Banks, on the other hand, creates characters for whom spaces have become places; locales overlain with meaning and value that stretch back over many years. This is especially true of Prentice, who at one point declares "I have a fascination with places people think powerful or important" (Banks 1993, 73).

Gainmeah Castle

One such place is Fergus Urvill's restored castle. We see Gainmeah Castle in its unrestored and restored state and it provides a setting for several key moments in the novel. The name of the castle is a nice Banksian joke — Gain-

Fig. 2. View of Oban, aspects of which are drawn on for Banks' Gallanach.

meah is Gaelic for sand. The Castle seems to me to be an amalgam of at least one real castle from the immediate region plus a dose of imagination. There has been some debate in the Banks' chat forums about the location but, judging from the evidence in the novel and the terrain the location puts it on the Bàrr an Fhithich, meaning hill of the raven from Bàrr (hilltop) and fithich (raven), on the northern slopes of the Cnoc Na Moine (peat hill):

Gaineamh Castle, home of the Urvills once again, stands amongst the alders, rowans and oaks that cover the northern flanks of the Cnoc na Moine, due south of the carbuncular outcrop that supports the First Millennium fort of Dunadd, and a little north-west of the farm rejoicing in the name Dunamuck. The castle, a moderately large example of the Scottish Z plan type, with canon shaped stone waterspouts, has a fine view through the trees and across the parkland and fields to the town of Gallanach [Banks 1993, 53].

This location is confirmed by the scene in which Prentice and Rory walk and look back across the fields towards the Dark Age fort at Dunadd:

Rory frowned, turning away a little and leaning back on the great stone. He folded his arms and looked out towards the steep hill that was the Dunadd [...]
I stood there, back at the same stone my Uncle Rory had rested against, a decade earlier. I'd left the castle and driven here to the stone circle shortly after we'd come down from the battlements.... I leant against the great stone, the way Rory had when he talked about the man betrayed, the man who'd seen — or thought he'd seen — something that hurt him. I looked ahead, out over the walls and fields and stands of trees. I shivered, though it wasn't particularly cold.
See, I said quietly, to myself.
Maybe Rory had been looking at Dundadd that day, as I'd assumed at the time. But beyond Dunadd, just a little to the right on this line of sight, I could see the hill where Gaineamh castle stood, its walls showing blunt and steel grey through the naked trees [Banks 1993, 411–12].

If Gainmeah Castle is "to the right" of the Dunnadd it is on the Bàrr an Fhithich, above and behind the outcrop shown to the left of the telegraph poles, seen in Fig. 3. There is, of course, no castle here but its features derive in the main from Carnassarie Castle, some seven or so miles north as the crow flies. This castle, though not a Z plan one, has the carved waterspouts and other features described when the children are playing hide and seek in the ruins:

The castle had dark, intact dungeons at ground level, and a stone staircase in a circular tower that rose to the open heart of the ruin, where a few jumbled stones and a floor of earth and weed looked up to the sky. The stairs wound further up inside the corner tower, pausing at each long collapsed floor above, where a doorway looked out onto the central well. Another stairway pierced through the walls themselves on the far side of the shell of the keep, rising through their thickness past another three doorways hanging like internal balconies, to a couple of small rooms at the top of dark chimneys which led to the base of the walls outside.
The castle held a variety of other dark nooks and shadowy crannies you could hide in, as well as windows and fireplaces set high in the thick walls, where you could climb if you were good at climbing, and if you were really good you could climb up from the circular stairs the very summit of the ruin, where you could walk, if you dared, right around the thick tops of the walls, over the weeds and

Fig 3. View from Dunchraigaig Stones to the Bàrr an Fhithich, proposed site of Gainmeah Castle.

the ivy, sixty feet or more above the ground. From there you could look out to sea, over Gallanach, or into the mountains to the north and the forested hills to the south [Banks 1993, 87].

Knowing the location of the castle may not seem that important but I would like to suggest a couple of reasons why being able to locate it so precisely is necessary. Firstly I think it is simply a matter of imaginative consistency; for Gallanach to work as a location Banks needs the Urvills to live somewhere between Lochgair and the coast. But given its pivotal role as a setting for action why not simply take advantage of the region's most obvious rocky outcrop and stick the castle on the Dunadd? The fact that Banks preserves the Dunadd, and then sets Fergus' castle on the hill due South of it hints that this Dark Age fort might have a significance in the text that is greater than its few appearances might suggest.

The Dunadd

The Crow Road is only intermittently interested in the land's very ancient history; its cairns, duns and castles being more often settings for action rather

Fig 4. Carnassarie Castle, interior.

than anything more symbolic. Yet in choosing to set the novel in this particular region, and in creating the town of Gallanach where he does Banks seems to me to have purposely set his text in a landscape whose symbolic resonance in the Scottish imagination is hard to overlook. Prentice's father tells the children the land's history:

> We learnt about the people who had made Scotland their home: the hunter gatherers of eight or nine thousand years ago, nomads wandering the single great wood and stalking deer, or camping by the edge of the sea and leaving only piles of shells for us to find; the first farmers, just beginning to clear the land of the blanket of thick forest a few millennia later; the Neolithic people who had built the tomb of Meas Howe before the pyramids were constructed, and the stone circle at Callanish before Stonehenge, in the thousand year summer of the third millennia; then came the Bronze Age and Iron Age people, the Vikings and the Picts, Romans and Celts and Scots and Angles and Saxons who had all found their way to this oceanically marginal little corner of northern Europe, and left on the place their own marks; the treeless slopes themselves, the roads and walls, cairns and forts, tombs, standing stones, souterrains, crannogs and farms and houses and churches and the oil refineries, nuclear power stations and missile ranges too [Banks 1993, 322].

We should note here how Banks conflates historical time and how this passage moves out from the geographic specificity of Argyll to embrace the whole of Scotland. It is from passages such as this that we can see evidence of Banks' interest in connecting his family saga to the wider history of Scotland; of using their story to tell a story about modern Scotland.

The children are casually familiar with the ancient sites "because we had lived here for most of our lives none of [...] us had bothered to visit half the places" (Banks 1993, 397) — and late in the novel Prentice, Verity and Lewis spend half a day visiting these sites and we get one of the few descriptions of the ancient clutter that is such a feature of this area:

> The land around Gallanach is thick with ancient monuments; burial sites, standing stones, henges and strangely carved rocks; you can hardly put a foot down without stepping on something that had religious significance to somebody sometime [....] We borrowed Fergus's Range Rover and went site seeing; trampling through muddy fields to the hummocks that were funeral barrows, looking up at moss covered standing stones, plodding round stone circles and chambered cairns, and leaning on fences staring at the great flat faces of cup and ring marked rocks [Banks 1993, 397].

Of particular significance is the placing of Fergus Urvill's castle close to the Dark Age fort of Dunadd, traditionally claimed as the capital of the ancient kingdom of Dalraida.

The Scots arrived in Scotland from Ireland in the fifth century, they were a Celtic people from the region of Ulster and their stronghold there was in

Dalriada, a part of today's County Antrim (Laing and Laing 2001). The name "Scots" is from the Irish and means "Bandit," reflecting the ways in which the tribe preyed upon Roman British settlements in North West England and South West Scotland. The Scots who arrived in what is today Argyll were led by Fergus mac Erc who founded a new kingdom of Dalraida from his stronghold at Dunadd (Daiches 2003). There is, then, a jokey allusion to ancient history to be seen in Banks' naming of his villain. The tribe soon came into conflict with local Celtic tribes, commonly known as Picts and the enmity would remain until the ninth century when the Scots and Picts were finally united under the leadership of Kenneth mac Alpin (Laing and Laing 2001, viii). Kenneth, then, is the first king of a united Scotland. Much of this ancient history is caught up in tribal myths and the circumstances leading up to Kenneth's accession are unclear but such ambiguity between fiction and fact creates apt terrain for a writer's imagination. We might see Kenneth's unexpected literary success as a latter-day version of his namesake's unexpected rise to power.

Whether it is productive to explore these parallels any further I'm not yet sure. Historians have argued that the Celtic culture of Dark Ages Dalriada was "tribal, rural, hierarchical and familiar," a society in which the family was more significant than its individual members and in which the position of women was relatively high (Laing and Laing 2001, 51). In Dalriada, leaders were often succeeded by their brothers and nephews, further suggesting the importance of the family unit. In ancient Dalriada "men of art": writers, craftsman and artists, had high social status. The Dark Ages have been described as "an age of migrations" and is very much the period in which modern historians see the early foundations of the modern Kingdom of Scotland being laid (see Lynch 1992). Michael Lynch in his recent history, notes that the Gaelic for great king is "ruiri," the overlord of a number of tribal kings, and Dunadd was home to the ruiri of Dalradia, Fergus's grandson Aedan, from 573. The Dark Ages history of Scotland is about the merger of Pictish and Celtic groups, a process that largely worked via intermarriage (Lynch 1992, 23). In a sense the founding of Scotland is then something of a family saga, founded upon quarrels and alliances that are essentially familial rather than tribal; just as Banks' *The Crow Road* tells the twentieth-century history of Scotland via the complex interactions of Urvills, McHoans and Watts.

Conclusion

It seems to me that the suggestive links between the characters in Banks' novel and some figures Dark Ages Scotland means that knowing more about where the book is set does add value to a reading, though I will be the first to say that I need to do more work on the period to turn suggestive allusions into plot drivers. Banks uses rural Scotland in a way that makes him part of that recent tradition in Scottish writing which we might trace back to Alasdair Gray's *Lanark* (1981) which is about "breaking significantly with the urban-fixated, anti-historicism of the post-war period" exemplified by James Kelman and those younger writers influenced by him like Duncan McLean and Irvine Welsh (Gifford, Dunnigan and MacGillivray 2002, 723). Banks' novel is a prose variant on Edwin Morgan's "Sonnets from Scotland" (1984) which critics have glossed as a text which offers "a rediscovered sense of the limitless imaginative possibilities of the *idea* of Scotland, or Scotlands, a matrix of myths, attitudes, possibilities, histories' (Gifford, Dunnigan and MacGillivray 2002, 733); a populist variation on Gray's *Lanark*, giving us a history of Scotland in all its contradictions. By challenging the idea that Scotland lacks a history writers like Banks turn to location to show how the past has shaped distinctive Scottish identities.

Notes

1. See especially Craig (1996), Chapter 7, "Posting to the Future," 207–225.
2. See especially Jackson (1989) Chapter 1, "The Heritage of Cultural Geography," 9–23.
3. Aspects of this work were presented at the Solstice E-Learning conference at Edge Hill University in summer 2008 — see http://www.edgehill.ac.uk/solstice/Conference2008/abstracts.htm#locative.

Works Cited

Armitt, Lucie. 2002. "The Crow Road." *The Literary Encyclopedia*. http://www.litencyc.com/php/sworks.php?rec=true&UID=1177. Accessed 27 February 2012.
Banks, Iain. 1993 [1992]. *The Crow Road*. London: Abacus.
_____. 2004. *Raw Spirit: In Search of the Perfect Dram*. London: Arrow.
Best, Steven, and Douglas Kellner. 1991. *Postmodern Theory: Critical Interrogations*. London: Macmillan.
Craig, Cairns. 1996. *Out of History: Narrative Paradigms in Scottish and British Culture*. Edinburgh: Polygon.
Daiches, David. 1993. *New Companion to Scottish Culture*. Edinburgh: Polygon.
Gifford, Douglas, Sarah Dunnigan, and Alan MacGillivray. 2002. *Scottish Literature*. Edinburgh: Edinburgh University Press.
Jackson, Peter. 1989. *Maps of Meaning: An Introduction to Cultural Geography*. London: Routledge.
Laing, L., and J. Laing. 2001. *The Picts and the Scots*. Stroud: Sutton.
Lynch, Michael. 1992. *Scotland: A New History*. London: Pimlico.
Patterson, Anna. 2002. *Scotland's Landscapes*. Edinburgh: Edinburgh University Press.

Imperfect Doubles
The Recasting of Place, Object and Character in the Dream Narratives of The Bridge

BETHAN JONES

The fact that Iain Banks' *The Bridge* (1986) is replete with doublings, mirrors and echoes is no surprise, given the novel's premise. As Tim Middleton has observed, "the novel is concerned with various processes of crossing over and transition" (Middleton 1995, 22), and this crossing over results in the doublings of location, object and character that I will explore below. The protagonist, Lennox, lies in a coma after a car crash on the Forth road bridge, and experiences a tangled mass of dreams-within-dreams; his subconscious playing over, jumbling and distorting the memories from his past life in Glasgow and subsequently Edinburgh. The ungoverned machinations of his unconscious mind create the "imperfections" arising from the disparity between lived experience and dream-narrative, in which events, places and people often correlate with their actual double but also appear transformed. Yet there is another layer of imperfect doubling, generated by the influence of Lennox's girlfriend, Andrea Cramond, on him and the progression of the novel. Andrea herself has an inveterate tendency to lead a double life and will not be content to settle for a conventional arrangement. Having moved to Paris for what is originally intended to be a three-year trip, Andrea finds a new partner (Gustave) and cohabits with him over an extended period; even when she comes to live in Scotland she frequently returns to Paris and to Gustave. Gustave functions as a curiously absent alter-ego of the protagonist: a distant double who shares his passionate love of a woman for whom neither is sufficient. Both are thus "imperfect," and the awareness of this imperfection infiltrates Lennox's persona as created within his coma-induced narrative.

Doubled Places

Ironically, in terms of physical attributes, the "imperfect" double Lennox creates for himself in John Orr reflects a degree of perfection that is lacking in his actual appearance and bearing. While Lennox has mousy-brown hair and a growing bald patch, Orr has glossy, black hair: thick, with a slight stylish wave. While Lennox is shorter than he would like, Orr is tall and imposing, with a gentlemanly poise and elegance. This ironic disparity between the physical types of these two versions of the same man are manifested when Orr watches the television screen on which a man in a hospital bed appears, describing him as "on the whole, a rather short, grey, ordinary looking man" (Banks 1990, 40): essentially non-descript. There are significant differences in their behavioral patterns and routines, too, though these are largely dictated by the curiously constrained and anachronistic environment which Orr inhabits. The narrative evoking the life of Lennox from childhood to early middle-age is firmly and logically rooted in chronology; as an adult, he lives in a society that discernibly reflects the political and sociological climate of the 1980s. The experiences and interaction of Lennox and his group of friends are perfectly in accord with this modern setting. He is raised in Glasgow as the son of a railway worker, experiences the thrill of liberation when he moves to Edinburgh to university and gives up on a Geology course to start one in Engineering Design. After his first sexual experiences, he then meets Andrea, who becomes the central figure in his life. Once together, they get drunk, smoke joints, have excellent sex and drive around together in the latest of a series of flashy cars that Lennox acquires.

The experience of the protagonist seems balanced between moments of sheer, transcendent joy, like the time when they are painting the new house in Leith (Banks 1990, 242) and he is struck by a euphoric sense of fulfillment, and the nagging sense of both envy and jealousy at the way Andrea is able to live. Orr's life in the infrastructure of the Bridge is also a hybrid of vague contentment and underlying frustration and discontent — though, interestingly, in the recasting of events by his subconscious, Lennox is never able to reproduce the moments of real exhilaration and transcendent joy. Orr tells Dr. Joyce that he is reasonably content with his life despite the blight of his amnesia: he dines with his engineer friends, plays rackets, visits numerous art galleries and is thinking of joining the yacht club. In his spurious status as a favored patient, he occupies the effortless role of a leisured gentleman, free to engage in his chosen pursuits without real responsibility. The world he inhabits is oddly and fascinatingly anachronistic, though comparable to the Thatcher era in its emphasis on division according to class and status. In the "real world" narrative, it is made explicit that Lennox is very much aware of this class issue. When he first meets Andrea and experiences the relative social elevation of her family, he becomes rather ashamed of his own parents and Glaswegian background (this possibly impacts on the representation of the thick accent and dialect of the barbarian within several dream sequences).

In the world of the Bridge, the upper echelons are reserved for the privileged and wealthy, while the workers are housed in small, bare rooms with shared bathroom facilities, below the train deck (this arrangement mirrors that of an old-fashioned cruise ship or ocean liner). While Lennox works for a living but experiences some of the advantages of relative prosperity (such as fast cars and expensive hobbies such as flying lessons), Orr is freed from the necessity to work by an unearned privilege. This life of privilege is one that is proved to be tenuous and temporal when all his possessions are removed from him (including the very clothes on his back). His fall from grace precipitates a sudden, brutal awareness of the treatment he will receive now that his elegant frock-coat and cravat have been replaced by workers' overalls. He is spurned by Dr. Joyce, who turns out to have been the author of his downfall; he is physically beaten by the doorman at Dissy Pitton's; he is made to forfeit half his allowance to pay for a handkerchief and a hat; and he has to give up his lavish apartment for a tiny room well below the train deck. Ironically, the man who helps him — Mr. Lynch — reveals himself in this act of kindness to be the only neighbor who has ever paid him attention or been friendly, since his arrival at the Bridge.

Orr persists in calling his new friend "Mr. Lynch" rather than Lynchy as instructed. His formal manner is characteristic of those inhabiting the higher reaches of the Bridge, and can be clearly distinguished from Lynch's more casual, "modern" vernacular:

> "Ye got to go somewhere, pal?" ...
> "Yes. I had best be off, actually. I'm going to see an old friend."...
> "No problem, pal. If ye want a hand tomorrow, give us a knock; it's my day off."
> "Thank you. You are a kind man, Mr. Lynch. Good day."
> "Aye. Bye-bye" [Banks 1990, 140].

The formality of speech and dress-code (Orr "performs his toilet") combine with the use of rickshaws and wagons to generate a surreal image of British (rather than oriental), antiquated elitism amid urban bustle. Yet this is not the whole picture, as aircraft pass ominously over the Bridge, people watch television in their rooms and huge, plush, room-sized elevators convey their human cargo from one level of the Bridge to the next. In this conjured world — imperfect and implausible — it is possible to discern a number of more localized doublings: a process in which the subconscious draws on specific images, objects and icons, yoking them together into a collective, confusing and imposing vision.

The Bridge itself is, of course, the most dominant and potent symbol, and the odd world created within its powerful frame serves as one of the most tantalizing and fascinating conundrums offered by the book on an initial reading. Its link with a more comprehensible reality is hinted at through the fragmentary narrative of the "Coma" section (balancing the more conventional "Coda" at the book's close), in which we may piece together enough strands to comprehend that a serious car crash has occurred on a road-bridge. It is not until near the end of the novel that we are presented with this incident conveyed in a coherent form: we discover that Lennox has taken the decision to drive his Jaguar back from Stewart Mackie's in Dunfermline to Andrea's house, after having smoked dope and consumed a considerable quantity of alcohol. Having been precipitated into a coma as a result of the injuries sustained during the ensuing collision with a broken-down, empty car, it seems symbolically appropriate that Lennox should be psychologically trapped — encased within the complex skeleton of the Bridge's colossal structure.[1] Yet the Bridge-world does not stem merely from this one association: it has its origins in Lennox's childhood experiences and subsequent events involving his relationship with Andrea.

Most significantly, the Bridge is indelibly etched on Lennox's mind through its association with an extremely painful event. On the night before Andrea departs for her three-year stay in Paris, she drives the two of them to the foot of the Forth Railway Bridge and they stand beneath it, with Andrea pulling him close and hugging him with an unprecedented and surprising force. The moment of intimacy is weighed down with imminent loss, and the embrace functions as a kind of entrapment. Lennox also experiences a heightened awareness of the bridge as it towers about them, so that the very structure becomes an intrinsic part of the experience (see Banks 1990, 178). Lennox recollects a time in childhood when he was brought to the bridge with his parents by his Uncle, and he sits on his father's shoulders, "his small hands open and grasping" for the red metal of the bridge (Banks 1990, 194). But this is a memory associated with conscious repression, as he remains silent, keeping it from Andrea. Once she has left, this spot becomes one to which he returns in order to brood. It is clearly an image of devastating power and a kind of terrible beauty, yet his connection with it is bound up with a sense of intense vulnerability and helplessness. It also acquires the association of disillusionment, when he discovers that the bridge is not steadily painted over a three-year span (as he told Andrea), but instead over a period ranging from two to six years, often with breaks. It enacts a minor betrayal in failing to conform to the romantic image he has of it; in this way, his relationship with it might be seen as an echo of his love affair with Andrea.

The railway bridge over the Forth finds its imperfect double in the colossal Bridge linking the City and the Kingdom in the coma-dream of the protagonist. The railway track of the original becomes the train deck of the dream-bridge, which forms the crosspiece of the A shape designating part of the Bridge's structure. Trains lie at the heart of this vision; it is significant that while the road bridge is the scene of his crash, it is the railway bridge (with all its complex associations for him) that provides the skeletal structure for the coma-induced dream. Just as the representation of the Bridge-world is regressive, harking back to an earlier period in history, so Lennox's subconscious fixation on trains and engines marks a regression to his childhood. His father was a railway worker, and would invite his son to accompany him to the railway shed where he worked. Perhaps Lennox's most pervasive childhood memory is of a locomotive being overhauled:

> [H]e remembered standing watching a massive loco on a static test working up to full speed on a set of buried, whining steel drums, its man-high wheels spinning in a blur, heat quivering from its metal plates, steam whirling about the strobing spokes; linkages and bars and piston rods flashed in the lights of the echoing, ground-shaken shed [Banks 1990, 110].

This is an image that gives him nightmares and instills in him fear and awe in equal measure. Arguably, this experience impacts on the horrific train crash that occurs on the train deck before Orr leaves the Bridge, once he has tended to the wounded. Even more strikingly, the image of the engine's power is reflected in Abberlaine Arrol's grotesque drawing in which she distorts the railway engines portrayed into malignant, vindictive agents of destruction. This picture, hung on Orr's wall, gives him nightmares in which he is being chased by a train, the parallel tracks moving and keeping pace even when he runs from side to side to escape them. When in terror he finally flings himself into a canal, finding momentary relief at the bottom where he can breathe within a pocket of air, he discovers another rail track and hears a train approaching in the distance. This nightmare within the coma-dream, deriving in part from the childhood experience described above, becomes bound up with Abberlaine (or Andrea) and his ambivalent feeling regarding her role in his life. The drawing is a treasured gift but it is also one that tortures him.

In a curious sense, the Bridge itself becomes Andrea's double. The intricate, geometrical architecture is variously described, but often using anatomical words and phrases. Orr finds himself within the bones of the Bridge; it is also described as arterial. Its red color acquires a number of associations: notably it is the color of dried blood, but it is also associated with the color of Andrea's hair. Abberlaine is another imperfect double as she only possesses some of the physical attributes of her original: she has the same fascinating crinkles beneath the eyes, yet her hair is not red but described as an imprecise "dark." She is unlike Andrea in the formality with which (like Orr) she feels obliged to conduct her relationship with him, yet she appears to have something of Andrea's creative and free-spirited zest for life. The rickshaw drive that Orr takes with her ends in a collision in which he is concussed: an indication of the way in which her zeal can have the undesired side-effect of damaging him. Ironically their roles are reversed here, as Lennox is the habitual speedster while Andrea prefers him to slow down. Abberlaine's need to hurtle from one place to another may be a way of subconsciously reflecting the restlessness of a woman who jets between countries to see her lovers, announcing herself at moments within these lovers' lives at her own convenience.

Just before Abberlaine arrives to see Orr in the apartment she lends him after his fall from grace, she tells him that she has been out partying. It is during this encounter that Orr and Abberlaine have sex for the first and only time. It is described in erotic terms (in some ways a classic seduction) and again the scene functions as a doubling of a "real" encounter: the cozy evening spent by Lennox and Andrea in the coast house at Gullane, when the fog outside keeps them from returning to the city. On this occasion, Andrea sits by the fire, combing and combing her red hair, as a type of pre–Raphaelite fantasy; in the recast dream-scene, Abberlaine allows Orr to comb it for her. Yet their first coupling becomes a travesty of that experienced in the Gullane house (and outside, when returning from the pub): Orr is beneath Abberlaine and feels an extraordinary weight pressing him down, almost to extinction: "Trapped. Crushed. Little death and that release. The girl holds me like a cage" (Banks 1990, 176). What Orr comes to realize is that this force is the weight of the entire infrastructure of the colossal Bridge above him, which he somehow supports. As well as functioning as a doubling of the evening at Gullane, this sex-scene also echoes the episode described above, in which Lennox is held by Andrea tightly but is aware of the immense weight of the Bridge above him. The dream version is pared down and brutal: it is stated quite unequivocally that Orr "felt as though he had just fucked the bridge" (Banks 1990, 176).

Doubled Objects

There are many instances of places or objects from within Lennox's pre-crash existence that find an equivalent in the world of the bridge. The Arrols' summer apartment, for instance, with its furniture draped with sheets and coverings is clearly a refashioned version of the house in Leith that Lennox redecorates with Andrea. There is a further echo, in that this experience evokes in him the memory of "standing in a wide roomful of sheet-draped furniture in the house at Moray Place a year earlier" (Banks 1990, 241). Another instance of transformed place or space is the rackets court which exists as an odd, rather fantastical version of a squash court.[2] In this game the equipment used in squash is subject to a literal doubling: the new game is played with two rackets and two pink balls, on a black court.

The vivid war imagery that occupies the narrative once Orr has left the Bridge is presumably a suitably traumatic and brutal response to the Falklands War and the Israeli invasion of Lebanon happening during the 1980s; we also learn that Lennox's brother has been conscripted (though he does return unscathed). In addition to places and world events, objects appear in an altered form in the bridge narrative, perhaps the most prominent being the scarf/handkerchief that functions as a love token in both narratives. When Lennox and Andrea visit the tower they glimpse while traveling between Jedburgh and Edinburgh, they climb to the top of some rather hazardous steps before making love in the small area near the viewing station at the top. Lennox is uncertain about this, knowing that Andrea's period has just started, but she merely laughs affectionately at his squeamishness and uses a white silk scarf to clean up. The scarf is left stained with a circle of blood and is lost for a while beneath a car seat. It is subsequently and expertly cleaned by Andrea and Mrs. Cramond — it is made as good as new — and remains a kind of talisman and memento to a transcendent moment. In the Bridge-narrative, the scarf becomes a handkerchief belonging to Orr, which he lends to Abberlaine to stem a nose-bleed. Like the scarf, the white handkerchief becomes bloodied and is then cleaned. Abberlaine has the handkerchief monogrammed with the letter O for Orr (just as Andrea has the scarf monogrammed with Lennox's initials). The monogrammed O is the stitched equivalent to the faint circle of blood that remains on the scarf after the initial rinsing: it becomes a more perfect, pristine and elegant version of the original and Orr is sentimentally attached to it. It is taken from him a number of times during his adventures, and always his priority is to retrieve it.

The letter O and the image of a circle permeate the novel, functioning as a *leitmotif* that knits a number of apparently disparate narrative strands together. The most frequent allusions are to the circular, aching bruise on Orr's chest which, in reality, of course, marks the place where his Jaguar's steering wheel hit him "like a circular sledgehammer" at the moment of impact (Banks 1990, 267). The recurrent awareness of this ache indicates the way in which physical sensation experienced during the coma infiltrates the Bridge-narrative as a kind of transferred pain. This also occurs, for instance, when Orr watches the man lying in his hospital bed on his television screen as when the man is injected he experiences what he thinks is vicarious or sympathetic pain. The pain also seems heightened during moments of intensified grief or trauma, and at one point he is said to experience the "echoing horror" of the old ache. Even when the circle on his chest is not associated with pain it seems to affect Orr's actions. After rackets, for instance, he showers and rubs foamy circles on his chest. Like the scarf and handkerchief, he seems branded by this mark, and is sporadically tormented by the residue of pain. He has, of course, been named as a result of the mark, and this remains his identifying label throughout the Bridge-narrative.

The circular brand also extends to various dream-representations of the Bridge itself. Orr considers the possibility that the Bridge may not be linked to land at either end, that it is possibly circular, and merely attached to itself. While the Bridge's architecture reflects the straight lines of an X or of an A, the trajectory of the Bridge itself may resemble a circle. During one vivid dream sequence, Orr imagines himself running along the Bridge to reach a group of women longing to have sex with him; taunting him with their sad eyes and overt carnality. Yet as he runs the Bridge rotates, keeping pace with him like the parallel rail tracks described earlier, so that he can never reach the women. At various points in the novel, Orr looks beyond the Bridge and sees this frustrating, perverse, circularity reflected in other bridges beyond.

Doubled Characters

The circular bridge that keeps pace with him is one manifestation of the impasse experienced in reality and echoed in the Bridge-narrative. Another representation of repressed progress — in this case a literal block or impasse — occurs near the beginning of the novel, in the episode invented as a dream by Orr to satisfy his therapist, Dr. Joyce. Here, Banks evokes a sinisterly fascinating scene in which Lennox is caught up in a sequence of doubled actions. He has just arrived by train at a "dark station" and is traveling in a carriage to an unspecified destination, conveying an unspecified but dangerous cargo. His carriage encounters another carriage, drawn by white rather than dark horses, and with a man driving, only faintly visible in the dark. Orr makes an attempt to pass on one side but is blocked. The two reach an impasse with every movement made by the one mirrored by the other. If one carriage shifts to its left, the other moves to its right, barring the way. If one man lifts a hand or begins to speak, the other does so too. Yet the process does not entail an exact mirroring: the protagonist recognizes that the two speak in different languages, and he is at one point relieved to find that his adversary does not have his own face. The other man is explicitly referred to as his "imperfect double" (Banks 1990, 24). Orr's frustration mounts to the point where he draws his pistol and attempts to fire and the other man does likewise, at exactly the same moment, but they hear only an ineffectual click as the guns fail to go off. The scene ends with the two turning back the way they have come in order to find another road.

Orr informs us that this "dream" is merely a fabrication: an elaborate part of an attempt to fool his doctor. Yet the fabricated story *is* still a dream, as it is part of the coma-induced Bridge narrative. It is a resonant episode that points to a number of the triggers that have produced it. In the context of the Bridge-narrative, of course, it might be seen to link to the blocked path of investigation that Orr pursues in his attempt to fathom the secrets of the Bridge. He has received no satisfactory replies, and a number of them are written in languages he does not understand. In the pre-coma narrative, however, the links are more clearly discernible. Gustave, his Parisian rival for the affections of Andrea, obviously speaks in a different language and has a different face from him. Yet figuratively he is his double: a version of himself that occupies the same role as he does in relation to the woman they both love. They block the path for each other, perhaps an idealized path leading them to a conventional relationship with Andrea involving marriage, perhaps children, monogamy and total commitment. As the pre-coma narrative progresses, Lennox experiences a number of epiphanies in relation to Gustave: revelations about the status of the two which seem to bring them together rather than highlighting difference. When it is discovered that Gustave has multiple sclerosis, for instance, Lennox wishes that he had not refused to talk about him to Andrea, creating a verbal impasse in which now the subject is taboo. He wishes that he had visited Paris, and he resolves to travel to Paris (which he has avoided doing throughout Andrea's association with the city) in order to meet him. He is jolted by the first realization that Gustave has never visited Scotland either. It brings home to him the fact that his rival not only occupies an equivalent position to him but also is likely to have similar feelings of exclusion at the way in which Andrea compartmentalizes her life.

If these two men are represented as the foiled carriage drivers, they also merge in the image of the stricken man lying supine in his hospital bed. Again, Gustave's diagnosis functions as an important trigger here: perhaps unsurprisingly, as it is a key, life-changing moment for Lennox and Andrea, and one that inevitably shifts the balance of their relationship. After hearing the news, Lennox dreams of Gustave lying in a hospital bed, surrounded by machines (Banks 1990, 251). It is easy to assume that when Orr watches his television and sees the comatose man he is experiencing a version of the classic "out of body" experience, in which he becomes aware of himself as a separate being who can be observed, as it were, from outside. In fact, the situation is more complex here, as the man observed is his imperfect double or rival as well as himself. The television switching itself on and imposing itself upon his attention certainly signifies his physical condition — his real body — breaking into his coma. It may also be an indication of the way in which Andrea's involvement with his rival forces itself into his mind when he would rather not be aware of it.

Arguably, the moment where the protagonist finds a room with a hospital bed in it and makes the conscious decision to walk through the door and get into it, indicates an attempt to "become" Gustave, occupying the role of the multiple sclerosis sufferer, as clearly Andrea will devote herself principally to the one who needs her most at any one time. Yet curiously this act also reflects a moment of surrender to the situation, an acceptance that if he wakes from his coma and begins to recover, Andrea will desert him for the other, sicker man. Interestingly, through, it is this moment of willed awakening that brings acceptance and a sense he might actually come to meet and know his imperfect double, without too much jealousy or resentment.

Conclusion

"Imperfection" in this novel ought, perhaps to be defined in two ways in order to understand some of its resonances and associations within *The Bridge*. Lennox and Gustave are "imperfect" doubles in the sense of inexact copies of each other: two men separated by place, language and appearance but occupying the same role. The places and objects doubled but transformed in the Bridge narrative analogously testify to this kind of imperfection. It is also the case the "doubler" or "doublee" is dogged with a sense of imperfection as a consequence of their inability to occupy a specific role singly: they are never quite enough — hence, for instance, Orr's problems with languages, stemming from Lennox's insecurities in this area. While Andrea reads and translates Russian, for instance, Lennox experienced frustration during their trip to the Soviet Union at his inability to speak more than a few words. Orr can speak only one language, while most people on the Bridge are at least bilingual. Sometimes this lack is of use to him, such as the time when he is considered an unthreatening steward on a train because he is essentially deaf and dumb. More often, his inability to communicate widely results in confusion or exclusion. But this inadequacy is merely one instance of his sense of imperfection when set against the benchmark of the woman he loves and with whom he wishes to possess an exclusive bond.

The figure "O," resonant with possibility, repetition and the opportunity to transform, would seem to triumph over the linear, angular and totalizing perspective offered by the Bridge. But it is also this "O" (a nothing, a zero) which Lennox recognizes as metaphor for his trapped existence; for being present in both realities, just as he is about to wake. At the close of the novel, we are not sure whether Lennox will embrace these opportunities and face his future positively or slide back into the restricting habits of his past. Insecurities thus surface as multiple imperfections within the Bridge-narrative, indicating fascinating ways in which the subconscious — given the chance — transforms and mutates elements of lived experience into a narrative as wayward as a dream.[3]

Notes

1. This is the case, of course, until he is able to escape on a train and experience life at one end of the Bridge, before struggling back to his old haunts before the final awakening.

2. We learn at one point that Lennox has taken up squash, which he does not really enjoy, in order to combat the middle-age spread that he is beginning to acquire. The game of double rackets in the dreamscape does not give him much satisfaction either.

3. I am grateful to Martyn Colebrook for his assistance with aspects of the reading for this essay.

Works Cited

Banks, Iain. 1990. *The Bridge*. London: Abacus.
Middleton, Tim. 1995. "Constructing the Contemporary Self: the Works of Iain Banks." In *Contemporary Fiction and National Identity*. Tracey Hill and William Hughes, eds. Bath: Sulis Press.

III. Genre

Textual Crossings
Transgressive Devices in Banks' Fiction

KATHARINE COX

The critical approaches brought together in this collection identify and analyze a series of concerns that unite Iain Banks' writing. In doing so, these essays read Banks' narratives as playful explorations of the relationships between space, place and identity, and find that these concerns are consistently present in his science fiction and mainstream writing. To refine this analysis still further, this essay's focus is to expose the "transgressive foundation" (Bataille 1962) that underpins his spatial interests. It is perhaps surprising to distil Banks' narratives down to a focus on transgression, especially given his investigation of a broad canvas of human, alien, machine and avatar experience.[1] However, each of his diverse and distinctive narratives features significant boundary crossing, resulting in a play of textual transgression. This essay will consider the concept of transgression and then use it as a way of considering Banks' ambiguous authorial position before finally analyzing examples of textual transgression in his writing, especially *Use of Weapons* (1990).

What Is Transgression?

This essay reads Iain Banks' work through an exploration of transgression as defined by Michel Foucault in his "Preface to Transgression."[2] Foucault's short essay addresses the carnal philosophy of Georges Bataille's writing, and has become an important interpretative framework for approaching transgression more generally. In it, he identifies transgression as an erotic language whose play emphasizes movement, limit and pleasure. The movement between these limits repeatedly reaffirms God's absence, as without the infinite there is an increased emphasis on limits. Foucault clarifies that this absence or death of God is not to deny his existence altogether, but rather to reaffirm his absence or lack. In this state of absence, the experience of wo/man is to be repeatedly defined by limits, boundaries and crossings.

To take this reading one stage further, the reader's position is itself seen to be transgressive. The interpretative function of the reader exceeds the limits of the text and plays within and without the interpretative network constructed by the author. For Bataille there is pleasure to be found in the reflection on the movement of the transgressive act, which can perhaps also be found in the interpretative acts of the reader: a type of *jouissance*. In Banks' writing, this is most obvious in the sections of sexual transgression[3] as well as in his textual games, where there is play between different genre constructions.

A focus on movement complements the etymology of transgression itself, which is sometimes overlooked by critics.[4] Returning to Foucault's work, his concept of transgression relies upon this etymology and describes the act of transgression as one that "involves the limit, that narrow zone of a line where it displays the flash of its passage" (Foucault 1964, 60). In describing the movement of transgression, the engagement and crossing of boundary would seem to hold equal sway with the movement itself. As such, transgression is essentially paradoxical: it both requires limits and the ability to transgress them, but in the act of transgression the limit itself is not eradicated, rather Foucault's "flash" serves to highlight and affirm the limit itself.

The concept as it is currently applied to literature is rather clouded and tends to be used by critics as a catchall term for subversion (see for example Booker 1991). There is a danger that transgression as it applies to a text becomes an interpretative game of "yes a text is transgressive" or "no it is not." Bataille and Foucault's approaches made this type of binary thinking problematic. Both emphasize the play inherent in the act of moving across limits in a manner that makes the relationship between the movement and the limit one of change but which results in reaffirming the limit. The etymological root of transgression clearly refers to a passing over or stepping across (*OED*) and as such the limit, movement and effect all combine, creating a result more complex than a simple dichotomy.

A focus on transgression is also a timely one given recent academic publications. These include a sociological study by Chris Jenks (2004) and Julian Wolfreys' 2008 analysis. Even more recently, a postgraduate academic conference held by the University of Stirling's English Studies Postgraduate Conference (May 2010) hosted Banks as a keynote speaker. Though the conference's application of the term tended to focus more on deviant behavior rather than Wolfreys' more nuanced determination of transgression (2008, 1), it is notable that Banks presented there. This perhaps reflects the appropriateness of reading his work in this critical framework and the interest in works on transgression which has grown rapidly since the early 1940s.[5] Using "Preface to Transgression," this essay will explore three aspects of Banks' writing: the categorization of Banks as an author, the classification of his writing into mainstream and science fiction categories, and finally an exploration of boundary crossings in his writing.

What's in a Name? Limiting Banks

Banks is an author repeatedly classified by publishing conventions. Despite work that is imaginative, prolix, and rarely expected, his publishing house Little, Brown Book Group have been complicit in the creation of two distinct yet apparently interrelated personae — that of Iain Banks and Iain M. Banks. Categorizing himself first and foremost as a writer of science fiction (his "genre of choice," Banks 2009), it was nevertheless his fantastic, non-science fiction novel, *The Wasp Factory* that was his debut novel in the United Kingdom, under the name Iain Banks. Following the *bildungsroman* of an unlikely protagonist, Frank, the novel's geography is that of a small planet, a microcosm of empire. Frank rules as despot of this liminal land (sometimes island when cut off by the causeway), having constructed complex processes of ritual, religion and warfare on his territory. Following its successful publication, Banks published the strange cross-genre novels *Walking on Glass* (1985) and *The Bridge* (1986) before beginning to publish his beloved science fiction. These first three fictional publications in the U.K. established Banks as an inventive and experimental writer who blended different genre elements in new and exciting ways. By 1993, Granta repeated its prophetic experiment to name the Best of Young British Novelists of a new generation and Banks was included along with a number of other (now distinguished) authors.

Despite this promising start, and although Michael Levy suggests that Banks' arrival on the publishing scene was one that "critics genuinely could not ignore" (Levy 2009, 161) there is little sustained criticism of his writing. He has been embraced by the science fiction community as a writer of intelligent space opera and there are some important articles which deal with his writing especially within a Scottish context, but this criticism does little to bridge his mainstream and science fiction outputs. To date (2013) there is no single-authored monograph that considers his work in general. This collection goes some way to address this.

Consider Phlebas is the first of his science fiction Culture novels (though a complete draft of *The Player of Games* was already finished before *The Wasp Factory*). The title is taken from T.S. Eliot's poem *The Waste Land* (1922) which he returns to for the title of *Look to Windward* (2000). Published in 1987 in both the U.K. and in America,[6] *Consider Phlebas* was made separate by being published under the name Iain M. Banks in both countries (the M. is short for his middle Scottish name, Menzies). Effectively, for publishing purposes the author enjoyed two constructions of his authorial identity with the second science fiction writing persona including a nod towards his Scottish identity. Publication of his science fiction has continued in the U.S. but this does not include all of his science fiction writing and in particular there are a number of his mainstream novels that have not been released there. Unlike the U.K. though, where Banks is published both with and without the "M," in the U.S. he is published solely with the "M." The marketing of his other mainstream fiction in the U.S. is now being addressed by the increased availability of his work through ebooks (such as Hachette's digital books).

Critics have repeatedly returned to these ambivalent names in interview (see for example Orbit 2002, Amith, 2009; Livingstone 2009). The names delineate difference, causing an artificial boundary between his mainstream and science fiction work and, as a result of these classifications, Paul Kincaid argues that they have "blunted some of the impact of his work" (Kincaid 2009, 179). However, even this simple division is problematic as fantastical elements and even science fiction conventions permeate his mainstream novels perhaps reflecting Banks' contention that "[t]hey're all just novels" (Banks qtd. Brooks 2002). In addition, it is problematic to refer to his mainstream fiction and science fiction as being distinct as in the U.S. Iain M. Banks has been solely marketed prior to 2012 as a writer of science fiction which presumably limits his mainstream readership in that country (the publications of *Stonemouth* 2012 and *The Quarry* 2013 has recently unsettled this). The classification of Banks has become even more blurred with the publication of *Transition* (a multi-verse traveling novel) which was published in Britain without the "middle initial" (Livingstone 2009). In America this was published as science fiction with the middle initial (Orbit). This is perhaps because in the U.S., Banks is predominantly known as a writer of science fiction and the publishers felt this novel could be better marketed in this vein. So publishers responding to different literary and market conventions categorize his work differently.

Textual Transgression: Science Fiction, Science Fantasy and Space Opera

Despite, or because of, the artificial classification of his writing into Iain Banks (mainstream) and Iain M. Banks (science fiction), Banks is repeatedly able to transgress the boundaries of science fiction within these classifications. In considering what makes up the recognizable structures of science fiction it is useful to first consider theoretical definitions of the form put forward by theorists who regularly explore the boundaries of the genre (see for example, Roberts 2000 and 2005; Landon 2002; Seed 2005; Bould *et al.* 2009). These critical investigations confirm, what is most simply expressed by Adam Roberts in his introduction to *Science Fiction: A New Critical Idiom*, that "[t]he term 'science fiction' resists easy definition" (Roberts 2000, 1). Critics such as James 1994; Parkin 1994; Spinraid 1993 (listed by Roberts 2000) proffer an economic classification of the genre constructed by publishing houses and book companies.[7] That the classification in the bookshop denotes genre is problematic for Banks whose "M" novels are regularly displayed alongside his mainstream work on the shelves of major U.K. bookstores (in Waterstone's, for example). Arguably his publishing house has continued this trend of "setting" what is science fiction by using the "M" in the first place. Such a definition therefore becomes increasingly difficult to maintain, and is clearly evident by the marketing of Banks' work. Postmodern science fiction in particular undermines the literary mainstay of genre still further, making it increasingly difficult to categorize (see for example the work of David Mitchell 2001, 2004; and Kazuo Ishiguro 2005).

For Robert Scholes (1975), Samuel R. Delaney (1984) and Damon Knight (1993 qtd. Roberts 2000), the role of the reader is a privileged one which, in interpreting the rule of the genre, recognizes the work as science fiction. There is a certain satisfaction as a reader of science fiction in recognizing the "triggers"[8] which alert the reader to the unfamiliar. This process, according to Gary Wolfe, creates a "tension" between the canny and the uncanny, the familiar and the unfamiliar, specifically, "between what is and what might be" (qtd. Landon 2002, 6). This tension is reminiscent of what Tzvetan Todorov termed the "hesitation" associated with the fantastic (1975) which he argues affects characters and readers alike. Both Wolfe's tension and Todorov's concept of hesitation are acts of transgression which rely on the crossing and re-crossing of lines of recognition.[9]

It is worth considering Darko Suvin's seminal work on science fiction which builds on Todorov's idea of hesitation, arguing that the literature of science fiction works on a principle of estrangement (or alienation). In stressing the unfamiliar as the boundary which is crossed by the reader, this crossing of the line is repeatedly negotiated and renegotiated over the course of the reading, and thinking about, the novel. Strikingly, Suvin considers this estrangement to arise from an authorial innovation (a "novum") or innovations ("nova") that are logically coherent or possible (Suvin 1979). Ultimately, the science of science fiction is that which arises from a rational or logical process, whether this is fully explained by the text or not.

Banks' writing is the writing of ideas but these are not always necessarily scientifically coherent (unlike his counterpart Alastair Reynolds) and there are numerous examples that might be more appropriate for a discussion on fantasy. As much as writers or readers of science fiction may wish the genre to be disassociated with fantasy it is possible for the fantastic to erupt from within science fiction, especially as they share a similar process of recognition. Banks' science fiction writing tends to explore family and emotional journeys that are not the usual fare of science fiction but of space opera, a sub-genre of the form.[10] Farah Mendlesohn refers to his science fiction as "romantic space opera" (Mendlesohn 2005, 556), combining the god-like sublimed races with the emotional overarching plots classically associated with science fantasy. Even in the representations of his machines, the sentient, capricious and god-like ships' minds, he visibly draws on ideas of myth and legend. Fantasy is a useful term when considering the deliberate ruptures in genre in his mainstream fiction as well. Whilst Banks' movement between these categorizations is obvious, there are perhaps two more nuanced areas in his writing that are masked by these labels. His mainstream fiction plays with fantasy, with alternant realities and impossibilities which are accepted as normal. Although this may have abated after he began to publish his science fiction Culture novels, his recent work *Transition* (2009) represents a willingness to explore science fiction genre in his mainstream work.[11] This was alluded to by the author in the discussions of this novel, where he links the settings to the world of *The Bridge* (in interview with Tim Haigh). To this group of novels I would add *The Wasp Factory, Walking on Glass, Whit* (1995), as well as the strange contemporary world of *A Song of Stone*. These novels operate to their own ascribed rules, are "worlds" in themselves and contrast with his other mainstream writing.

In an added preface to the 1992 edition of *The Wasp Factory* (Abacus), Banks makes explicit the constructed world in which Frank roams. The remoteness and isolation of the Cauldhame home creates the ecological and societal environment for the warped protagonist to pursue his personal vendettas against nature, his father and other family members. The violence of the novel coupled with the twist at the end has caused some readers to question whether the murder episodes have been dreamt up by Frank/Frances. The reality of the situation is further undermined by the ethereal character of Eric, Frank's unstable brother, who is only ever seen or alluded to by Frank. This central character lifts the novel above the narrative technique of the unreliable narrator and causes it to border on the realm of science fiction. His ritualistic device enables Frank to predict future incursions into his homeland: "[t]he Factory had said it twice [....] Everywhere I turned was fire" (Banks 1984, 125). This technology combined with the numerous taboos that Frank constructs in relation to his home suggest a realm over which Frank has power. Frank demonstrates this power through extreme acts of violence which punish transgressors. Ironically, it is Frank who is revealed as the principle transgressor having been socialized as a boy (albeit a castrated one) who is then revealed to be female at the end of the narrative.

The Bridge is reputably Banks' favorite novel (see Wilson 1994 and Haigh 2009, for example) and, as he notes, has been occasionally mistaken for science fiction. "It's been reviewed as a science fiction novel, even though it wasn't published as such. It's certainly non-realistic enough to be bordering on SF. There are one or two SF bits and pieces in there" (qtd. Wilson 1994, n.p.). The early parts of the novel in particular contain a number of trigger functions which might suggest the otherworldly to the reader. The bridge structure appears total in these early parts of the novel, with the only sight of land contained in the rocks at the base of its structure and in a landscape painting.[12] The society of the bridge is familiar yet unfamiliar. Its structure is rigidly hierarchical, appears vaguely dystopian with no apparent social mobility (though the character of John Orr is able to circumvent this as he is an amnesiac, feted by his doctor). Strange legalities surround sexual contact (Banks 1986, 50), and both religion and politics seem not to exist. Even simple acts like the playing of sports is rendered unfamiliar by the invention of a type of rackets game that require dual rackets and two balls (Banks 1986, 27). The dominant frame of the narrative is contained within the otherworldly dystopia of the Bridge and as Lennox wakes it is far from clear which reality will remain dominant. Though it appears that he is "back," at the end of the novel, this is far from established, and its ambiguity suggests that any resolution will be provisional and temporary. By linking the futuristic world of *Transition* to that of the Bridge, Banks has deliberately increased the sense of this work as science fiction, and again causes the unsettling categorization of both.

In addition, the novels *Complicity* (1993) and *Canal Dreams* (1989) also seem to border on fantasy, as their descriptions of bodily violation render them otherworldly. This is particularly true of *Canal Dreams* as Hisako Onoda, a professional cellist, transforms herself into an avenging "superhero" in the strange luminal space of a hijacked ship, trapped in the Panama Canal.

The life of the loose-living protagonist of *Complicity*, Cameron Colley, descends into a Dante-inspired spiral of hell whereby assaults and bloody murders reflect the imagination of his psychotic best friend. Both of these novels function around a series of bodily transgressions. The action of *Canal Dreams* occurs around the unreality of a ship marooned in the Panama Canal during a revolution. There are two sets of climaxes in the novel, the scenes where Onoda is repeatedly raped and the doubling of this when she takes her revenge and murders the entire crew. The carnage of the novel is intensified by the limited proximity over which the action occurs, which causes the ship itself to be read as another self-reliant world.

As these examples demonstrate it is both attractive to limit and categorize Banks' work but the act itself is also fraught with difficulty. Mainstream fictions reveal fantastical and otherworld realities, science fiction vies with space opera and science fantasy making Banks' writing difficult to pin down. Prose novels are interspersed with poetry and genre distinctions are undermined and repositioned. From a textual perspective, his work is transgressive, typified by the movement of play.

Bodily Transgression: Use of Weapons

Banks' science fiction novels are lengthy, with the exception of the short story collection *The State of the Art* (1991), and often explore the dominant forces at play in the Culture universe. Social taboos are usually made explicit through the Culture's dealings with other races and species. Although Banks moves forwards and backwards along the timeline of their "race," one of the problems with the Culture is that, as they have eliminated risk and taboo, the Culture hubworlds tend to be rather boring. Without the usual demarcations of social taboo it is usually up to the alien races the Culture encounters to provide some fun. Culture individuals tend to limit themselves to rock climbing, drug and gland modification, liberal and often group sex. Perhaps the lifting of these typical taboos frees the reader to engage with the Culture. In doing so, the reader passes over the limits of their own individual context while maintaining the knowledge of these limits. It is the encounter with the other alien species that heightens the reader's sense of transgression as the reader is party to the Culture's uncertain response to the transgressions of these other races which the reader often recognizes as being close to our own. Despite Banks' enjoyment (perhaps flippant) of the Culture utopia, which he terms "my secular heaven" (CNN 2009, n.p.), it is often these other alien environments that provide the opportunity for transgression as the Culture appears to be without limit. It is no coincidence that in one of his strongest novels and the one he claims to be one of his favorites of the science fiction genre, *Use of Weapons*, the Culture play a relatively minor and conciliatory role.

The tense narrative centers on a brother Cheradenine, his two sisters Livueta and Darcksense, and their male cousin Elethiomel. The figure of Elethiomel/Cheradenine Zakalwe is the enigmatic protagonist at the centre of the novel who obeys his Culture cooperative Diziet Sma's directives in order to receive help to return to, and apparently to regain an association with, his sister Livueta. Throughout the novel Elethiomel/Cheradenine regresses his memories trying to locate a terrible transgression in his past. For a while the reader may be lulled into thinking this transgression is the sexual conquest of Darcksense which her brother Cheradenine inadvertently witnesses:

> Elethiomel sat, trousers round his ankles, hands on Darckense's naked hips under her bunched up dress, and looked calmly at him.
> Elethiomel was sitting on the little chair that Livueta had made in her carpentry class, long ago [Banks 1990, 184].

The use of Livueta's name is significant here as Banks implicitly makes the reader aware of her absence and yet creates a metonymic connection to her. In doing so, all four are physically or metonymically present in the room. Further to this, the four characters are structured and defined in relation to one another. The "two boys and the two girls" (Banks 1990, 356) are literally interchangeable as Elethiomel/Cheradenine demonstrates by taking his cousin's name after his death. Identity is changeable as the characters play out their roles in this game. In this sense, Darcksense is the object through which the violation of the family unit is played out. Obviously distressed at the witnessed sexual act, her tears and confusion complete her as a receptacle of transgression as she feels the shame of the act unlike the laughing Elethiomel.

Elethiomel is psychotic and repeatedly acts out of self interest and for power. His desire to win is all consuming as he notes on the verge of his second death: "*The point is to win [...] Everything must bend to that truth*" (Banks 1990, 363; author's emphasis). Although he has sex with Darckense and later abducts her, he claims that "Livueta was his real desire" (Banks 1990, 339). Elethiomel is able to make sexual claims on the women that Cheradenine does not, for fear of this act of transgression. Though Cheradenine appears to concur with Elethiomel's preferences and hold Livueta in higher esteem he is unwilling to transgress familial relationships.[13] Livueta remains aloft and inviolable unlike her sister who has been injured in a riding accident, shot by intruders as a child, and deflowered by Elethiomel before her elaborate death at his hands. Her treated bones trace the impact of some of these encounters while a bone fragment from when she was shot perversely penetrates

Elethiomel just above his heart so until his first death (a beheading) and regeneration he bears a physical reminder of this shame.

Livueta functions as an idealized woman in this text. She embodies the aloofness of the woman that cannot be violated. Prior to learning what happened to Darckense, towards the end of the novel, her figure is depicted as being widow-like as she dresses "always in dark clothes now-days" (Banks 1990, 345) and she ultimately retires to a life of a nurse, working in "a clinic in the slums" (Banks 1990, 357). She also represents the type of woman that Cheradenine must protect and that Elethiomel wishes to possess.

Cheradenine's desire to respect and protect his family, represented by Darckense's kidnapping, results in his misreading of Elethiomel's intentions. He, and especially Livueta, do not recognize their situation as a war game and that Elethiomel is prepared to obliterate the bonds of family in order to win it. The horror at the center of this work is the use of Darckense as a psychological weapon. After reducing Cheradenine's capacity to function as a commander with her abduction, Elethiomel extends this further by killing her, making her bones into a chair, and sending it to his cousins:

> [H]e came closer and slowly closer to the chair, he saw that it had been made out of the bones of Darckense Zakalwe [....] They had tanned her skin and made a little cushion out of it; a tiny pink button in her naval, and at one corner, just the hint, the start of some dark but slightly red-tinged hair [Banks 1990, 350].

Elethiomel finally and fully objectifies his cousin, turning her metaphorical use as a vessel of his transgression into an object and weapon of war. The stark image of the chair recalls Vincent Van Gogh's repeated and perhaps obsessive depiction of a singular chair (see for example Van Gogh 1888), and the image is one that returns to haunt Elethiomel/Cheradenine. In addition, the horrific use of human flesh and bone to recreate a domestic object recalls the stories of Nazis using human parts to create lampshades. Elethiomel's complete dehumanization[14] of his victim enables him to murder her in this way and yet he heightens her humanity through his choice of representation. In re-constructing the chair, Elethiomel makes a link to their prior sexual encounter witnessed by Cheradenine, both through the choice of furniture but also though the hint of pubic hair. It also links to Livueta as it was she that crafted the original chair. The production of the chair is compounded further by the knowledge that Elethiomel would have been unable to fashion this alone (her murder, skinning, construction of the chair, her tanning and making of the cushion and so forth) so her body is further violated by the "they" who helped (Banks 1990, 350).

The Culture's role in this story is initiated by Diziet Sma who, in bringing Elethiomel/Cheradenine[15] to Livueta, demonstrates the tenuousness of their interference. Though they are engaged in the wide-scale regime manipulation and change across the universe how can the Culture achieve their intentions to work for the greater good if they are unable to provide the same care of consideration at an individual level?

Conclusion

Banks' fiction is repeatedly revealed as transgressive. This process of transgression is realized in Foucauldian terms: through the movement, limit and passage across boundaries, and is mirrored by the response of the reader when reading his work. Typically, transgression is most explicit in the play of his authorial persona, his genre-crossing fantastical fictions and the exploration of his textual and sexual games. This essay argues for the prominence and persistence of transgression among his writing and, in so doing, contends that transgression will remain an important factor in the analysis of his writing into the future.

NOTES

1. To simplify to the extreme, Banks' writing ranges from the manipulative minds of sentient space craft (*Excession*), the concerns of ageing rock star (*Espedair Street*), political and corporate subterfuge in *The Business* to the ambiguous gender of Frank/Frances in *The Wasp Factory*. This collection endeavors to give voice to the variety and breadth of his writing.
2. So much of Foucault's work is categorized by a preoccupation with space, from the uncanny experience of the heterotopic, to the otherness of clinical and prison confinement and the act of moving between different spaces itemized by his late work "Of Other Spaces." For a detailed analysis of this work in relation to sexuality see Sally R. Munt's *Queer Attachments: The Cultural Politics of Shame* (2008).
3. Sexual transgression pervades much of Banks' writing whether this deviant practice is societal, physical or both. His concentration on family in his mainstream writing lends his work a similar epic and dynastic intensity to his science fiction. The family connections in this writing are not straight forward. In his depictions of first cousin sex in *Use of Weapons, Against a Dark Background, A Steep Approach to Garbardale,* the attempted intergenerational rape in *Whit*, and brother and half-sister incest in *A Song of Stone*, Banks repeatedly reworks and probes the safety of the family.
4. Critical discussion of transgression can be quite loose, and has been applied simply as a catchall for subversion in such volumes as Kenneth W. Graham (1989) and Deirdre Lashgari (1995).
5. I'm grateful to Nicholas Willmott whose work on transgression identified this expansion in critical works on the subject, he notes that in the British Library Integrated Catalogue (2010), "'Transgressive' in the title field currently shows 64 titles. These date from 1941 (a work on geology) to 2010. There are five titles from the 1980s, thirteen from the 1990s, with the remainder published on or after 2000" (2010).
6. This novel is published by Orbit as an imprint of Little Brown Book Group in the U.K. and by Orbit an imprint of Hachette Book Group in the U.S.

7. Roberts' exploration of the genre is very straightforward and useful. See Roberts 2000.

8. Significantly, in George Orwell's opening sentence of *Nineteen Eighty-Four* (1949) the clocks striking thirteen or the use of depilatory soap in Frederik Pohl and C.M. Kornbluth's novel *The Space Merchants* (1953) as noted by Tom Shippey (2005, 13) function as triggers at the time of publication but have since been overtaken by changes in cultural practice which lessen the effect of these triggers to such an extent that they may no longer function as such. In part this process reflects the prophetic or guiding inspirational principles behind science fiction to inform popular culture and science.

9. My reading here is a rebuttal of Roger Luckhurst's metaphor for science fiction as a series of deaths, as a result of this genre boundary crossing (see Luckhurst 1994). Luckhurst's polemic closes down the possibilities inherent in both science fiction and transgression and, while I do not see this transgressive movement as ultimately liberating, the play and pleasure affording by this boundary crossing is effaced in Luckhurst's model.

10. Although his novels are sometimes sprawling dynastic affairs Banks' maintains a comedic or deft touch. For example, see *The Algebraist* where the diamond-toothed baddie speeds towards war only to become utterly irrelevant upon arriving (rather like an extended version of the dog swallowing the alien invasion force in Douglas Adams' *The Hitchhiker's Guide to the Galaxy*).

11. In the U.S. this represented a continuation of his science fiction writing although this time outside of the domain of the Culture.

12. Obviously realistic in our frame of reference but imagined and possibly fictional for the people inhabiting the structure of the Bridge (see Banks 1986, 43).

13. Though we might not find this initially surprising, this sexual and societal taboo repeatedly acts as a stimulus in Banks' writing.

14. Although all these characters are all alien it seems most relevant and less confusing to refer to these humanoid characters as human.

15. Another way in which the disorientation of transgression is apparent is in the connections between his novels. This has been extended further by the return of particular characters such as the enigmatic Elethiomel Zakalwe in *Surface Detail* (2010), which again unsettles our knowledge of him.

WORKS CITED

Amith, Aidan. 2009. "Interview: Iain Banks—A merger of two banks." *The Scotsman*. 13 September 2009. http://news.scotsman.com/interviews/Interview-Iain-Banks—A.5640948.jp.

Banks, Iain. 2009. "In Conversation with Tim Haigh." *Tim Haigh Reads Books*. http://tim haighreadsbooks.com/.

Bataille, G. 1962. *Eroticism, Death and Sensuality*. Trans. Mary Dalwood. Reprint, San Francisco: City Lights.

Booker, M. K. 1991. *Techniques of Subversion in Modern Literature: Transgression, Abjection and the Carnivalesque*. Gainesville: University of Florida Press.

Brooks, Libby. 2002. "The Word Factory." *The Guardian*. 26 August 2002. http://www.guardian.co.uk/books/2002/aug/26/fiction.iainbanks.

CNN. 2009. "Author Iain M. Banks: 'Humanity's future is blister-free calluses!'" *CNN*. http://edition.cnn.com/2008/TECH/space/05/15/iain.banks/.

Foucault, Michel. 1964. "A Preface to Transgression." In *Religion and Culture* [1999]. Manchester: Manchester University Press, 57–71.

Hardesty, William H. 2000. "Space Opera Without the Space: The Culture Novels of Iain M. Banks." In *Space and Beyond: The Frontier Theme in Science Fiction*. Gary Westfahl, ed. Westport, CT: Greenwood, 115–22.

Jackson, Rosemary. 1981. *Fantasy: The Literature of Subversion.* London: Routledge.
Jenks, Chris. 2004. *Transgression.* London: Routledge.
Jervis, J. 1999. *Transgressing the Modern, Explorations in the Western Experience of Otherness.* Oxford: Blackwell.
Livingstone, Ken. 2009. "The Books Interview: Iain Banks." *The New Statesman.* 17 September 2009. http://www.newstatesman.com/books/2009/09/livingstone-interview-culture.
Lowe, Greg. 2008. "Iain Banks — Interview." *Spike Magazine.* March 24, 2008. http://www.spikemagazine.com/iain-banks-interview.php.
Mitchell, Chris. 1996. "Iain Banks: *Whit* and *Excession*: Getting Used to Being God." *Spike Magazine* http://www.spikemagazine.com/0996bank.php.
Mitchell, David. 2001. *Number9dream.* London: Hodder and Stoughton.
_____. 2004. *Cloud Atlas.* London: Hodder and Stoughton.
Orbit. 2002. "Interview with Iain M. Banks." SSFworld.com. http://www.sffworld.com/interview/2p0.html.
Roberts, Adam. 2005. *Science Fiction: The New Critical Idiom*, 2d ed. New York: Routledge.
Surkis, Judith. 1996. "No Fun and Games Until Someone Loses an Eye: Transgression and Masculinity in Bataille and Foucault." *Diacritics*, vol. 26, no. 2: "Georges Bataille: An Occasion for Misunderstanding" (Summer 1996): 18–30.
Suvin, Darko. 1979. *Metamorphoses of Science Fiction.* New Haven: Yale University Press.
Williams, Owen. 2009. "Iain M Banks Talks Culture." *Empire.* 2 November 2009. http://www.empireonline.com/news/story.asp?NID=26180.
Willmott, Nicholas. 2010. "'Is Literary Transgression Stupid Stuff?' An Examination of the Usefulness of Transgressive Literature as a Literary Genre." Unpublished MA thesis.
Wilson, Andrew. 1994. "Iain Banks Interview." *Textualities.* http://textualities.net/andrew-wilson/iain-banks-interview/.
Wolfreys, Julian. 2008. *Transgression: Identity, Space, Time.* Hampshire: Palgrave Macmillan.

"Still magic in the world"
Banks and the Psychosomatic Supernatural
Kirsty A. Macdonald

> Oh I know there's goodness in the world, too, Cameron, and compassion and a few fair laws; but they exist against a background of global barbarism, they float on an ocean of bloody horror that can tear apart any petty social construction of ours in an instant [Banks 1993, 302].

In Banks' 1993 novel *Complicity*, serial killer Andy places his own crimes within the context of a post–Thatcherite, post–Regan world that is for him horrific. There is nothing supernatural in the very real, very corporeal crimes that Andy commits. However, when it comes to the ethereal, Banks' depiction is rather more sympathetic. The supernatural in his mainstream, realist fiction is not horrific but usually a positive, ennobling force, concerned with reconstructing social bonds. There is enough horror in this world for Banks without projecting it into the otherworld also. The supernatural occupies a key space in a number of his realist novels, in particular *The Wasp Factory* (1984), *The Crow Road* (1992) and *Whit* (1995). Within these texts it is a productive, creatively ambiguous presence.

Theorizing the Psychosomatic: Realism, Fantasy and the Fantastic

While Banks' work has been readily examined through the lenses of fantasy and science fiction, the presence of the supernatural in his realist fiction has not been fully analyzed, theorized or categorized. It has become a cliché to cite the recurrence of the supernatural as a characteristic of Scottish literature more widely. However, in keeping with the ostensible realism of this branch of his fiction, the origins of the supernatural phenomena portrayed are not wholly unquestioned. This internal contradiction — incorporating the ambiguously unreal — subverts realism from within, pushing the boundaries of the novel. Moreover, the possibility of a disrupted psyche supports the notion that Banks' fiction is concerned with a postmodern fragmentation of the self, calling for a move away from the individual and a return to the communal. This is what Cairns Craig refers to as "heterocentricity," the value underlying specifically Scottish left-of-center traditions in politics (Craig 2002). This type of supernatural will be referred to here as "psychosomatic," a term derived from the field of medicine, in which it is vaguely and variously defined. Generally, definitions point towards a conjunction of the corporeal and the psychological, "involving or depending on both the mind and the body" (OED 1989, 770), mirroring the co-presence of interpretations and sustained ambiguity in these texts. "Psychosomatic" will be used to designate a *seemingly* real supernatural being or event, which is connected to the body and casts an influence over events, but which also may be the projection of a troubled mind. Ultimately, these episodes are consistently ambiguous in terms of their existence and origins.

With regard to genre, this sustained ambiguity in literature has been labeled "the fantastic." However, Banks is a notorious player of games when it comes to literary categories. Craig argues that, "all of his novels, in either mode, are explorations of the possibilities of combining or disrupting the expectations of particular genres" (Craig 2002, 23). Banks does indeed often only acknowledge genre boundaries in order to transgress them. However, a distinction can fruitfully be drawn between the three novels examined in this chapter and his other "otherworldly"realist fiction. Novels such as *Walking on Glass* (1985), *The Bridge* (1986), *The Business* (1999) and *Transition* (2010), blend a world recognizable as a fictional representation of our own with dystopian, utopian, satirical or parallel worlds beyond, be they "real" dimensions or dreamscapes. We might term these opposing worlds "real" and "fantasy." However, *The Wasp Factory*, *The Crow Road* and *Whit* do not offer this distinction, and moreover do not offer a full acceptance of the otherworldly or supernatural within our world. In this respect, they cannot be labeled either magic realist or fantasy texts. Within magic realism the supernatural is an accepted phenomenon and causes no hesitation or uneasiness for characters or author; the supernatural becomes just another part of the fictional reality, in much the same way as it does in fantasy.[1] Fantasy refers to the representation of tertiary worlds and alternative social orders, however referential they might be to the reader's own.

The field of "fantasy" theory in general is confusingly large, and, in terms of genre distinctions, often dubiously overlaps with that of "the fantastic." Critics as prominent as Rosemary Jackson, Neil Cornwell, Kathryn Hume and Lucie Armitt use "fantasy" and "the fantastic" interchangeably, illustrating a general lack of discrimination in terminology in the field.[2] Due to this lack of specificity and the fact that, according to the definitions I favor, the fantastic denotes any kind of supernatural ambiguity and not just that involving potential psychological explanations, the term will not be widely used here, in favor of the "psychosomatic supernatural." However, if the lucid but limited definition of the fantastic provided by Tzvetan Todorov in his study, *The Fantastic: A Structural Approach to a Literary Genre* (1975 [1970]) is temporarily adopted, it can be seen that fantastic literature represents a stronger interrogation of realism than other non-realist modes such as fantasy, science fiction and magic realism. Todorov would define these modes as "marvelous," while Rosemary Jackson argues that they "have recourse to compensatory, transcendental otherworlds" (Jackson 1981, 180). Jackson's phrase is loaded with judgmental meanings, but it is fair to say that these genres do provide a degree of reader satisfaction and passivity in the reading process not available in the fantastic. Todorov's formulation of the fantastic involves a supernatural manifestation that remains entirely ambiguous, drawing reader and often characters into an unnerving hesitation between natural and supernatural explanations. According to Todorov: "The fantastic is that hesitation experienced by a person who knows only the laws of nature, confronting an apparently supernatural event," yet it only lasts as long as the hesitation does, "it is the hesitation which sustains its life" (Todorov 1975, 25, 31). Chris Baldick concurs, arguing that the fantastic is "a mode of fiction in which the possible and the impossible are confounded so as to leave the reader (and often the narrator and/or central character) with no consistent explanation for the story's strange events" (Baldick 2008, n.p.).

Realism represents the illusion of a world that is whole and self-sufficient. Fantasy, with its tertiary worlds, and magic realism, with its unequivocal magical manifestations, also represent such an illusion due to the acceptability of the supernatural within the altered codes of their literary contexts, governed by the laws of a reality removed from literary mimesis. These genres do still comment, however covertly, on the realities of our world, and can have profound political implications, yet in the fantastic the very nature of representations of the "real" is called into question. The sustained doubt regarding the actuality of the supernatural plays upon, as Jackson states,

[T]he difficulties of interpreting events/things as objects or as images, thus disorientating the reader's categorisation of the "real" [....] It takes the real and breaks it [....] The fantastic exists as the inside, or underside, of realism, opposing the novel's closed, monological forms with open, dialogical structures, as if the novel had given rise to its own opposite, its unrecognisable reflection [Jackson 1981, 20, 25].

The fantastic elements in these three novels are evident in relatively fleeting episodes. Moreover, they have a specifically psychological relevance, as noted above, whereas the fantastic as a literary genre as defined by Todorov may also refer to the tension between dream and reality rather than just madness and reality. Therefore, the more specific term of psychosomatic supernaturalism is employed here as the most pertinent.

Whit

While Banks in general is a relatively under-researched writer, the 1995 novel *Whit* is one of his least critically discussed texts. *Whit* is essentially a quest novel, following the literal and metaphorical journey of central protagonist Isis Whit. Isis is a member of a hybrid religious sect that incorporates elements of Christianity, Buddhism and Hinduism in particular — the Luskentyrians — and we follow her as she attempts to locate her cousin Morag and discover the origins of her community's belief system. Despite the novel's unusual and entirely invented subject matter, it does still pertain to realism by evoking actual places in Scotland and beyond. The sect is based in the countryside outside the town of Stirling, it takes its name from its original home in Luskentyre on the island of Harris in the North West[3], and Isis travels through the cities of Edinburgh, Glasgow and London during her search for "the truth." This is a self-conscious allusion to realism as a genre, which was first defined in 1826 as "the literature of truth."[4]

Isis holds a significant position within the community as a second-generation Leapyearian, born on February 29 as daughter to a father born on the same day a generation before. She is also grand-daughter of the sect's founder, Salvador. This, she initially believes, is the source of what she refers to as her Gift. She tells us that as a child she was in a house fire that killed her parents: "I know the fire changed me. My memories begin with that vision of aching, empty blueness, the smell of dampened smouldering and the sound of my great-aunt's grief; the Gift of Healing came upon me two years later" (Banks 1995, 256). This power to heal via the channeling of energy through her body is undoubted in Isis's mind initially, and is witnessed and respected by others. Early on in the novel, she relates how she and her brother Allan discover a dead fox that she is able to re-animate:

> I felt the flow of life, in me and in the animal. A strange tension built in up me [sic], like a blessed opposite of bottled-up anger, germinating, budding and blossoming then flowing out of me like a glowing beam of vitality and being.
> I felt the animal quicken and stir in my hands.
> In a moment it jerked, and I set it down on the ground again; it wobbled to its feet and shivered once, looking shakily around. It growled at Allan and then leaped away, vanishing into the ditch before the hedge. Allan stared at me wide-eyed with what appeared to be horror and — for all that he was the boy and two years my senior — looked very much as though he was about to cry [Banks 1995, 3–4].

It is possible to interpret this incident as perfectly natural, the fox perhaps having been asleep or unconscious and simply brought round by the noise and touch of the siblings. However, Allan is terrified, we are later led to believe, as he resents anything more powerful than him, particularly when that power may have purer and less selfish motives behind it than he does: both we and Isis eventually discover that Allan has been exploiting the community for financial gain and plans to take over its leadership. He shares Isis's belief in her powers, but for him this is something to be feared. However, the reader is free to assume that these powers are as false as the religion on which they are built and, in keeping with the fantastic, the ambiguity is sustained until the end. It is only when Isis learns that her faith is built on very shaky foundations that she herself begins to question her Gift. She discovers that her grandfather Salvador was an army deserter and has consistently manipulated those around him in order to keep various secrets hidden. The faith and subsequent community he founded first in Harris has been constructed on his "visions," made-up powers giving him the special status he needs to conceal his problematic past and gain the trust and faith of his followers. While considering whether or not to disclose this information to the community, Isis reflects:

> Was my Gift real? Was it genuine? Could I be certain? All these questions — or that one question in those different guises — had come to depend, in my mind, on the precise physical state of that small wild animal, that summer's day with Allan in the stalk-stubbled field, when I had been a child.
> I had never known the answer. For a time I had thought that I might come to know it, but I could accept that I never would, and in that acceptance found a liberating realisation that it didn't really matter. Here was what mattered; here, looking out over these stunned, bewildered, awed, even fearful faces, *here* was action at a distance, here was palpable power, here was where belief — self-belief and shared belief — could truly signify [Banks 1995, 455].

Isis' epiphany comes when she faces her community, not yet sure whether she will tell them that their faith is built on a series of lies. What she feels is a responsibility towards them, as she acknowledges her part in the communality of their shared existence. Via recognizing the multiple interpretations of a component of herself, she is led to the realization of her role within a shared belief system, within a collective of selves, and one in which she cannot act alone. Regardless of its origins, her Gift has always been about others, about healing and helping those around her. Furthermore, the ambiguity of her Gift suggests that within herself she is not one but many, and this is extrapolated to a community level. This disallowing of the conventional, ruggedly individual and coherent Romantic self and subsequent return to commonality is again characteristic of how a positive postmodernism operates in Banks' fiction.

The Wasp Factory

Similarly, Banks' first published novel, and more frequently examined, *The Wasp Factory* is primarily concerned with belief and concealed truths. Central protagonist Frank, whose sincerity of belief is foregrounded by his very name, creates a religion of the self, which he firmly believes endows him with the preternatural ability of second sight. He ritualizes his life as a means of desensitizing himself to and normalizing the often horrific and violent deeds he commits, justifying his actions as transcendentally sanctioned. His religion comes complete with temple (the World War Two bunker), altar, omens and artifacts, such as the eponymous wasp factory, the intricate machine Frank creates in order to prophesy the future. These also include the skull of Old Saul, the dog he has been told "castrated" him when a child, family pictures and totemic "sacrifice poles," incorporating the putrefying heads of ritually killed animals. He invests these symbols with a metaphysical power, claiming to be able to sense things through them. At one point he attempts to telepathically contact his brother Eric via this power. Frank relates:

> I knelt in the pungent darkness before the altar, head bowed. I thought of Eric [...] I leaned forward and put my right hand palm down on the top of the old dog's cranium, keeping my eyes closed. The candle was not long lit, and the bone was only warm [...] I felt my stomach clench itself involuntarily and a wave of what felt like fiery excitement swept up from it. Only acids and glands, I knew, but I felt it transport me, from one skull through another to another. Eric! I was getting through! I could feel him; feel the aching feet, the blistered soles, the quivering legs, the sweat-stuck grimy hands [Banks 1984, 125–126].

This is one of the few times Frank drops his personal defenses enough to fully empathize with and feel a bond with another being. The reader can dismiss this episode straightforwardly as the delusions of a troubled mind, however sincerely related by the subjective first person voice. Yet Frank firmly believes in the potency of his "supernatural" powers, and so invests in them. It is Frank's belief that is significant, as well as the probability that this belief will be questioned, along with others, following his discovery of the Gothic family secret, that he is biologically she, and the unhinging of identity that occurs as a result.

If the supernaturalism of the novel, including Frank's assumed quasi-spiritual connection with his habitat, is unresolved, providing questions without answers, then the conventional image of the North as otherworldly is in turn subverted. Banks exposes this through exaggeration and ultimate rejection. Craig notes this when he states that

> *The Wasp Factory* is shocking precisely because it turns the conventions of Gothic fiction, which readers are used to treating as belonging in a purely imaginary realm, into the assumed realities of ordinary life in the North of Scotland [Craig 2002, 24].

As with *Whit*, Banks is at pains to suggest the reality of events by setting them in potentially real places, explaining their geography in detail.[5] The supernatural, primitivism bordering on the barbaric, madness and eccentric family relationships (often portrayed as characterizing the Highlands as well as being traditional motifs in Gothic fiction) are, however, gothically exaggerated to the point of grotesquery. This excessiveness becomes part of the critique, as hyperbole undermines the possibility that such characteristics have a rooting in reality, and consigns them to the imaginary. Moreover, this is reinforced by the fact that the entire narrative is related in Frank's voice, unreliable to say the least.[6] However, the novel's overall message is clear when Frank, concluding his narrative, muses that

> our destination is the same in the end, but our journey, part chosen, part determined — is different for us all, and changes even as we live and grow. I thought one door had snicked shut behind me years ago; in fact I was still crawling about the face. *Now* the door closes, and my journey begins [Banks 1984, 184].

Conventions and indoctrinated beliefs are restrictive and dogmatic. Freedom of identity comes when these are interrogated and undermined, or simply left behind. In the novel, the myth of the North, like the myth of constructed gender identity, is rejected and the potentialities for the self are optimistically proliferated. Frank's conclusion above is comparable to Isis's in *Whit*: whatever happens next, it is likely to be an improvement on the previous basis of family secrets and false beliefs. Questions of free will and predestination accumulate in both novels, and also the idea of what you take with you on such journeys.

Both Isis and Frank must ultimately recognize but move towards abandoning their encumbering ancestries and inheritances, in order to forge new relationships. This is underlined at the end, as Frank cradles her brother's head in her lap and is already moving towards forgiving her father.

The Crow Road

Prentice McHoan's quest in *The Crow Road* is a similar journey of self- and familial-discovery. An encumbering weight of ancestry or inheritance is again apparent, and the traditional Highland associations, self-consciously alluded to in both *Whit* and *The Wasp Factory*, are initially maintained only to be ultimately questioned. The opening paragraph of *The Crow Road*, narrated by Prentice himself, reads: "It was the day my grandmother exploded. I sat in the crematorium, [...] and I reflected that it always seemed to be death that drew me back to Gallanach" (Banks 1992, 3), his Argyllshire hometown. Again, the ostensibly realist nature of the novel is foregrounded by the use of actual place names.[7] Death generates the journey north, in this case the death of his grandmother, the matriarchal and ambiguously supernatural Margot McHoan. Again, the supernatural, the Highlands, and death (all gateways to an "other" world) are correlated and exaggerated, and therefore exposed to potential interrogation. The use of the term "crow road" itself is a symptom of simultaneous acceptance and rejection of convention. Its first meaning is signified by an archaic folk saying for death: "away the Crow Road [....] It meant dying: being dead. 'Aye, he's away the crow road,' meant, 'He's dead'" (Banks 1992, 126). Death is represented as a journey along the "crow road" to some final but tangible destination. Yet the Crow Road is also the title of Prentice's Uncle Rory's pre-humus unfinished collection of writings, literarily sophisticated and eloquent, and also a bustling main street in Glasgow's cosmopolitan west end in close proximity to the university. It is when these meanings collide, involving the abject moment of distortion of boundaries entailing centre and other, that modern rational awareness and the associated perceptions of the North are deconstructed. As Colin Manlove argues, the supernatural is evoked to depict "sophisticated people being variously confronted by the primitive, the mysterious and the suppressed [... as a counteraction to] too much knowledge" (Manlove 1994, 216). Knowledge is interrogated, and the resultant ambiguity combined with a dubious supernaturalism destabilizes certainties.

Frank's conviction in *The Wasp Factory* that he possesses a degree of second sight is echoed by Margot McHoan's belief in her ambiguous and unresolved ability in *The Crow Road*. When discussing the disappearance of Rory eight years previously, around which the narrative pivots, Margot tells Prentice, "I think he might be dead," explaining that she bases this belief on her extrasensory moles: "I can tell what's going on in this family by my moles. They itch when people are talking about me, or when something [...] remarkable is happening to the person." Rory's melanomic representative, located on Margot's wrist, has emitted: "Not a sausage [...] for eight years, not a hint, not a sensation" (Banks 1992, 12–13). Margot's conviction proves to be true when we discover towards the conclusion of the novel that Rory was indeed murdered eight years ago, but her supposedly paranormal ability to know this remains unexplained. The ambiguity is underlined by Prentice's narratorial comment: "I stared at the dormant eruption with a sort of nervous respect, mingled with outright disbelief" (Banks 1992, 13). His sophisticated modern self dictates disbelief, while the primitive, superstitious and suppressed element of his psyche cannot help but have a grudging respect for something that in times past would have been wholly accepted. Armitt has interpreted Grandma Margot's mysterious moles as a straightforward example of magic realism. She states:

> This is a motif which would not be out of place in a Salman Rushdie novel and which is proven to be a correct gauge in the context of Uncle Rory's death [....] Magic realism is a disruptive, foreign, fantastic narrative style that fractures the flow of an otherwise seamlessly realist text [...] its etymology is one that looks to return to the real and reinvest realism with its own magic [Armitt 2000, 305].

Yet, firstly, the novel is far from "otherwise seamlessly realist." It is strewn with magic and potential ghosts in the form of haunting past memories represented as analepsis, and depicted through a carefully cultivated unfolding structure involving past and present scenes punctuated with dead Rory's writings, which appear regularly in chapters eight, ten and twelve. Secondly, magic realism leaves no room for hesitation or consternation regarding the supernatural; it requires belief and acceptance, something that neither Prentice nor the reader are prepared to give to Margot's perceived powers.

Additionally, Armitt ignores the distinctively Scottish and folkloric quality of Margot's ambiguous ability. Her moles exist in the realms of lore and superstition as witch-marks. Traditionally, these were the bodily indicators of the practice of witchcraft, much relied upon as evidence in the spate of witch trials in Scotland in the late sixteenth and early seventeenth centuries. They appeared, as Robert Kirk states, as: "a small mole, horny and browncoloured," through which the devil or some familiar was supposedly to have suckled milk or blood.[8] Margot is witch-like in that she yields a degree of power, and performs the role of family guru whose wise yet ambiguous advice is often sought. Moreover, her personal moral code is somewhat unconventional for an elderly Highland lady. She smokes because, as she says herself, "I'm seventy-two years old now, and I don't give a damn" (Banks 1992, 10), and talks about sex to her grandson: "The last time I had sex was on that back seat [....] Don't look so shocked, Prentice" (Banks 1992, 6). She is one of Margaret Elphinstone's characteristically Scottish literary "dangerous women," refusing

> to become quite ideologically sound. She is too sinister for that. She has appeared since the ballads as the daughter of the otherworld, with all the danger and glamour that that implies [...] with the other world open to her, she becomes more than subversive, she is perilous, and perhaps, in terms of accepted moralities, downright evil. She has a long and questionable history [Elphinstone 1992, 42–59, 47].

Elphinstone's reference to the Ballads is important here. When Armitt argues that in contemporary literature, "what we find in magic realism (particularly at the dark end of its spectrum where it meets the Gothic) is a double-edged frisson which oscillates around the disturbing aspects of the everyday" (Armitt 2000, 306), she could be describing the supernatural elements of the Ballads, which have existed orally in Scotland for centuries. The Ballads often feature the unexplained and persistently ambiguous entry of something magical or even evil into a prosaic setting, and just so Margot brings an element of magic into the most commonplace context of a woman advising her grandson during a stroll.

The sinister and subversive edge comes when we realize that what she is referring to is the mysterious and obscure death of her son. He himself acts as an almost supernatural presence in the novel. His narrative voice appears regularly throughout the text as a kind of voice from beyond the grave, an ambiguous ghost. This was literalized in psychosomatic supernatural form in the 1996 television adaptation of *The Crow Road*. Screenwriter Brian Elsley translates Rory into the new medium as an ambiguous ghost, appearing only to Prentice in order to advise and provide clues as to his mysterious disappearance. Banks' narrative technique is a more subtle approach, allowing Rory's presence to be fully ambiguous: is he a "ghost writer" whose voice reaches us from the "other side," or is this a straightforward embedded first person voice emanating from the late Rory's pre-humus papers? We cannot know. What we can know, however, is the inter-familial bonds that Margo personifies will be inherited by Prentice, as he finally acknowledges the interconnectedness of events and people that can and do operate outside conventional religious structures. Prentice reflects towards the end that "we continue in our children, and in our works and in the memories of others; [...] it was only a sort of sad selfishness that demanded the continuation of the individual spirit in the vanity and frivolity of heaven" (Banks 1992, 484) The novel ends with him holding his baby nephew and standing with his brother and cousins, facing an unknown future optimistically. Through Prentice's journey Banks illustrates a new humanism.

Conclusion

Both supernatural and psychological explanations operate simultaneously in relation to the fantastic episodes in all three novels. The supernatural phenomena potentially exist within the private world of the self and also outwardly in the shared world of the real. The refusal to identify a single centre of truth, in terms of interpretation of events, leads on to a refusal of the solitary, and by extrapolation an advocation of the communal. A crucial tenet of realism is the false idea of closure and resolution towards the end, whether positive or negative, for the satisfaction of the reader. In these texts, resolution is not possible, and in a postmodernist sense elides the dichotomy of real/unreal in a politically pertinent way. As Terry Eagleton argues, "to be inside and outside a position at the same time — to occupy a territory while loitering skeptically on the boundary — is often where the most intensely creative ideas stem from" (Eagleton 2003, 40). This creativity, for Banks, allows him to celebrate a return to effective and beneficial social constructions such as family, community and humanity. In the world depicted in these texts, there is still the potential for magic, for wonder and for meaningful interactions with others.

NOTES

1. Amaryll Beatrice Chanady carefully defines and differentiates categories in her 1985 study, *Magic Realism and The Fantastic: Resolved Versus Unresolved Antinomy*. She defines magic realism thus: "In contrast to the fantastic, the supernatural in magical realism does not disconcert the reader, and this is the fundamental difference between the two modes. The same phenomena that are portrayed as problematical by the author of a fantastic narrative are presented in a matter-of-fact manner by the magical realist. Since the supernatural is not perceived as unacceptable because it is antinomious, the characters and reader do not try to find a natural explanation, as is frequently the case with the fantastic" (Chanady 1985, 24).

2. See for example: Armitt's *Theorising the Fantastic* (1996), Cornwell's *The Literary Fantastic: From Gothic to Postmodernism* (1990), Hume's *Fantasy and Mimesis: Responses to Reality in Western Literature* (1984) and Jackson's *Fantasy: The Literature of Subversion* (1981).

3. The sect's origins in the North West are significant, and tap into a Scottish literary trope associating the North with the Other: a regional Other within a nation already the Other for its southern neighbours. The association between the Highlands of Scotland and the Otherworldly has a long and notable literary history. A summary might include: James Macpherson's late-eighteenth century Ossianic verse; portrayals in some of Walter Scott's *Waverley* novels, including *Waverley* (1814) itself and *The Bride of Lammermoor*

(1819); Robert Louis Stevenson's 1887 story "The Merry Men"; J.M Barrie's 1932 novella *Farewell Miss Julie Logan*; and into the late-twentieth century and the present day with a large number of fiction, film and television portrayals, from *Brigadoon* (1954) to the BBC comedy series *Little Britain* (2003–).

4. The term was first used in relation to literature in France in 1826, in the periodical *Le Mercure Francais*. It was defined as "the literature of truth." For a full discussion of the origins of the mode see Carsaniga's *The Age of Realism* (1978, 9).

5. The town of Porteneil, near which the Cauldhame family home and its tidal island lie, is fictional, but the novel suggests that it is located on the Moray Firth somewhere near Inverness in the North East Highlands.

6. For a fuller consideration of Frank, his mental illness and his position as the classic unreliable narrator, see Martyn Colebrook's 2010 essay, "'Journeys Into Lands of Silence': *The Wasp Factory* and Mental Disorder."

7. Gallanach is a settlement just outside of the North Argyll town of Oban. Banks adopts the name and transports it to a fictional village in Mid-Argyll, which lies next to real places such as Loch Fyne, Lochgair, and Kilmartin.

8. See also Coleman O. Parsons' *Witchcraft and Demonology in Scott's Fiction* (1964, 147).

WORKS CITED

Armitt, Lucie. 1996. *Theorising the Fantastic*. London: Arnold.
_____. 2000. "The Magic Realism of Contemporary Gothic." In *A Companion to the Gothic*. David Punter, ed. Oxford: Blackwell.
Baldick, Chris. 2008. "The Fantastic." *The Oxford Dictionary of Literary Terms*. Oxford: Oxford University Press. http://www.oxfordreference.com/views/ENTRY.html?subview=Main&entry=t56.e448. Accessed 21 April 2011.
Carsaniga, G. M., ed. 1978. *The Age of Realism*. Hassocks: Harvester Press.
Chanady, Amaryll Beatrice. 1985. *Magic Realism and The Fantastic: Resolved Versus Unresolved Antinomy*. New York: Garland.
Colebrook, Martyn. 2010. "'Journeys Into Lands of Silence': *The Wasp Factory* and Mental Disorder." In *Demons of the Body and Mind: Essays on Disability in Gothic Literature*. Ruth Bienstock Anolik, ed. Jefferson, NC: McFarland, 217–226.
Cornwell, Neil. 1990. *The Literary Fantastic: From Gothic to Postmodernism*. Hertfordshire: Harvester Wheatsheaf.
Craig, Cairns. 2002. *Iain Banks's Complicity: A Reader's Guide*. New York and London: Continuum.
Eagleton, Terry. 2003. *After Theory*. London: Allen Lane.
Elphinstone, Margaret. 1992. "Contemporary Feminist Fantasy in the Scottish Literary Tradition." In *Tea and Leg-Irons: New Feminist Readings from Scotland*. Caroline Gonda, ed. London: Open Letters.
Hume, Kathryn. 1984. *Fantasy and Mimesis: Responses to Reality in Western Literature*. London: Methuen.
Jackson, Rosemary. 1981. *Fantasy: The Literature of Subversion*. London: Methuen.
Kirkpatrick Sharpe, Charles. 1972 [1884]. *Witchcraft in Scotland*. Raymond Lamont Brown, ed. Wakefield: S.R. Publishers.
Manlove, Colin. 1994. *Scottish Fantasy Literature: A Critical Survey*. Edinburgh: Cannongate Academic.
OED. 1989. *The Oxford English Dictionary*, vol. XII, 2d ed. Oxford: Clarendon Press.
Parsons, Coleman O. 1964. *Witchcraft and Demonology in Scott's Fiction*. Edinburgh: Oliver and Boyd.
Todorov, Tzvetan. 1975 [1970]. *The Fantastic: A Structural Approach to a Literary Genre*. Richard Howard, trans. Ithaca: Cornell University Press.

Teaching Banks
The Wasp Factory *and* Frankenstein

EMILY GARSIDE AND KATHARINE COX

This essay will explore the experience of teaching Iain Banks' *The Wasp Factory* (1995) as part of a higher education module, focused on twentieth-century literature, and in particular the pairing of this novel with Mary Wollstonecraft (Godwin) Shelley's *Frankenstein: Or, The Modern Prometheus* (1818). The essay uses a framework which draws on practitioner insight, critical perspectives, reflection, analysis and input from students to consider the worth of teaching *The Wasp Factory* on an undergraduate syllabus. Banks' first novel has an important presence in Higher Education beyond its mainstay on Scottish literature courses. It appears on English literature modules considering British twentieth-century literature and contemporary literature as well as modules considering gender. Ben Knights, in his capacity as the Director of the HEA (Higher Education Academy) for English, champions the importance of the novel in the English Subject Centre Seed Guide (in Gibson 2011). This Seed Guide situates Banks alongside such canonical writers as William Shakespeare, Jane Austen, Charlotte and Emily Brontë and Oscar Wilde. In viewing him among his contemporary peers in the Guide, teaching advice on Banks is represented alongside exercises on Andrea Levy, Graham Swift and Nick Hornby. In Knights' exercises he uses the novel's representations of animals, the narratives of male apprenticeship and the geography of the island as starting points; all engaging subjects for a seminar discussion.

Context for the Teaching Session

In this particular context, Banks' novel featured on a module entitled "Modernism to Postmodernism." It is a year-long twentieth-century module, with *The Wasp Factory* as the penultimate text "representing" the 1980s.[1] The students studying this module were all from joint honors degrees (English plus a creative subject such as contemporary media, creative writing or drama). Though the module sits within the English literature side of the programs, it was important to the course team that the fiction encouraged the students to explore connections with their creative subjects which was realized through a creative option in the modular assessment. Over the course of the module, the students engaged with a number of key concepts in the development of twentieth-century literature; these included changes in narrative style and technique, the role of the unreliable storyteller, and representations of reality. Though part of the module's aims were to explore connections between the joint degrees, the course team also wanted the students to make links between modules on the English degree; especially to consider and reconsider earlier literature in light of twentieth-century writing. For this reason the team paired up novels from prior modules; such as Jean Rhys' *Wide Sargasso Sea* (1966) so that students could locate their earlier reading of Charlotte Brontë's *Jane Eyre* (1847); or discussing Angela Carter's *The Passion of New Eve* (1977) alongside Virginia Woolf's *Orlando* (1928). Studying *The Wasp Factory* gave the students an opportunity to reconsider their knowledge and approach to Shelley's *Frankenstein*, read as part of a Gothic literature module.

Students were introduced to Banks via a one hour lecture which included basic biographical information on Banks and placed him in context as a Scottish writer. This overview included the renaissance of Scottish literature from the 1980s onwards, identifying the significance of the writing of Alasdair Gray, James Kelman, Banks and Irvine Welsh. It also positioned Banks as a political writer, which follows on from the majority of critical texts on Banks which include him as part of a Scottish movement.[2] The lecture also outlined Banks' writing as an author of both mainstream and science fiction, before considering representations of fantasy and the fantastic within his mainstream fiction.

The content, designed for the two hour seminar to accompany the work on Banks' novel, was changed due to the reaction the novel elicited prior to teaching it. At the beginning of the module the module leader and tutors opened a discussion using the University's VLE (Virtual Learning Environment), Blackboard. The discussion board function in this module is intended to support the work undertake in seminars whereby seminar questions extend and remind students of discussions they have undertaken in class.

However, the discussion of *The Wasp Factory* preempted its session on the VLE and went "viral" on Facebook with students discussing this "sick" book.

The precedent for this response is perhaps contained in the initial critical reviews that accompanied the novel as well as the clever use of these by publishers Little, Brown Book Group. A host of negative reviews are included in the Abacus edition which highlights the violence and gore of the novel; coupled with this is a very personal reaction from reviewers, capturing their indignation and revulsion. As the infamous quotation from the Sunday Telegraph confirms, "Enjoy it I did not" (qtd. Banks 1990, preface). Any reader who picks up the novel, reads the blurb and the reviews, is aware of its transgressive status and these quotations can work as perverse textual sound bites even before the novel is read. The impact of this on the class was evidenced via the initial on-line reaction and followed up by the preparation the students undertook. As a result, the majority of students had read the novel prior to the seminar which made for a very vocal and detailed discussion. This impetus to read the book was elicited by the students (rather than by the tutor's timely reminding about the reading list). We have had a similar consensus to complete the reading prior to class in detective fiction seminars where students preferred to be in the know about the end of the book, rather than have the knowledge imparted to them over the course of the lecture. There's a possibility that the knowledge of a "twist" at the conclusion of the novel (alluded to in the VLE) also helped precipitate this reading.

Violence in the Novel

Given the students' interest we were concerned that there may be a tendency to valorize the violence in the novel. However, in the initial group discussions it became apparent that some of the students had read the violence in the novel as symbolic (and perhaps fantastical or imagined).[3] They argued that the use of violence functions as a literary technique and not as a derogatory element of Banks' writing which situated their reading in opposition to some reviewing critics. It was then a simple matter to make this response explicit as the starting point for an argument and one that challenged existing critics. In the culminations of their discussion, they read violence in the novel as a strength of Banks' abilities and not as Gavin Miller, in *Edinburgh Companion to Scottish Literature*, views Banks, as merely aping the "non canonical popular and pulp horror authors" (Miller 2007, 202). Perhaps there was also a desire from the students to rescue Banks from the clutches of critics who did not understand the irony of popular culture references, such as the so-called "video nast[ies]" (Sunday Express qtd, Banks 1990, preface). Though the students seemed keen to claim Banks as a writer of youth experience there was also a need to balance this to ensure that these responses remained critical and distanced.

The Wasp Factory is a very rich text that lends itself towards a discussion of gender and theoretical notions of anti-essentialism. However, having studied a variety of texts that depict aspects of anti-essentialist theory, such as Carter's *The Passion of New Eve*, we were keen to augment this focus and guide the students into discussions of the monstrous in the novel. Taking a cue from the Gothic work the students had already completed, we worked within the relationship between Shelley's *Frankenstein* and *The Wasp Factory*, in particular the relationship between creator and monster, humanity and monstrosity.

Using Banks' statement about the writing process that writers "stand on the shoulders of [a] particular giant, write something initially similar but developmentally different, so that the field evolves and further twists and turns are added" (Banks 2011, n.p.), we encouraged the students to think about whose shoulders Banks might be writing. This led to some interesting discussions drawing on the connections with Carter in particular before one of the students mentioned the similarity of Frank's name which could be short for Frankenstein. This was a defining moment in the seminar which caused the class to think about Shelly's novel and in particular her monstrous creation. Building on this, we asked the students to consider these similarities in small group work. During the course of the session, they mentioned a rich variety of connections, including Frank's quasi-scientific process which satirizes empirical enquiry, the narrative of maturation (*bildungsroman*) for both "monsters" and the idea of progenitor/creator. This was this final area, the relationship between creator and monster, that we most wanted to explore as it seemed to make such an obvious connection to Shelley's novel.

Exploring the Monster/Creator Dynamic in The Wasp Factory *and* Frankenstein

The following analysis draws on student observations and seeks to evidence this through additional critical material. It would be useful in future to build on these discussions and perhaps create an on-line Wiki of materials for subsequent groups. In doing so, it would be interesting to note the following year's responses to the enthusiasm of this earlier group; whether perhaps they would view the appropriation of the text in the same way or if they would want to distance themselves from this earlier discussion.

In both *Frankenstein* and *The Wasp Factory*, students addressed the ambiguity and the blurring of the roles of monster and creator. In *Frankenstein* the creature accuses Frankenstein and names him explicitly as his creator:

> Ye you, my creator, detest and spurn me, they creature to whom thou art bound by ties only dissoluble by the annihilation of one of us [Shelley 2008, n.p.].

In this exchange the doctor expresses clear ownership of the creature offering to "extinguish the spark which I so negligently bestowed" (Shelley 2008, n.p.). It becomes clear after the creature's unusual education that he understands the role of his creator to nurture him and, finding him wanting from the ideal, rejects him based on his neglect. As the creature blames his own creation on the doctor, Frankenstein comes to take on that responsibility, naming himself monster. In the battle that ensues, "let us try our strength in a fight, in which one must fall" (Shelley 2008, n.p.), the violence and anger of master and creator become indistinguishable. In Shelley's text it seems inevitable that only one can remain, either creator or monster, and this can also be seen in Frank's relationship with his father.

In *The Wasp Factory* the lines between monster and creator are also blurred and complex in terms of what is created. Frank is part of a pseudo-scientific and a social experiment instigated by Angus, his father. Through drug-induced hormonal treatment Angus creates Frank, who is as Schoene-Harwood illustrates

> [a] manufactured, entirely fictitious creation, obsessively overcompensating for a patriarchally inflicted lack of natural manliness by pursuing an extremist ideal of violent masculine perfection [Schoene-Harwood 1999, 133].

The association between manliness and this hyper-violence is a problematic one which was leap on by the students. Though Schoene-Harwood is perhaps being deliberately contentious there are some big assumptions that were voiced in class about masculinity and violence that this quotation allowed us to explore further. This was a particularly spirited aspect of the discussion and led to some interesting points about the representations of masculinity in this and the other novels studied. It was valuable also to be able to point students towards contemporary work on masculinity and its positioning in relation to feminism. It was pleasing to see the roundness of the discussion here partially as a response to work on feminism and how some students (two male students in particular) reflected on this later as "something for them" in their self-assessment portion of their summative submission. Despite some of the unlikely positivity surrounding this representation of gender, the class nevertheless seemed to appreciate the exaggerated and extreme nature of this representation which we discussed as monstrous. The exaggerated aspect of

Banks' writing helped here as this part of the discussion could have been overly heated or rendered generalist.

In his essay concerning *The Wasp Factory*, Alexis de Coning articulates the persistence of monsters in literature in the arts in which he claims the monstrous is an indication of "the significance of the monstrous as a social and cultural trope" (de Coning n.d., 2). In considering Frank and his father in *The Wasp Factory* students were asked to evaluate them as examples of literary monsters and in particular to explore the relationship between creator and monster. From this position, students were able to draw on the work they had completed on *Frankenstein* and, in so doing, a comparison between Shelley and Banks' characters began to develop. There are obvious parallels that Banks develops such as the father-figure of Angus, himself a scientist, which draws clear parallels with doctor Frankenstein, as does the suggestive naming of Frank. The students successfully identified these obvious allusions and then explored some of the thematic concerns with more detail.

Both texts explore the boundaries between life and death, and man's ability or opportunity to influence life and exert power over it. In numerous ways Frank is able to take life; in addition to his routine and regular destruction of wasps and rabbits, his murders of humans are enacted over a number of years and qualify him as a serial killer. It is in death that Frank identifies his power:

> My dead sentries, those extensions of me which came under my power through the simple but ultimate surrender of death, sensed nothing to harm me or the island [Banks 1995, 20].

Such rituals are linked to his imaginary castration. In part, his ritualizing mirrors the process by which he has "become" male. Frank forms an identity through his rituals in the way he has been denied forming of his own sex (for even if Frank views himself as male he is an atypical one due to his "castration"), and perhaps as a compensation for this. The make-up of his body, his hormones and the internal struggle between nature and nurture, gender and sex becomes manifest in Frank through expressions of violence and a desire for power over life. In particular, Frank's response to death is cavalier:

> Two years after I killed Blyth I murdered my young brother Paul, for quite different and more fundamental reasons that I'd disposed of Blyth, and then a year after that I did for my young cousin Emerelda, more or less on a whim. That's my score to date. Three. I haven't killed anybody for years, and don't intend to ever again. It was just a stage I was going through [Banks 1995, 42].

Frank's detachment from the murders he commits indicates the drive to kill is abstracted, related to the power; to the act itself rather than a crime of passion against those he murders. This is a crucial consideration for discussion with the students as it is pivotal that the students are able to articulate Banks' reasons for representing violence and death in this way. As has been previously noted, this group's exploration of the novel was sensitive and was perhaps born as a response to the generalized reviews they'd already encountered. The human victims for Frank are aligned with his animal victims: the dead hare or wasps in his factory. The mechanisms of death, as with the rituals that imbue his life, are what fuel Frank's murders; it is not the pursuit of death itself but the power and feelings of validation which accompany it. In Frank's case this stems from a need, conscious or otherwise, for control over his life; his castration has robbed him of control over his own body, he therefore exerts control over the bodies of others through the power of life and death.

However, it is his father Angus who gives life to his creation: Francis Leslie Cauldhame. The descriptions of Angus' rooms and references to his scientific past seem redolent with allusions to the nineteenth-century scientist figure of which Frankenstein is arguably most prominent. In considering Angus' creative and scientific impulses, students were able to make tangible connections here to both Frankenstein's as progenitor of his monster as well as the figure of Dracula. This led to a discussion of the male mother or the "terrible mother" which they'd also encountered in critical work on D.H. Lawrence's *Sons and Lovers*. These many asides in seminars often serve as a starting point for students' own research, as it proved here with a number of students working up this concept in their essays.

Banks resituates Frankenstein's drive to create life in Frank. Whereas Frank desires to bring death and destruction, Frankenstein toils to make life:

> After days and nights of incredible labor and fatigue, I succeeded in discovering the cause of generation and life; nay, more, I became myself capable of bestowing animation upon lifeless matter [Shelley 2008, n.p.].

Students quickly realized that Frankenstein is consumed by his work in much the same way as Frank obsessively undertakes a ritualized life which leads to the murders. Both novels explore the unhealthy nature of these scientific obsessions and the dire consequences of these.

Victor Frankenstein begins with grand aspirations about what his power over life and death can do, but the reality of what he creates (the creature) crushes this. Frankenstein's monster goes on to commit horrible deeds; he murders and terrorizes with a seemingly removed attitude brought on by his indifference to the human race. Angus in *The Wasp Factory* also appears satisfied with the success of his creation in Frank after his "pilot" attempt with his brother Eric. Though it could be argued that Angus' success is crushed first by the nature of the son he has created and then by Frank's discovery of the truth, in some ways Angus' experiment worked. Angus creates a son who embraces a type of extreme hyper-masculinity and who ultimately guesses wrong about his father's experiments, believing his father to be a woman. Angus ultimately confesses the truth but also reveals a number of further scientific proofs at his disposal should he have been challenged:

> He was going to confront me with the specimen-jar [containing a fake wax penis and testicle] if I ever started to query whether I really was castrated [Banks 1995, 181].

Banks describes the deconstruction of the myth around Frank's castration. Here Frank instructs his father to "tell me" (Banks 1995, 178) followed by his father's acquiescence which we do not hear directly from Angus but rather as a synopsis version via Frank. Power is shifted to Frank when he holds the specimen jar aloft which had held power over him throughout his life. The identity of Frances/Francis shifts when he gains power over his father at this point.

The revelation at the conclusion of *The Wasp Factory* illustrates the level of Angus' experimentation:

> [Angus] started dosing me with male hormones, and has been ever since [the accident] ... what I've always thought was the stump of a penis is really enlarged clitoris [Banks 1995, 240].

This renaming of his/her body repositions the relationship that Frank has with his/her identity. It is useful to consider Judith Butler's discussion on male and female pronouns at this point, as one which alters from:

> an "it" to a "she" or a "he" and in that naming, the girl is "girled," brought into the domain of language and kinship through the interpellation of gender [Butler 1993, 7].

When Frank "girls" himself he gains control and power putting himself in control and so in the role of creator. Still at this point he is skeptical, and this passage which signals a changed notion of identity is problematic as "[e]ven now I can't be sure he told me everything" (Banks 1995, 181).

Though Frankenstein is also concerned, consumed even, by similar drives of power (of life over death) his actions and thoughts as presented by Shelley draw distinction from Frank. Frankenstein reminds the reader that "[he] is not recording the vision of a madman" (Shelley 2008, n.p.). In comparison, Frank is unreliable and a partial narrator,[4] whose sanity as a character the reader is often forced to question. The fantastical elements of his story as well as the nonchalance of his murdering "stage" do allow the character to be read as an unreliable one which coupled with his brother's psychiatric problems again challenges his credibility. The implications of this were forensically considered by the group. The creative writing students in particular were very familiar with the construction of an unreliable narrator and their discussions focused on the technique of "showing" rather than "telling" via the narrator. This technical discussion was balanced by an investigation into the implications of this unreliability. Did it cause the reader to deal flippantly with the deaths? Did these deaths even happen? A number of students pointed to the hyperbole of the narrator and the farcical manner of these killings to argue that these were all imagined. One student drew on his reading of Brett Easton Ellis to suggest that his work *American Psycho* (1991) also unsettles the reader with similar questions. Though this was not set reading, others in the group has also read *American Psycho* and were keen to discuss this line of comparison to the extent that it threatened to engulf the existing topic to consider *The Wasp Factory* in partnership with *Frankenstein*. It is perhaps important to note both texts' satirical depiction of violence and also the popularity of both of these novels with the students. It has led the teaching team to reflect on the possibility of developing a module that would consider this aspect of contemporary story telling; however, there would be a need to ensure that this did not become gratuitous. Given the thoughtful and often sophisticated response to these texts here though, the idea is perhaps a promising one.

Conclusion

The ambiguity of the novel is evident in the final line of Banks' novel and forms a valuable creative aspect to have the students consider what will happen next:

> Poor Eric came home to see his brother, only to find (Zap! Pow! Damns burst! Bombs go off! Wasps fry: tsss!) he's got a sister [Banks 1995, 184].

Considering this final declarations the parallels between the two texts remain apparent, each is sketchy on exactly what will become of the "creation"; will Frankenstein's creation die as he asserts? How will Frank's life change now following this alternative revelation of self? Will his/her murderous impulses cease? By selecting the creative option for assessment students who were interested were able to explore the novel's themes and concerns further (namely through a creative writing exercise and accompanying critical reflection). Intriguingly, the students who chose this option explored earlier aspects of the novel rather than fulfilling a "what happened next" approach (though it is hoped that subsequent students might follow this angle). The creative responses tended to follow some of the tangential concerns from the seminar which had obviously fired the students' imagination. In particular, one of the English and Drama students explored the idea of Eric as an imaginary character imposing a first person narration that demonstrated that he and Frank were one and the same (the critical reflection that accompanied this was very well articulated). In addition, there was evidence of students playing with unreliable narrators, drawing out aspects of the monstrous and using the first person to approach the task. The themes present in their work reflected the discussions undertaken in the seminars but they pushed their thinking through further by constructing a creative piece from which to view and review the original. Each heeded Banks' advice to write "something initially similar but developmentally different, so that the field evolves and further twists and turns are added" (Banks 2011, n.p.). In following the original quotation, it is arguable whether Banks' writing can be considered that of a "giant" as yet but this collection goes some way to demonstrate his significance and variety as a contemporary author of importance.

The worth of teaching Banks' novel can be usefully drawn from a commentary on teaching *Frankenstein* by Gladys Veidemanis (1986). In discussing the teaching of *Frankenstein*, Veidemanis notes the importance of teaching a novel that students find both "interesting [and] intellectually stimulating" (Veidemanis 1986, 61). The observations made about *Frankenstein* as a novel could also be applied to *The Wasp Factory*, as Veidemanis notes, the novel: "[c]ompels the reader to such philosophical questions as the nature of humans, the origins of good and evil" (Veidemanis 1986, 61). These questions that Veidemanis indicates as vital for teaching *Frankenstein* form the backbone of the questions considered for Banks. So it is that standing on the canonical shoulder belonging to Shelley we can approach this twentieth-century novel. In so doing, *The Wasp Factory* has the potential to become both a classic but also that rare thing that is a text that is both interesting and intriguing for students.

Notes

1. Although the seminar did not situate the novel within an historical context this might be usefully achieved through a mediation on Thatcherism and the politics of the Falklands War.
2. See for example Duncan Petrie (2004) and Cairns Craig (2002).
3. There was a very interesting digression about whether Frank had imagined the whole thing and that even Eric could be read as a side of this unreliable narrator.
4. Banks regularly explores this idea of an unreliable narrator. His work in this area is most explicit in *Transition* where the opening lines of the novel state: "[a]pparently I am what is known as an Unreliable Narrator, though of course if you believe everything you're told you deserve whatever you get" (Banks 2009, 1).

Works Cited

Banks, Iain. 1995 [1984]. *The Wasp Factory.* London: Abacus.
_____. 2009. *Transition.* London: Little, Brown.
Banks, Iain M. 2011. "Science Fiction Is No Place for Dabblers." *The Guardian.* 13 May 2011. http://www.guardian.co.uk/books/2011/may/13/iain-banks-science-fiction-genre.
Butler, Judith. 1993. *Bodies That Matter: On the Discursive Limits of "Sex."* London: Routledge.
De Coning, Alexis. n.d. "Sympathizing with a Monster: An Exploration of the Abject 'Human Monster' in Iain Banks' *The Wasp Factory.*" Google search "De Coning Sympathizing with a Monster."
Schoene-Harwood, Berthold. 1999. "Dams Burst: Devolving Gender in Iain Banks's *The Wasp Factory.*" *ARIEL: A Review of International English Literature* 30, no. 1, 131–148.
Shelley, Mary Wollstonecraft. 2008. *Frankenstein, Or The Modern Prometheus.* Project Gutenberg. www.gutenberg.org.
Veidemanis, Gladys V. 1986. "Frankenstein in the Classroom." *English Journal* 75, no. 7, 61–66.
Miller, Gavin. 2007. "Iain (M.) Banks: Utopia, Nationalism and the Posthuman." In *Edinburgh Companion to Scottish Literature.* Berthold Schoene-Harwood, ed. Edinburgh: Edinburgh University Press, 202–209.

IV. Gender, Games and Play

Contesting Gender in *The Wasp Factory*, *Whit* and *The Business*

SARAH FALCUS

Gender is a complex subject in the "mainstream" novels of Iain Banks. It is not unusual to find women as victims of male sexual aggression (see, for example, Morgan in *A Song of Stone* 1998). Whilst this may highlight the repression and dangers of patriarchal masculinity and exposes women's subordination in this system, it nevertheless runs perilously close at times to the traditional portrayal of women as little more than sexual objects, perhaps producing a vicarious pleasure in the reader. However, this is not the whole story. Women are very often strong and determined in Banks' novels.[1] This might suggest that Banks is insistent on a simplistic position of gender equality. This approach is signaled near the end of *The Business* as Kate considers her decision to move to Thulan and states that "[j]ust in the last few generations, finally able to control our own fertility, have we been able to act more like men and contribute more with our brains than our bodies" (Banks 2000, 388). This approach fits in with the way that women in many of these novels are forced to deny the specificity of female experience in favor of a stereotypically male role.

But, again, this is not the only way to read Banks' work. Berthold Schoene-Harwood, in his discussion of gender in *The Wasp Factory*, argues that Banks is intent on exposing and ridiculing the whole patriarchal system; in this case in his tale of a violently masculine young man who turns out to be a young woman (Schoene-Harwood 1999, 132). In this essay, I argue that these various ways of approaching gender in Banks' work are held in tension in *The Wasp Factory*, *Whit* and *The Business*. These novels do not offer easy or unproblematic narratives of women in men's worlds, but explore what happens and what is sacrificed when women try to take up positions of power in patriarchal social systems. In these texts, gender, like identity, is not stable, and the conclusions of the novels present both concepts as a process of negotiation. This can be related to Cairns Craig's analysis of Banks' novels in terms of game playing:

> The conflict between being a player and being played upon, and the difficulty of discovering the rules of the game in which one is playing, are the insistent themes of Banks' fiction [Cairns 2005, 233].

The question here might therefore be: can women change the rules of the game? In these three texts women are the narrators of their own stories. Immediately, I have to introduce a caveat: at times this narration does take on a ventriloquist nature; for example, when it is a vehicle for the author's own political or social beliefs, or for his overtly witty satire. This can be problematic, as in Isis' narration, for example, when the ironic tone makes us question the naivety of the narrator. Indeed, this lack of distance between author and protagonists in many of Banks' texts has been identified by a number of critics.[2] Nevertheless, it is significant that these women, who are bound in different ways to ultimately patriarchal systems, are given the chance to tell their own stories in narratives that are often ironic and ambiguous, signaling dawning awareness in the women of the positions in which they find themselves.

Context

There's no doubt that in these three novels women are strong and determined. Frank's father's hormone- and lie-induced experiment produces a girl who believes she is a castrated boy. Frank therefore "invents" himself as a male and along with this "a whole religion and cosmology which will explain and justify the microcosmic barbarian world he imagines himself to be the centre of" (Sage 1996, 25). Frank's strength leads to a bizarre and ritualistic system of macabre beliefs and practices, which includes three well-planned and carefully executed murders. The result is, as Victor Sage describes him, "a supermale, an insular warrior, whose enemies are Women and the Sea" (Sage 1996, 25). In this way, the world he creates mirrors his psyche; as Sage states, "[t]he topography of Frank's little world of death and retribution is the topography of his own unconscious self-denial" (Sage 1996, 25). Frank's defensive need to take and remain in control and present a super-masculine persona, means that he rejects anything he identifies as feminine or weak, ironically becoming a male barbarian figure, while, of course, being a woman. This makes clear that gender is a construct, with (excessive) masculinity the outcome of a fiction; an experiment. As Schoene-Harwood argues, this darkly amusing exploration of the construction of gender leaves open the possibility that Frank's personality may be a result of his upbringing, the hormones his father feeds him, or a mixture of the two, but it nevertheless presents gender in the performative (Schoene-Harwood 1999, 131–2).[3] In opposition to this, Frank's father is presented (by Frank of course) as weak, particularly towards the end of the novel when he tries to avoid the return of Eric: "[t]hat lying old shit, trying to lure me away from the house just because *he* was too frightened to face Eric [....] Call himself a man!" (Banks 1984, 168). Of course, this is also an example of the duality created by the narrative voice in this text: Frank's idealization of a retrograde manliness becomes ironic and humorous in the light of the text's conclusion. Whilst Kate in *The Business* and Isis in *Whit* are, of course, gendered female from the beginning of the texts, they nevertheless also present similarly determined and strong characteristics, asserting a dominance that in many ways appears learned. And, again, men in *The Business* and *Whit* are reflected as weak and, often, unprincipled.

Many of the set pieces in *Whit* illustrate Isis' fearlessness and willingness to defend her beliefs. For example, she throws Tabasco sauce in the faces of BNP thugs when they taunt Boz with racist insults (Banks 1996, 180). Of course, the whole narrative of her long and rather torturous (given the approach of the sect to the modern world) journey to London and beyond, followed by her besting of Allan and her ultimate success in taking control of the sect, demonstrates her strength and resourcefulness. This is underlined in the novel by the fallibility of the men around her: Zeb and Boz make no attempt to join her when she stands up to BNP supporters, or confronts the dog in La Mancha; Salvador turns out to be a thief and Allan a scheming capitalist. This is a clear reversal of traditional gender associations, with Isis the strong, determined, resourceful and principled woman, and the men weak, scheming, unprincipled.[4]

Kate in *The Business* is similarly strong, right from the opening conversation, where she deals with an employee of the Business (her junior) who is struggling to make an important business meeting because he has had half his teeth extracted. Kate enjoys the fact that men such as Rix and Henderson are afraid of her when she visits the Silex plant (Banks 2000, 21). And, in one of the most amusing examples, she uses that symbol of masculinity (if not midlife crisis), the red Ferrari, to symbolically castrate Adrian and turn him into a whining fool. Linking this to the incident in *The Wasp Factory* when Frank's mother knocks his father over with a motorbike, symbolically castrating him too, and leaving him literally holding the baby, Banks seems to have a penchant for setting up the downfall of men at the hands of their own machines, as well as women.[5]

Therefore, there is a clear desire in these novels for women to be seen as just as strong, if not stronger, than the men around them, reversing the traditional binary of gender associations. Kate and Isis may be seen as pseudomen in many ways, as the reactions of other characters suggest at points, echoing the more literal "man-acting" of Frank. But of course this can be problematic, suggesting that the qualities these women exhibit are the very characteristics most to be admired, producing a simplistic assertion of female equality. However, this is obviously tempered in these novels by the fact that these women are all clearly women within men's worlds and that these worlds are the focus of critique and interrogation in the novels. Frank, most obviously, is at the heart of a world controlled by the twisted lies of his father. As Schoene-Harwood argues, this extends even to language, as Frank's father teaches him that Pathos was one of the three musketeers or that Vitreous was a town in China (Schoene-Harwood 1999, 141–2.). Even Frank's independent system of beliefs, with its own geography of sacrifice poles, bunker and wasp factory, is ultimately formed within the patriarchy espoused by his father and therefore "his supposedly alternative existence replicates in minutest detail the symbolic order he aims to replace" (Schoene-Harwood 1999, 142).

It is not difficult to see that Kate and Isis are in very similar positions. Isis is in the sect set up and controlled by her grandfather and based upon the mythology he continually revises in his *Orthography*. Just as Frank lives his life according to the lies fed him by his father, so Isis lives her life, even to her sexual and reproductive future, as a Luskentyrian, following the malleable rules of her grandfather. Kate's position in the Business similarly dictates her life, even to the denial of faith in favor of capitalism.[6] So the positions of equality, if not dominance, achieved by these women are based upon traditionally male attributes such as strength, power and resourcefulness, and success is measured in competitive terms. Isis is therefore proud of her status as a "tough cookie," with the implication being that such a quality is unusual in a woman (see Banks 1996, 181). The men around her often admire her strength, again stressing its oddness in a woman. Kate is similarly admired in *The Business*, and also feared, as though an unknown quantity. Incidentally, in both texts, men find this sexually attractive.

Absence of Mothers

In order to achieve power, therefore, these texts suggest that women sacrifice the specificity of feminine experience in favor of the valorization of stereotypically male values. One of the ways that the texts present this exclusion of female experience is through the absence of mothers in all three novels.

On one level, this absence underlines the fact that these women are social rather than genetic constructions, with learned gender behavior. All three of the narrators are raised in non-traditional ways, with biological mothers absent, dead, or lacking control over their daughters' lives. The most obvious example of this is of course Frank, who is a modern Frankenstein's monster (gothically without mother), created by his father to believe that he is a castrated man. And so the mother is something Frank must deny and repudiate in order to follow his Oedipal path. Frank creates a system in opposition to his "greatest enemies [...] Women and the Sea," linking the two as uncontrollable (Banks 1984, 43). Of course, the irony of this is that Frank is simply playing out the psychoanalytic narrative of the female child as a little man, to use Luce Irigaray's description of this position (see Irigaray 1985, 27). Frank's attitude to women points to the way that the assumption of power and control is predicated on the denial of the feminine, making clear that this text aims to undo and expose the Law of the Father that oppresses female experience.

But this can also be seen in a less explicit way in *Whit* and *The Business*. Isis' parents died when she was very young and she is brought up in the sect with what she sees as lots of love and pseudo-parenting, but what this ensures is that she is not a product of a maternal heritage, but of a paternally ordered society, in which, however, she is central as a future leader. Isis, like Frank, is at the centre of a world of ritual and symbol; and, as Frank's father is responsible for Frank's position, so Salvador, Isis's grandfather, dictates hers.

In *The Business*, Kate's mother is weak, providing love, but also introducing the young girl to domestic violence and the privations of a poor, Glasgow home. Again, she experiences another form of mothering, this time from Mrs. Telman. This is maternal, but also paternalistic: Mrs. Telman visits regularly but not frequently, bringing presents for both Kate and her mother, and directing their lives, even finding Kate's mother a new job. This assumption of the paternal role is clearly suggested at Kate's mother's funeral, where Mrs. Telman steers Kate away from her presumably alcoholic biological father, signaling her control over Kate and her "fatherhood" of the girl (Banks 2000, 34). Mrs. Telman is also representative of the Business itself and is preparing Kate for her role in this. The sense of indoctrination into the system is echoed in the bland and yet slightly menacing reference by Tommy Chongolai to the Business' control of Suvinder's nephew as a way of insuring control over Thulan:

"If he [Suvinder] has no children, there is a ten-year-old nephew who is next in line. He is in one of our schools in Switzerland." Chongolai smiled. "He is making good progress" [Banks 2000, 166].

As this suggests, for the Business, children are simply part of the capitalist system; Kate is therefore a product of Mrs. Telman and the Business, not of her mother.

More generally, there is a scarcity of mothers in these novels: in *The Wasp Factory*, Frank's mother is absent; in *The Business*, Mrs. Telman cannot have children and Kate's mother dies; in *Whit*, Isis is surrounded by mothers (though her own is dead), but the care of children cannot be limited to one mother, Yolanda has lost her daughter (Isis' mother), and even Sophi's mother died giving birth to her. Whilst the absence of mothers makes clear that the daughters are products of social systems and could also be said to highlight the way that the patriarchal system oppresses the mother, it also has more problematic connotations; for example, it is associated with the gothic and women as potential (sexual) victims without the protection of their mothers. And, more crucially, these texts could be said to contribute to the effacement of the mother. Mothers are reduced here to symbols or fairytales. Isis' mother is part of the long story of the cult, dying in a fire from which Isis' father saved his daughter by throwing her from a window. Frank's mother is also part of family lore, roaring away on her motorbike after leaving her second child on the island. Even Kate's mother is part of a story of the past; that of the rags-to-riches tale of the little Glasgow girl found making a profit selling sweeties to her friends (Banks 1996, 252; Banks 1984, 107; Banks 2000, 22–30). In these texts, the real mother is effaced in favor of the mother of myth. And this extends into the lives of the daughters, none of whom are mothers and all of whom have difficulties with their own sexuality and potential motherhood.

Frank is obviously, once again, the most extreme example of this. His defensive denial of the feminine extends to a hatred of the mother: "I can't remember my mother because if I did I'd hate her" (Banks 1984, 66). This further exemplifies his playing out of the Freudian scene. But, Kate is also not a mother and though having had fertility tests, insists to Luce that she does not want to be a mother (Banks 2000, 284). Isis is also struggling with the possibility of motherhood, which is the desired outcome of her participation in the festival of love. This is of course linked to her difficulties with her sexuality, and to the commodification of motherhood in the sect, where it is controlled by the community and integral to the future of the sect. For all three women, motherhood is something that cannot be countenanced. In different ways it threatens the identities of all three: Frank's excessive masculinity; Kate's role as high flyer; Isis' sense of self.

Sexuality and Relationships

These women also have problems with their sexualities. Kate takes a stereotypically masculine approach, with sex as a commodity. This is particularly clear in her approach to Raymond, the chauffeur, and her delight at the way he is able to compartmentalize his roles as her lover and her servant. This attitude to sex fits in with the Business' capitalist ethos, as made clear when beautiful women are available for men during the meeting at Blysecrag. But Kate is also in love with Stephen, who is unlike the other men in being faithful to his wife. On one level, this suggests that the only man Kate can love is one who is not a typical man, pointing to the possibility of a different order of things, where equality works both ways and is not unproblematic. However, it's also possible that there is a compensatory quality to this, as though Banks is trying to prevent Kate from being simply a ventriloquized man and offering her more feminine attributes. March argues that Banks does include "reconciliatory narrative gestures"— into which we could place this affair— in order to avoid this sense of women just acting as men, but that these "suggest the very gender typing Banks hopes to avoid" (March 2002, 100). Whichever way we read this, it is clear that Kate's sexuality will not be allowed free expression as long as she wants to keep her position in the Business, as the Business's surveillance of Stephen's wife suggests.

Isis' relationship with sexuality is even more problematic. This ripples through the text, from her relationships with Morag and Sophi (whom she does not want to see marry), to her feelings at watching the porn and her worry about the festival of love. The plot against Morag involves the idea that Isis is sexually obsessed with her, and Morag does not seem to have found this too hard to believe. Isis' physical appearance in the early part of the text, with her parson's clothes, short hair, and boyish figure, seems to symbolize her desire to deny her sexual identity. Her naivety itself, which comes out clearly at points in the narrative, could also be seen as a form of self-defense, preventing her having to deal with her sexual desires. Sexuality is something commodified and formalized in a sense by the sect, with Isis knowing that she is expected to produce another child to be a leapyearian. Isis theoretically and often makes clear her support of free love, but she does not indulge herself and always seems to be the object of inappropriate sexual desire rather than the communion of which she speaks. As Isis says to Yolanda: "I don't know what I want. I don't know who I want. I don't know *that* I want" (Banks 1996, 234).

Further complicating the presentation of sexuality in *The Business* and *Whit* is the fact that Isis and Kate are both victims of sexual advances, from a number of men in the texts, but most specifically from older, male relatives: Kate, Uncle Freddy; and Isis, Salvador. Even though the women seem very able to cope with these events, these incidents leave a lingering sense that Banks is unable to escape entirely the presentation of women as potential sexual victims and objects of sexual desire rather than subjects exploring their own desires.

Just as relationships with mothers are weak or absent entirely in these texts, so relationships with other women more generally can be difficult. In *The Business*, Kate's relationships with other women seem to be limited to that with Luce, bar the few conversations with Miss Heggies and Madame Tchassot. And she admits that she gets on best with Luce on the telephone (Banks 2000, 326). Their relationship is antagonistic and tense, and there is little sense of mutual support. Power for Kate does mean isolation from other women.

Women, on the other hand, do help Isis and bring her success, and her relationships with women are generally more positive than those of Kate. But she is largely rejected by the women of the sect after Allan spreads lies about her, suggesting that they are victims of the sect's ideology and hierarchy; unable to pull away from what is, despite its espousal of (divine) equality, a fairly patriarchal system, in which even maternity is controlled. In this system, female friendship is difficult to sustain. The women that do help Isis are those from outside of the sect: Sophi the lion tamer; Yolanda the straight-talking American; Morag the happy whore. There's an affirmation of the strength of women in these stereotypical figures, but their politics are questionable, particularly Morag's supposedly innocent enjoyment of her role in porn films. Her childlike enjoyment of the flumes[7] is meant to counteract her role in the sex industry, but this is a rather trite sidestepping of the complexities of women and sexual exploitation, interrogation of which is limited to Isis recognizing that free love and prostitution might not be the same thing and not altogether positive (see Banks 1996, 126–127). It is also notable that despite this help from women, Isis sees her task very much as her own, in the manner of the traditional male hero, echoing Kate's largely individualistic battle with members of the Business. She determines to be cold and hard, seeking the truth:

> Within me there was now set in place a cruel desire; a will, a determination to seek the lode of truth amongst this flinty wilderness of lies [Banks 2000, 333].

Therefore power means isolation from other women, in Kate's case. In Isis' case, relationships with other women are only supportive outside of the sect and power within the sect is something she must hold alone.

A Sense of Self

These factors all suggest that the position of equality for women within these men's worlds is predicated on a denial of the feminine in favor of the support of a traditionally masculine value system. Nevertheless, the texts do present the possibility of other roles for these women, particularly as they reach their conclusions. By the end of all three texts the systems that created the narrators have been exposed as questionable. Frank has found out the truth about his childhood and his status as a woman. Kate has come to doubt the ethical position of the Business and also come to see what she has lost in her desire to be the best. Isis, like Frank, has found out that her beliefs were false and based on fiction. In these texts, the religious/ethical/philosophical systems have been found wanting and the women find that their identities must be remade. The reiteration of identity is constant in *The Wasp Factory*, as Frank asserts his sense of self in the catechism before using the wasp factory, in his dreams about the man he might have been, and as he imagines himself as a city (Banks 1984, 120, 48, 62). Isis too asserts a sense of self often in the early part of her narrative, making clear the way that her identity is bound up in the mythology of the sect: "I am The Blessed Very Reverend Gaia-Marie Isis Saraswati Minerva Mirza Whit of Luskentyre, Beloved Elect of God, III" (Banks 1996, 82). But as Isis' narrative continues there is more and more sense of her playing a part, which comes from the breakdown of her long-held beliefs and her sense of herself and her place in the world. She admits this when she returns to the community from her travels: "I felt that I was somehow playing the part of the unjustly accused, even though that was exactly what I was" (Banks 1996, 300).

Whilst in Thulan, Kate plays a different role from that of powerful executive. Thulan is associated throughout *The Business* with a less technological and more caring, humane way of life. Poetic interruptions to the main narrative underline this idea that life in Thulan runs according to a different timescale and order. It is only here that Kate can take on a pseudo-maternal role, seen in her dealings with the children of Thulan, when she wipes their noses and holds their hands (Banks 2000, 242–243). The symbol of the monkey is also significant here. Kate carries this on her travels and it is the only constant in her life, suggesting that it is a symbol of home. It is also a symbol of her movement to the Business as it contains in its base the coin given to her by Mrs. Telman in their first meeting (Banks 2000, 47). She gives this to a Thulan child, connecting her to this country and expressing a desire for home, but also perhaps suggesting that she has not renounced the woman who made her, even if she now doubts the philosophy of the Business. At the end of the text, Kate agrees to marry Suvinder and live in Thulan, accepting the role of wife and potential mother. This choice of a traditional wifely role over that of a businesswoman suggests that Kate has been forced to give up one role in order to take up the other. Even Kate acknowledges the potentially gendered nature of this as "another example of the same old sad self-sacrificial martyrdom crap I've lamented in my gender throughout my life" (Banks 2000, 388). But, as this example makes clear, Kate's reflections on her decision to move to Thulan are an attempt to ameliorate the interpretation of her choice as a typical gendered fate for woman, providing a metanarrative comment on the conclusion of the text. And these reflections also make clear that Kate sees her decision as one of social responsibility as much as individual choice because she is also moving to Thulan to help the country prepare for the inevitable influx of technology and the changes this will bring. March argues that Banks "often presents the ambiguous role of technology" in his work and we see this here (March 2002, 87). Thulan may have been presented throughout the text as the "other" of the Business, but it is a place unable to escape the influence of capitalism and global technological advances. More insistently, the Business presumably still controls and educates Suvinder's nephew, making the issue of Kate's potential motherhood one of political and national importance.

Therefore, the conclusion of this text can be read as a complex expression of female identity. Kate has certainly recognized the limitations of her life in the Business and actively sought other options, options that are predicated in many ways on her feminine identity, particularly her role as potential mother. This bears out the thesis that she must leave the Business in order to explore roles not based upon masculine and patriarchal values, that traditionally feminine roles must be sought in other places. Nevertheless, the text makes clear that she is not beyond the reach of the Business and Thulan is certainly not an idyllic other-world that unproblematically offers the positive exploration of the feminine. It is a principality based firmly on traditional monarchical values, where Kate's fertility will become a matter of prime concern, where her feelings about Suvinder mean that she is unlikely to find the fullest expression of her sexual desires, and where she is likely to face opposition in the form of the stereotypically monstrous mother of Suvinder. In some ways, she has simply traded one game for another.

Like Kate, Isis too plays the game to get what she wants, in her case control of the sect. Isis' gift is eventually revealed to have come through the female line, with the visions that founded the order having been largely those of Zhobelia and not Salvador, and she plays Allan at his own game and wins. Unlike Kate, she is left in a position of power within her social system, having effectively overruled the men around her. This suggests that her conclusion is a more optimistic one, as she can take over the running of the sect, introducing more democracy and dismantling its totalitarian ethos. Like Kate, she turns to community and social responsibility as the way forward. Craig argues that Isis therefore learns to play "consciously and better" a game in which she did not initially know she was a player (Craig 2005, 234). At the end of the novel, Isis asserts the value of truth and concludes the novel by beginning another story. It is not clear from this how much of the truth she will tell her people and whether or not she is prepared to risk destroying the order by telling the female-centered truth of its conception and the tale of Salvador's former life as Moray Black. The danger here is that Isis is willing to set up another grand narrative to replace that she has undermined. Given the emphasis throughout the novel on the negotiable nature of truth, belief and the past, something built into the structure of the novel according to Stephen R. Jones, this conclusion is a very uncertain thing (Jones 2004, 384–385). This is true also of Isis' gender identity, with her sexuality and her attitude to motherhood remaining unclear. Having been primarily an object rather than a subject in the sexual scene, Isis has resolved not to enter the festival of love, but she has not yet found a way to negotiate her own sexual difficulties, nor to come to terms with her potential motherhood. Therefore, Isis may have discovered a place for herself within a maternal rather than a paternal line, but the possibility of a positive feminine identity is posited rather than realized by the end of this novel.

In the final image of Frank cradling his brother's head Duncan Petrie sees Frank embracing the feminine. He suggests that this can be read in terms of the national psyche, "with *The Wasp Factory* positioned as a fable about the need to move beyond self-defeating myths rooted in masculine hardness and violence" (Petrie 2004, 121). The image is certainly a recovery of a feminine, even maternal, force that has been suppressed in the world of the text, and the novel undoubtedly reinforces the need to move beyond the barbarian and the assertion of a violent code of misogynistic masculinity. To achieve this, Frances recognizes that she will have to leave the island, moving away from that spatial representation of her masculine identity. Significantly, however, as Schoene-Harwood points out, the house has not been destroyed, suggesting perhaps that though Frank may leave her home and its deceits, it will continue to exist (Schoene-Harwood 1999, 147). As Cairns argues, Frank recognizes even at the end that escaping this game leaves him still trapped, as we all are:

> Had she been Frances, however, she would have been no less insistently trapped in a world of games, like the Freudian theories of "penis envy" which her supposed castration ironically mirrors [Craig 2005, 233].

Frank knows that "[e]ach of us [has] our own personal Factory" (Banks 1984, 183). Frank may leave the island and find himself seeking his destiny back on the face of the factory, but this does not suggest that he is free or that systems of containment, of gender and identity, do not still exist.

Conclusion

In the end, this is something that all three texts accept. These texts do explore the possibility of equality and also its limitations if women accept the rules of the patriarchal game. There is the chance for Isis to change these rules at the end, as there is for Frank, but these endings are inconclusive. The acceptance of the limited nature of personal choice, our personal factories, suggests that these three women are trapped in whichever system they choose, with whatever gender expectations that brings: Kate now in Thulan; Isis in the Luskentyrians; Frank in a new gender, but carrying the weight of his past with him. The three texts make clear that these women have not found Hélène Cixous' "new world," but have traveled to places where they see the possibility of a different exploration of feminine identity while they continue to negotiate the shadows of the systems that they were nurtured within (Cixous and Clément 1986, 72). The game must continue to be played.

Notes

1. As many critics, such as Christie L. March, recognize (see March 2002, 99–100).
2. See, for example, Victor Sage (1996, 24) and Richard Todd (1996, 156).
3. Schoene-Harwood is drawing upon Judith Butler's theory of performative gender here.
4. In some ways this reflects the strength of her namesake, the Egyptian goddess Isis, who is repeatedly seen to act alone and even embarks on a quest to consolidate the parts of her dismembered husband (eds).
5. See Banks (2000, 365–72) and Banks (1984, 107).
6. As in many of Banks' novels, skepticism about faith and capitalism permeates *Whit* and *The Business*.
7. This is something that is obviously satirical, as the narrative makes clear in its references to the effect of flume rides on the body. See, for example, Banks (1996, 358).

Works Cited

Banks, Iain. 1990. *The Wasp Factory*. London: Abacus.
_____. 1996 [1995]. *Whit*. London: Abacus.
_____. 1998. *A Song of Stone*. London: Abacus.
_____. 2000 [1999]. *The Business*. London: Abacus.
Cixous, Hélène, and Catherine Clément. 1986. *The Newly Born Woman*. Betsy Wing, trans. Manchester: Manchester University Press.
Craig, Cairns. 2005. "Player of Games: Iain (M.) Banks, Jean-François Lyotard and Sublime Terror." In *The Contemporary British Novel*. James Acheson and Sarah C. E. Ross, eds. Edinburgh: Edinburgh University Press.
Irigaray, Luce. 1985. *Speculum of the Other Woman*. Trans. Gillian C. Gill. Ithaca: Cornell University Press.
Jones, Stephen R. 2004. "Action at a Distance: Narrative Structure and Technique in *Whit*." *Studies in Scottish Literature* 33.1.
March, Christie L. 2002. *Rewriting Scotland*. Manchester: Manchester University Press.

Petrie, Duncan. 2004. *Contemporary Scottish Fiction: Film, Television and the Novel.* Edinburgh: Edinburgh University Press.
Sage, Victor. 1996. "The Politics of Petrifaction." In *Modern Gothic: A Reader.* Victor Sage and Allan Lloyd Smith, eds. Manchester: Manchester University Press.
Schoene-Harwood, Berthold. 1999. "Dams Burst: Devolving Gender in Iain Banks' 'The Wasp Factory.'" *Ariel* 30.1.
Todd, Richard. 1996. *Consuming Fictions: The Booker Prize and Fiction in Britain Today.* London: Bloomsbury.

Games Playing Roles in Banks' Fiction

Will Slocombe

> One can be the player, or one can be ... played upon [Banks 1993, 222].

Games have always been an aspect of fiction, from stories such as *The Book of One Thousand and One Nights* (c.850), through most detective fiction, to the mind-bending and often absurd games of postmodern writers. To see games as playing a role in such narratives is not difficult: they act as parallels for wider narrative developments, foreshadowing tools, or thematic devices. Banks' writing, both "straight" fiction and science fiction, certainly uses games in these ways, but what is most interesting is that he modulates the traditional literary use of games as a reflection of, or escape from, reality. Firstly, Banks endeavors to show that reality (or at least our understanding of it) works through games; they do not just reflect reality but inherently color our perceptions of it. The choice is not *whether* we play the game or not, but *how* we play. Moreover, the way in which we play the game reveals more than just our understanding of its rules: it reveals who we are. Secondly, Banks' fiction highlights the fact that most games are about control, about "winning," because, as the opening quotation suggests, "One can be the player, or one can be ... played upon" (Banks 1993, 222). If games embody the idea of competition, of agonistics, then how we compete reveals our ethical stance towards others, the extent to which our strived-for victory is due to, or at the expense of, others.

Throughout his fiction, Banks returns time and again to these two issues, offering different interpretations of games to explore more fully how they interrelate. *The Player of Games* (first published 1988) and *Walking on Glass* (1985) are the two most obvious texts to analyze in this respect as both are predicated upon an awareness of games and how they work, and the numerous plot threads and schemes of characters are represented in terms of gameplaying. Furthermore, although Banks' works do not always bring games to the fore in terms of content, they almost always use games in structural terms; *Complicity* (1993), *Excession* (1996), *The Steep Approach to Garbadale* (2007), and *The Quarry* (2013) are obvious examples of Banks' ability to use games as plot devices, and *The Bridge* (1986) is also constructed as a kind of intellectual game with the reader. What follows is an exploration of the games in Banks' fiction, and the way he plays them.

"Iambs an' Ink": Gaming Plays with Iain M. Banks

"Games" is a broad description of any number of activities yet all games have certain key features. There have been a number of key debates on the nature of games, such as a 1968 special issue of *Yale French Studies* edited by Jacques Ehrmann, Roger Caillois's *Man, Play, and Games* (1961) and, more relevantly to this essay, Peter Hutchinson's *Games Authors Play* (1983). This debate has been extended in recent years following the rise of computer games. Such analyzes often focus on how the narrative element interacts with gameplay, seen in the works of critics such as Gonzalo Frasca, Espen Aarseth, and Barry Atkins. One of the most important areas of all these works is the crucial distinction between "play" and "game," as Hutchinson explains:

> "Games" may involve sustained or intricate play, but they may also be seen as specific examples of play where some sort of rule can be seen in operation — such devices as allegory, parody, prefiguration — in which a clear method is adhered to. "Play" is less organised and less controlled [Hutchinson 1983, 14].

Put simply, games emerge when a number of "plays" are given direction and order; a set of rules. For example, in *The Bridge* there are obvious puns and word plays that have little overall narrative impact:

> Behind each knee an H, from behind her behind a +, her nostrils were ,s (hope this isn't getting too confusing for you), her waist was)(, and pride of place went to V (in plan, prone), and ! (front elevation). Then of course she digested all this and pointed out that she also had a : and regular .s (though these were puns, not signs — like I say, she was a woman of letters). Never mind; at that ! I went i (she went O) [Banks 1999, 188].

Using letters and punctuation to describe this woman of letters, Banks challenges the reader to understand exactly what actions and bodily parts he is describing. This is not a game as such, however, because it does not in itself develop the narrative. Thus, this is a "play" in the narrative's overall game.

The second important point about games, and one more debated than the first, is that games have a purpose and, as a result, an outcome. This outcome is usually associated with victory, or, as Gonazlo Frasca defines it, "*games have a result: they define a winner and a loser; plays do not*" (Frasca 1999, n.p.). This idea is debatable because, as Hutchinson summarizes,

> "rules" suggest competitive play, but Suits (as well as Huizinga and Caillois) refrains from using the concept of "winning." He sees the aim instead as "an attempt to achieve a specific state of affairs." In literature, too, the emphasis is rarely on triumphing at the expense of another: it is on the pleasure which is derived from analysis and recognition, on the pleasure of *mastery* over a text which has been presented as a specific form of challenge [Hutchinson 1983, 7].

The element of competition is certainly central to the notion of a game, although I am not as convinced as Hutchinson that this does not involve some sense of victory. He would rather use the term "mastery" than winning, yet dominance is still an integral part of the game.

Dominance informs many of the games in Banks' fiction. Most of the names of games involve pain, dominance, and control, such as Damage (*Consider Phlebas* 1987), Stricken and Possession (*The Player of Games*), Despot (*Complicity*), and Empire! (*Steep Approach to Garbadale*). Furthermore, Banks' most famous game, Azad, is deliberately designed to intensify and pyschologically embed the desire for domination: "Whoever succeeds at the game succeeds in life; the same qualities are required in each to ensure dominance" (Banks 1999, 76). Banks not only makes a link between games and reality here, a link that endures throughout his fiction, but also demonstrates that dominance is a key factor in why games are played. Of course, Azad is pre-programmed to encourage competitive and dominant behaviour, as Jernau Morat Gurgeh, the eponymous Player of Games, later realizes:

> He hadn't realised how seductive Azad was when played in its home environment. While it was technically the same game he'd played on the *Limiting Factor*, the whole feeling he had about it, playing it was where it was meant to be played, was utterly different; now he realised ... now he *knew* why the Empire had survived because of the game; Azad itself simply produced an insatiable desire for more victories, more power, more territory, more dominance [Banks 1993, 200].

This is a continual feedback loop; the game was created within a hierarchical and violent society and so is a reflection of that society and as such reinforces these character traits, ensuring that those who prosper in the game prosper in society. This is an element of all games (they reflect the material and cultural conditions of a society), as Banks tells the reader: "Gurgeh never ceased to be fascinated by the way a society's games revealed so much about its ethos, its philosophy, its very soul" (Banks 1993, 30).

Despot is of especial interest here as this game is not only modelled on dominance, but also based on a real-world game, *Civilization*. Most players of *Civilization* (and its sequels) will recognise elements of the game in Banks' description of *Despot* (see *Complicity* 1998, 261-62), and Banks has clearly admitted the source in an interview with Ed Ricketts in 1996. In fact, as early as 1989, in an interview with David Garnett, he discussed his fascination with games, including his attempts to create his own.[1]

Both these interviews offer a view of Banks as "The Player of Games," revealing that, by linking the process of writing to the act of playing, the true games are the texts themselves. The references to games are in a sense the "plays" he makes; from these plays it is possible to establish the rules behind them, thereby allowing us to discover what game Banks is writing. That is, if plays are isolated elements that are united by a rule to become a game, then by looking at instances of games across his fiction we can begin to determine the rules behind their inclusion; the games are not important in and of themselves, but how they are used is. Thus, we reach the point at which the relationship between "Iambs an' Ink" become relevant. Banks "writes" games, using the text as the board and the characters as pieces. This is a game between reader and author that is encoded in the explicit game references in the narrative; such references serve as stresses in whatever narrative they appear, acting as parallels to the unstressed content of the plot, with both elements finally providing clues to the ongoing game that is the text itself.

Use of Weapons: Enigmas, Parallels, and Devices

The use of games in fiction resides not just in the inclusion of games in a narrative, but in the structure of the narrative itself. A number of literary games have been identified by Hutchinson, who subdivides them into three key techniques: enigmas, parallels, and narrative devices (see Hutchinson 1983, 23). Enigmas are the mysteries of the text, those elements that add suspense to the narrative and force the reader to ask questions about the narrative. Parallels are specific instances of games that mirror the ongoing narrative developments. Finally, narrative devices are the structural elements of a text in which the author plays games with the reader, including choice of narrator, timeframe, or perspective.

Enigmas necessitate the reader asking a question to which the text then responds. *Complicity* is an obvious example of this as the narrator, the journalist Cameron Colley, seeks to discover who is murdering certain important people. As the narrative progresses, the reader, alongside the narrator, draws closer to discovering who the culprit is. Nevertheless, other texts force the reader to ask different questions to those traditionally addressed by the detective story. Other uses of enigmas become clear on a brief survey of the titles of Banks' works. *The Player of Games* may ask us who the narrator is, but the more profound question that readers ask is "Who is 'the Player of Games?'" Gurgeh is obviously one player, but is he really the eponymous Player of Games? The narrator is equally a player, hiding his identity from the reader, as are the unnamed Culture Minds that set the entire narrative in motion, not to mention the author of this text, Iain M. Banks, or the reader of the story trying to work this out. *Use of Weapons* (1990) also plays games with identity, but in this case it is the protagonist's identity that is under question, and the title is again enigmatic. Elethiomel/Cheradenine Zakalwe has "[such] consummate skill, such ability, such adaptability, such numbing ruthlessness, such a use of weapons when anything could become a *weapon*" (Banks 1993, 350); he is the Chairmaker, the person for whom anything can be a weapon, but he is equally a weapon of the Culture. Thus, the story does not end with Zakalwe, but with the recruitment of a new Culture "weapon," Mr. Escorea. Equally, the central enigma of *The Bridge* is not in fact the identity of the narrator (although that is again an issue) but what the bridge itself means — is it the psychic construct of a coma patient, the real Forth Rail Bridge, or the literary technique that unites the three different stories together?[2]

Such enigmas are often highlighted through the use of parallels. In *Complicity*, *Despot* and *Xerium* (a.k.a. *Xerion*), relate to broader plot developments.[3] The main discussion of *Xerium* is in terms of "how to beat the game," with Andy telling Cameron how to pass a particular level in a "sneaky" way (see Banks 1998a, 135–36). Banks foreshadows how capable Andy is at playing games in the real world through his description of game-playing skills. Later, on the brink of the revelation that Andy is the murderer, Banks describes the destruction of the narrator's civilisation in *Despot*; here, the destruction of a computerised civilisation finds parallels in the approaching collapse of the narrator's world. It is no surprise that, by the conclusion of *Complicity*, Cameron "can't be bothered with games just now" (Banks 1998a, 312). Other parallel games are evident in *Consider Phlebas* (1987) and *The Steep Approach to Garbadale*. In *Consider Phlebas*, the game of Damage appears at the moment of Horza's escape from the Culture and his journey to Schar's World. In the course of this journey, all who follow him die, lives lost as a result of the game he is playing, lives given to save his life (one of the key elements of Damage; see *Consider Phlebas* my edition Banks 1993b, 195). At the end of the narrative, Horza dies and it becomes clear that he is not *the* player after all, but played upon by the Culture. This kind of technique is obviously a parallel, but the text as a whole functions in these terms; *Consider Phlebas* plays with T. S. Eliot's *The Waste Land* in terms of tone and mood, narrative action, and intertextual/extratextual references.[4] There are even, as Carolyn Brown notes in "Utopias and Heterotopias" (1996), evident links between the Culture/Idirian war and the Crusades, implying that Banks is also playing games with history here. Equally, in *The Steep Approach to Garbadale*, *Empire!* is an obvious and immediate parallel for the takeover of the Wopuld family's business (which created the game) by Spraint Corp, and also the way the way in which Win, the family matriarch, seeks to control and manipulate events within the family.

Hutchinson's third subdivision of games, narrative devices, are Banks' main weapon in his arsenal and enables all of the other games to ensue. Hutchinson's idea of narrative devices is suitably broad, incorporating many of the traditional techniques of rhetoric including ambiguity, paradox, puns, and symbols, but, in terms of Banks' fiction, it is perhaps best defined in terms of three key areas: structure, narration, and language.

The most difficult structure within Banks' fiction is clearly found in *The Bridge*, which uses a series of chapters and subchapters. It opens on a short section, Coma, that introduces the central action of the story before it is divided into three main sections, Metaphormosis (introducing the main symbols), Metamorpheus (the omnipresence of dreams), and Metamorphosis (the final changes in the dream landscape). The structure of the novel involves three interlinked stories, one of the narrator, and another two in his unconscious involving the Forth Rail Bridge and a Glaswegian barbarian. Throughout each of these strands, events mirror each other (such as the blood-stained handkerchief), intertextual references proliferate (the barbarian's dagger is actually a copy of one of the Culture's knife-missiles and the barbarian enters the Underworld only to accidently assist Sisyphus, kill one of the Gorgons, and petrify Charon), and plays are made on words, punctuation (as seen earlier in the description of the woman of letters), and events. However, as the narrative progresses, the sections merge into geological periods and epochs, indicating to the reader the gradual evolution of the narrative from split strands to a coherent, unified story. The structure of *The Bridge* is evidently based upon the structure of the earlier *Walking on Glass* (1985), which is split into three different stories that remain in parallel throughout the novel. In *Walking on Glass*, although there are numerous indications of blurred boundaries between the three stories (internal parallels to the action of another story), these are much less complex than those of the interlinked structures of *The Bridge*.

Furthermore, some Culture stories also incorporate innovative structures. In order to defer the revelation of Zakalwe's true identity, for example, *Use of Weapons* introduces another split-narrative under three larger headings, one in which the narrative progresses in numerical order (One, Two, Three...) and another that works in reverse (XIII, XII, XI...). Other plays include the narrator of "The State of the Art," Skaffen-Amtiskaw (from *The Player of Games*), structure the story told by Diziet Sma (from *Use of Weapons*) into chapters and sub-chapters named after ships produced by the *Infracaninophile* (loosely translated: "lover of the underdog") and the "State of play" sections of *Consider Phlebas*, where Fal'Ngeestra — one of the few humans able "to forecast and assess on a par with a well-informed Mind" (Banks 1993b, 87) — predicts Horza's actions before he does, allowing the reader to see this as a game, with players trying to steer the decisions of their opponents.

In terms of narration, aside from the aforementioned enigmatic narrators and protagonists, Banks also plays with narrative perspective. Whereas most of his novels use third-person narration, *Complicity* uses first- and second-person perspectives; Cameron's story is always first-person ("I") while the murderer's is second-person ("You"). This allows a more direct contest to emerge between murderer and detective while maintaining their complicity. There are two main sections, however, where Banks uses this narrative technique to further his game. The first is during the fake-rape sex-game played by Yvonne and Cameron, where only the first-person narrative perspective allows the reader to see that this is not the real murderer at work (see Banks 1998a, 125–30). The second occasion is at the conclusion of the narrative, where the perspective shifts and Cameron — hitherto "I" — becomes "You." Cameron's gaming days might be over, but Banks implies that Cameron and Andy might be closer than the (biased) first-person narration suggests; after all, many of Andy's targets profit Cameron and we learn of an occasion, five years ago, where Cameron experiences "something that was you and was not you, was a threat and not a threat, an enemy and not an enemy, but possessed of a final, expediently functional indifference more horrifying than evil" (Banks 1998a, 310).

Finally, Banks' language is clearly an important part of his game-playing. Instances such as the aforementioned woman of letters aside, Banks' love of language is evident throughout *The Bridge*. When the narrator is jealous of Andrea's facility with Russian, he resorts to playing with his native tongue: "[He'd] lost her to a language (and to a foreign tongue, he thought bitterly; he knew there was someone else in Paris)" (Banks 1999b, 196). Other linguistic plays emerge in *The Bridge*, from the phonetic spelling of the barbarian's story, highlighting his ignorance (as with the later *Feersum Endjinn* 1994), to the aeroplanes that write in Braille. Language is in fact central to an understanding of how games function in Banks' fiction, a point alluded to throughout the Culture novels. For instance, Gurgeh understands Azad through language:

> [The] moves could become a language, and Gurgeh thought he could speak that language now, well enough (tellingly) to lie in it [....] There was no single message, but rather a succession of contradictory signals, pulling the syntax of the game to and fro and to and fro until the common understanding the other players had reached began to fatigue and tear and split [Banks 1993a, 148].

The realisation that a game is a language allows Gurgeh to confuse his opponents, but this is not only true of the link between Azad (the game) and Eächic (the language). Banks also alludes to this in connection with Marain, the language of the Culture, which is "like the best games, essentially very simple but offering almost infinite possibilities" (Banks n.d.). Likewise, Banks starts out from basic premises and then adds layers of complexity, beginning with language, complicating narrators, and finally works the structure to create a game that the reader has no choice but to play. His "use of weapons" is such that he uses any and all means at his disposal to set up plays and games at all layers of the narrative.

Outside Context Problems: Playing by a Different Rulebook

If we are to properly acknowledge the roles that games play in Banks' fiction, then it is important to understand the principle of Outside Context Problems. This term, taken from *Excession*, reveals that games are there to show that it is impossible, in many respects, to ever truly win. There is always somebody else playing a meta-game, of which your game is only a part. This is the essence of an Outside Context Problem, as Banks explains:

> An Outside Context Problem was the sort of thing most civilisations encountered just once, and which they tended to encounter rather in the same way a sentence encountered a full stop. The usual example given to illustrate an Outside Context Problem was imagining you were a tribe on a largish, fertile island; you'd tamed the land, invented the wheel or writing or whatever, the neighbours were cooperative or enslaved but at any rate peaceful and you were busy raising temples to yourself with all the excess productive capacity you had, you were in a position of near-absolute power and control which your hallowed ancestors could hardly have dreamed of and the whole situation was running along nicely just like a canoe on wet grass ... when suddenly this bristling lump of iron appears sailless and trailing steam in the bay and these guys carrying long funny-looking sticks come ashore and announce you've just been discovered, you're all subjects of the Emperor now, he's keen on presents called *tax* and these bright-eyed holy men would like a word with your priests [Banks 1996, 71–72].

Of course, for "these guys carrying long funny-looking sticks" the Culture would equally be an Outside Context Problem and this is precisely the point: an Outside Context Problem occurs when we see games on a cultural level. One culture plays a particular kind of game, involving domesticating animals and inventing the wheel, and can comfortably be seen to be winning, while another, which has normally been playing the game longer, has produced ironclads and muskets. The point of an Outside Context Problem is that a culture can only play the game *on their own terms, on a particular level*. The Culture is usually the Outside Context Problem for most cultures and games are at the heart of this realisation: "The Culture aimed to stay roughly as it was and change at least a proportion of those lesser civilisations it discovered, while acting as an honest broker between the Involved — the more developed societies who made up the current players in the great galactic civilisational game" (Banks 1996, 87). The purpose of *Excession* is to highlight that Outside Context Problems can also happen to more advanced races. The Culture plays its games, having set up the Pittance weapons store to come into the area of the galaxy in which they are at war against the Affront (who are only at war because of a conspiracy within the Culture Minds), while all the major galactic civilisations try to take possession of the unknown entity, the Excession. Unfortunately, the Excession plays by different rules, having access to universes both beneath and above the one these cultures inhabit. Thus, it deigns to play by their rules, although it cannot possibly do so: "*It does what you do. It absorbed those ultimate absorbers, the Elench; it leaves alone and watches back those who come merely to watch in the first place*" (Banks 1996, 430; author's emphasis). An Outside Context Problem occurs when you discover that you are only playing on a smaller board, and that somebody is playing the meta-game.

In *The Steep Approach to Garbadale*, Banks deliberately highlights such meta-games, as the protagonist, Alban, explains after playing *Empire!* and losing deliberately in order to teach his opponent a lesson: "there was the game, and then there was the meta-game. Even without a league lasting all year long, there was always the meta-game, the game beyond the game; you had to think of that, too" (Banks 2007, 297). In fact, the meta-game is the key to Banks' use of games; games can be visualised as a series of concentric circles, with the smallest games being played closest to the centre, but which are themselves part of a larger game, and with that game part of a still-larger game, *ad infinitum*. It is therefore no surprise that this reflects Banks' model of reality: "The expanding universe lay inside a larger one, which in turn was entirely enclosed by a bubble of space-time with a still greater diameter. The same applied within the universe you happened to find yourself in/on; there were smaller, younger universes inside it" (Banks 1996, 270). This form repeats itself in *Matter*, where the artificial Shellworld, Sursamen, is a series of concentric globes shielding those living within it from the machinations of the Involved, or "In-Play" (Banks 2008, 166), galactic races. This is precisely what Banks does in his fiction: smaller language games/plays nestled inside larger structural or narrative games, nestled inside the game-text, nestled in the context of his other works, and so on.[5]

To see this more clearly, it is worth considering *Walking on Glass* in these terms. Quiss and Ajayi are imprisoned in the Castle of Bequest for failures during the Therapeutic War. To escape they have to answer a single question:

> [They] had to play a series of odd games, working out the rules for each one in turn, playing each one to a conclusion, without cheating or colluding. At the end of each game they had one chance and one chance only to answer the riddle they had been set [....] The question was: What happens when an unstoppable force meets an immovable object? [Banks 1999a, 44].

The game as narrative device is evident here; they must play one game to be given the opportunity to play another. Ostensibly, this is a simple procedure, but the games are close to impossible; One-Dimensional Chess, Open-Plan Go, Spotless Dominoes, and Chinese Scrabble. In each case, they have to work out the game's rules, and then play a game through to the conclusion. The games, all based on the subject planet's games (clearly Earth), get harder to play as they progress through them.

This is only the first game-level in the text, however. Later, it is revealed that the entire Castle functions around games, as Quiss discovers when trying to intimidate a servant. The servant tells Quiss: "We've started a new regime to make things more interesting down here. When people ask us a question some of us always tell the truth and some of us always tell the opposite. Some of us give correct answers, and some of us give incorrect answers, but we're always consistent, you see?" (Banks 1999a, 82). This is a revised knight/knave problem in which Quiss should think strategically rather than bully the servants, yet Quiss cannot do this. Eventually, when the Red Crow shows him the room in which former prisoners of the Castle decide to play the roles of earlier inhabitants of Earth, Quiss, believing that he has no chance of escape, gives up hope. Quiss's discovery of the room is significant, as it opens up the Quiss/Ajayi narrative into Steven Grout's narrative (who may be himself a former prisoner at the Castle; see Banks 1999a, 217, 227). It is Grout who finds the solution to their problem:

> McGuffin's
> ¡ZEN BRAND!
> matches
> average contents: $\sqrt{2}$
>
> Steven didn't understand. He turned the matchbook over and read the riddle printed on the back. He didn't understand that, either. He read out the words slowly to himself. "Q: What happens when an unstoppable force meets an immovable object? A: The unstoppable force stops, the immovable object moves" [Banks 1999a, 217].[6]

Quiss never stays in the room long enough to find this matchbook, and instead lapses into despair.

Ajayi's response to the games is different. After finding that the walls of the Castle are made of books, she begins to learn the languages of Earth and uncover the meaning behind the Castle itself. Rather than play the games as the rules imply, she is actually searching for the rules *behind* the games, the meta-game. After Quiss destroys the games table at which all games must be played, and therefore with only one chance to provide the answer, Ajayi discovers something interesting:

> She noticed that the legs of the small table had been made out of books [....]
> "*Titus Groan*," she read, talking softly to herself. "*The Castle, Labyrinths, The Trial...*" And another book, which had the title page missing. She glanced over the torn remains of the first page instead, and frowned.
> [...]
> She sat down.
> She started reading.
> After all, what else was there to do?
> The story began:
> He walked through the white corridors... [Banks 1999, 232–33].

As the reader is aware, this is the opening to *Walking on Glass*. The question is whether this version of the text contains the solution to the riddle (that is, the one contained in Grout's narrative), or if this is only Graham Park's story, which opens *Walking on Glass*. This opens the Ajayi/Quiss narrative to the third narrative strand, in which Sara and Slater are playing with Graham, although he is never fully aware that he is being played. Thus, there are two potential methods out of the Castle: Quiss can play at being human until he finds the matchbook (Steven Grout's story) or Ajayi can read the unnamed novel, which may contain her own and Grout's story within it. In this manner, the layers of the game expand throughout *Walking on Glass*, and the different strands continually bleed into each other, therefore equating metalepsis indicating the movement between different game levels. The game table is not important *per se*, past getting the opportunity to answer the riddle for the first time; rather, it is the rationale behind the games, the rules upon which the Castle is constructed, and all this is controlled by the one who we assume is the ultimate player of games: the author himself.

The Player of Games: Iain "Morat" Banks

A text is a contract between reader and author and by accepting that Banks plays games with his fiction, it is clear that he equally plays games with his readers: when we read his works we agree to play by the rules of his game.

In *The Bridge*, for example, readers must follow the difficult path through the various narratives, decoding numerous puns (plays) in the hopes that they will finally uncover the "point" of the text (the rules of the game). Equally, in *Walking on Glass*, the reader's task is to look for points of intersection in the three different strands, decoding implied links and rejecting those that might be irrelevant. Who, finally, wins these games? Who is the player and who is played upon by the conclusion of the novel? Who retains control in this game?

There are, perhaps, no conclusive answers to such questions. Still, in this game between author and reader it is important not to forget the game that occurs behind this one, the meta-game in which all other games are played. It is not insignifcant that both *Walking on Glass* and *The Bridge*, the two works by Banks that most exemplify his game-playing traits (they not only play games in the text, but blur the boundaries between genres, and between fantasy and reality), finally conclude on short pieces outside the game of the text. In the "Truth and Consequences" section of *Walking on Glass*, Banks moves beyond the traidic structure of the rest of the text as Graham finally leaves behind the earlier games of Sara and Slater. In a burst of indignation, Graham gains "a total allergy syndrome directed at everything around him" (Banks 1999a, 238), looking at the works of mankind and seeing nothing more than a series of moves designed to perpetuate humanity's cruelty and horror. Throwing his drawings of Sara, the adult magazine, and the murdered animal into the canal, "he walked off; away down the canalside, back up towards the little gate, towards the city again" (Banks 1999a, 239). Likewise, the "Coda" of *The Bridge* concludes with the patient rejecting the fantasies of his coma and accepting the alternative:

> The choice is not between dream and reality; it is between two different dreams. One is my own; the bridge and all I made of it. The other is out collective dream our corporate imagery. We live the dream; call it American, call it Western, call it Northern or call it just that of all we humans, all life. I was part of one dream, for good or ill, and it was half-nightmare and I almost let it kill me, but it hasn't. Yet, anyway [Banks 1999b, 283].

It is important to note here the ambivalence of which dream almost killed him — the Bridge or Western ideology — for he realises, like Graham, there is one dream that we must accept, one game that must be played. How we play it is up to us; it is our choice not to play the game as we are told to play it by all the corporate imagery, the "carefully civilised savagery of the technology of pain and the economies of greed" (Banks 1999b, 238).

This is a view equally enacted in *Matter*, where Banks brings the meta-game to potentially its highest level, when Hyrlis (a former Special Circumstances operative) meditates on the nature of reality:

War, famine, disease, genocide. Death, in a million different forms, often wreteched and protracted for the poor individual wretches involved. What god would so arrange the universe to predispose its creations to experience such suffering, or be the cause of it to others? What master of simulations or arbitrator of the game would set up the initial conditions to the same pitiless effect? God or programmer, the charge would be the same: that of near-infinitely sadistic cruelty; deliberate, premeditated barbarism on an unspeakably horrific scale [Banks 2008, 339–340].

Hyrlis' logic dictates that this amorality, in the final analysis, comes down to "matter":

By this reasoning we must, after all, be at the most base level of reality — or at the most exalted, however one wishes to look at it. Just as reality can blithely exhibit the most absurd coincidences that no credible fiction could convince us of, so only reality — produced ultimately by matter in the raw — can be so unthinkingly cruel. [Banks 2008, 340].

It is thus through this logic that Banks reveals to us the purpose of these meta-games; not to play (or be played), but to show that there is always a choice, even here in the world of Involveds and hyperspace "whether we are all in a still greater game" or not, as Hyrlis notes, the larger games can hinge on the just one action, just one choice: "We may all be mere particles, but we are each fundamental!" (Banks 2008, 348). Thus, no "matter" is worthless, and no matter the game, Iain "Morat" Banks plays games in his fiction to point to the wider game, in which we have a choice. The moral of the story is that outside of the petty games of dominance and control is a larger, more complex game. It may not always be pretty, or pleasant, but it is the game that matters above all others ... look inside for evidence.

Notes

1. See *PC Format* (June 1996) for the Ricketts interview and *Journal Wired* 1 (Winter 1989) for the Garnett interview. An article entitled "The Player of Games," in *The Banksoniain* 7 (2005), offers a useful summary of the Garnett interview given the problems of availability of the original.

2. The identity of *The Bridge*'s narrator, otherwise unnamed, is indicated only at two points in the text; once when he dates a girl called Nicola and people "made jokes about their names, called them imperialists, asked them when they were going to claim Russia back" (196) and another when "a group called the tourists had some success; their lead singer went on to become half of the Eurythmics. People would ask if he was related to her" (242).

3. *Xerium* is "also known as" *Xerion* because the name is altered later in *Complicity* (see Banks 1998a, 135, 261). Is this accidental or just another of Banks' games with readers? This question also applies to the intertextual references to "The State of the Art" in *Use of Weapons* (1990). Twice in the text it is implied that Diziet Sma has visited Earth prior to the narrative action of *Use of Weapons* which corresponds to the short story "The State of the Art" (1991). These instances occur in the mention of Petrain (Banks 1998b, 37) and

in the mention of "cruel and unusual punishments" (Banks 1998b, 230), and yet when Zakalwe mentions "inflation," she does not know what it means (Banks 1998b, 105).

4. See Gary Wilkinson's "Poetic Licence" for a more detailed reading of the links between Eliot's poem and *Consider Phlebas*. This literary game is also continued in *Look to Windward* (2000), a "sequel-of-sorts" to *Consider Phlebas*, and again uses lines from the "Death by Water" section of Eliot's *The Waste Land*.

5. Although there is not space to consider it in this article, it is also worth considering the nature of cheating in relation to these meta-games. In *The Player of Games*, Gurgeh is blackmailed by Skaffen-Amtiskaw because he uses the drone to cheat at Possession; this can be compared to the drone's observations of the Azadian justice system, where the Labyrinth Prison, ostensibly a moral maze, is subverted by the rich or where females and males are allowed to play Azad, but are never taught to play well; the game is part of a larger (biased) cultural game in which the rules of the game are modified. Equally, in *Excession*, the Culture lures the Affront into war. Are such examples cheating or merely playing the long game?

6. The reference to "McGuffin" is important here, as a McGuffin is a plot element "initially presented as being of great significance to the story, but often having little actual importance for the plot as it develops" (*OED*). In reflexive terms, Banks both highlights this matchbook as a vital plot element, linking the Quiss/Ajayi and Grout narratives together, yet this is also dismissed by Grout and, indeed, plays no further significance in either narrative. The reader has to determine whether this is a red herring, a true McGuffin, or neither ... another game on another level.

Works Cited

Banks, Iain. 1993a [1988]. *The Player of Games*. London: Orbit.
_____. 1993b [1987]. *Consider Phlebas*. London: Orbit.
_____. 1996. *Excession*. London: Orbit.
_____. 1997 [1991]. *The State of the Art*. London: Orbit.
_____. 1998a [1993]. *Complicity*. London: Abacus.
_____. 1998b [1990]. *Use of Weapons*. London: Orbit.
_____. 1999a [1985]. *Walking on Glass*. London: Abacus.
_____. 1999b [1986]. *The Bridge*. London: Abacus.
_____. N.d. "A Few Notes on Marain." http://homepages.compuserve.de/Mostral/artikel/marain.html. Last accessed 17 August 2007. First published in *The Culture* [now defunct fanzine].
_____. 2007. *The Steep Approach to Garbadale*. London: Little, Brown.
_____. 2008. *Matter*. London: Orbit.
Brown, Carolyn. 1996. "Utopias and Heterotopias: The 'Culture' of Iain M. Banks." *Impossibility Fiction: Alternativity, Extrapolation, Speculation*. Derek Littlewood and Peter Stockwell, eds. Amsterdam: Rodopi, 57–74.
Frasca, Gonzalo. 1999. "Ludology Meets Narratology: Similitude and Differences Between (Video)Games and Narrative." *Ludology.Org: Videogame Theory*. http://www.ludology.org/articles/ludology.htm. Last accessed 17 August 2007.
Garnett, David S. 1989. "Interview: Iain M. Banks." *Journal Wired* 1 (Winter), 51–69.
Hutchinson, Peter. 1983. *Games Authors Play*. London: Methuen.
"The Player of Games." 2005. *Banksoniain* 7 (August), 4–5. Available online at http://www.banksoniain.netfirms.com/banksoniain_07.pdf. Accessed 17 August 2007.
Ricketts, Ed. 1996. "Interview with Iain Banks." http://www.futurehi.net/phlebas/text/banksint15.html. Accessed 15 August 2007.
Wilkinson, Gary. 1999. "Poetic Licence: Iain M. Banks's *Consider Phlebas* and T. S. Eliot's *The Waste Land*." http://www.fearful-symmetry.co.uk/poeticl.htm. Accessed 17 August 2007.

Digital Souls and Virtual Afterlives in the Culture Series

Joseph Norman

Iain M. Banks' long-running Culture series is notable, among other things, for helping to invigorate the science fiction sub-genre of space opera, previously seen as the "despised child of SF" (Mendlesohn 2005, 556), and contributing to establishing British science fiction at the forefront of the genre as a whole, as part of the so-called "British Boom" of the 1990s and 2000s (Butler 2003, n.p.). The Culture itself, a post-scarcity anarchist/socialist techno-utopia, incorporates elements of utopian fiction into a traditionally conservative, rightwing sub-genre, and helped to "reclaim space opera for the left" (Jamneck 2011, n.p.).

While the ways in which Banks draws upon space-opera and utopian fiction in the Culture novels has been addressed at length elsewhere (see Guerrier 1999), the influence of more recent science fiction sub-genres on his work, such as Cyberpunk, have received relatively little attention. In *The Blackwell Companion to Science Fiction,* Farah Mendlesohn, argues that

> at the beginning of the 1990s Cyberpunk had dominated the external face of science fiction. In a world of fractionalized peace, and a huge displacement of money and power, Cyberpunk reflected the despair of many westerners at the mass exodus of manufacturing jobs to the developing world, and the threat suggested in the rise of computer networks [...] Banks refused to accept the inevitability of capitalism posited by Cyberpunk and earlier space opera [....] SF mostly reflects the social and economic mores of the contemporary world — it is actually very difficult to think outside the box — but in this one area, Banks simply disposed of the box [Mendlesohn 2005, 556].

Banks' Culture is clearly a utopia, and so it seems that Mendlesohn would not consider these novels to be truly Cyberpunk texts as they offer a more optimistic vision than the dystopian outlook of traditional Cyberpunk. The Culture novels do, however, incorporate several other familiar Cyberpunk tropes, such as powerful artificial intelligences (AIs), advanced virtual reality environments, and forms of technologically adapted (post)human cyborgs, familiar to most from William Gibson's famous *Sprawl* trilogy,[1] or through films that bear its influence, such as Mamoro Oshii's *Ghost in the Shell* (1995),[2] *The Matrix* (1999),[3] and *TRON*[4] franchises. Indeed, Banks and Gibson have expressed a mutual appreciation of each other's work. In *Arena* magazine, Banks chose *Neuromancer* as one of his top ten science fiction novels (Banks no date),[5] and Gibson has described Banks as "a phenomenon" (Gibson qtd. Banks 1993, n.p.).[6]

This chapter addresses the influence of Cyberpunk on Banks' work particularly in reference to the various depictions and functions of souls in the Culture series. I draw upon several Culture texts in my analysis, including *Excession* (1996) and *Look to Windward* (2000), but mostly *Surface Detail* (2010; the penultimate Culture novel published), as souls play a particularly vital role in its complex narrative.

Souls

In the Culture universe, all forms of sentient life, including AIs and non-humanoid life forms, have what Banks calls a soul. The term "soul" itself is somewhat slippery, involving a variety of different definitions in the fields of theology and philosophy, and can be understood both in religious and secular terms. According to the *Oxford Dictionary of Philosophy*, the soul is "the immaterial 'I' that possesses conscious experience, controls passion, desire, and action, and maintains a perfect identity from birth (or before) to death (or after)" (Blackburn 2005, 346). The *Encyclopædia Brittanica* adds that "in theology, the soul is further defined as that part of the individual which partakes of divinity and often is considered to survive the death of the body" (Encyclopædia Britannica 2011).

In *Surface Detail*, souls are described as "mind-states [...] dynamic full-brain inventories" (Banks 2010, 66). The focus, therefore, is placed upon the secular definition of souls as the contents of the mind, or the combination of personality and memories that Banks understands as consciousness. Most importantly, souls in the Culture universe can be converted into, or captured as, *digital* information, in a similar manner to Case from Gibson's *Neuro-*

mancer, who is able to explore cyberspace in a disembodied, virtual form. In his 1964 text *Understanding Media,* Marshall McLuhan argued that many of "our (post)modern technological capabilities function as 'the extensions of man.'" In summarizing his argument, Scott Bukatman states that: "the proliferation of the technologies dedicated to information and communication comprise an extension, outside the body, of the central nervous system: that elaborate, electrical message-processing system" (Bukatman 1998, 70).

In the Culture universe, an individual's soul can be "backed up," effectively saved in a similar manner to saving a file onto a USB or other data-storage device in our world, by technologies designed to connect directly with an individual's central nervous system, often referred to as "Soulkeepers." The most sophisticated kind of Soulkeeper is known as a "neural lace." Neural laces are used widely in the Culture, especially among operatives of its "black ops" division Special Circumstances. This device, a hybrid of organic and electronic components, often adopted by its bearer at a young age, "grows with the brain it's part of, it beds in over the years, gets very adept at mirroring every detail of the mind it interpenetrates and co-exists with" (Banks 2010, 78), and makes the process of "soul-saving" automatic. Should anything happen to the individual who bears the neural lace that may potentially damage their soul (such as severe brain damage, or bodily death), a "copy" of it may be obtained from the lace; this version will exactly replicate the mind, but only up until the point at which it was last backed up.[7]

The total separation of mind and body in this manner corresponds with the famous notion of substance (or Cartesian) dualism, as popularly explicated and defended by French philosopher Rene Descartes. For Descartes, the soul exists in an entirely immaterial, non-physical state, fundamentally distinct from the material state of the body (Descartes 1998, 58). Another model of consciousness proposed by philosophers and neuroscientists that builds upon Descartes' theory is the Mind/Computer analogy, which, while the details vary slightly between different theorists, revolves round the idea that the body and brain are related in a similar manner to a computer's hardware and software: the brain is a computer, which "runs" the software of the mind; the mind controls the processes of the body.[8]

Soulkeeper technology in the Culture novels enables individuals to transcend the physical world and have their "essence" encoded as pure information, which crosses over into the virtual, digital environment. This ability enables souls to exist in various different forms in both the physical universe and in computer-simulated environments. When a soul transfers from one state of being to another, it is often (though not exclusively) as a result of physical bodily death, because, despite the potential for a kind of immortality presented by the backing up of individuals' souls, most species in the Culture novels chose to "die" eventually: "It was quite a rare species that naturally generated individuals capable of being able, or wanting, to live indefinitely" (Banks 2010, 128). If an incident occurs that requires a soul in pure digital form to be removed from its neural lace container, such as severe damage to, or destruction of the body of the mind's owner, one option is for the soul to be transferred back into another body in the physical universe, known as "Revention."

Revention

Surface Detail provides perhaps the most important exploration of Revention in the Culture series. As with many of Banks' Culture novels, *Surface Detail* interweaves several narrative threads that mix the personal and the political in a complex relationship, which is only made fully apparent at the novel's conclusion.

The novel's protagonist Lededje Y'breq tries and fails to escape her captor Joile Veppers, which results in her violent murder at his hands. Fortunately for Lededje, due to a favor that she granted an eccentric Culture Mind (a highly advanced AI) many years in the past, a neural lace was allowed to develop in her brain, as its gift to her in return. Lededje, however, was unaware of this fact, because, when asked about compensation for her trouble, she flippantly replied, "Whatever you think fit. Surprise me" (Banks 2010, 89). Lededje is subsequently resurrected by the Culture, and her soul revented and "brought back to life in a physical body in the Real" (Banks 2010, 91). Lededje's resurrection back into the Real (used in Banks' novel to describe a real-life physical environment as opposed to a virtual one) is far from messianic: her choice to be brought back into the physical world seems motivated purely by a desire for revenge against Veppers.

Without the existence of Soulkeeper and Revention technology, Lededje would be unable to feature in *Surface Detail* in exactly this manner. This story begins with her "death," and in most narratives this would be problematic. In order to be able to feature Lededje as a fully fledged protagonist after her death, the author would usually have to rely upon some kind of potentially inappropriate or unconvincing supernatural "beyond-the-grave" element, which would make her quest for revenge almost impossible. In this manner, *Surface Detail* enables a unique and unusual narrative to be told, which would not be possible in many other genres. In doing so, Revention takes the notion of Cartesian dualism to a logical, if extreme, conclusion: if the soul is (or can be made to be) entirely separate from the body, then, theoretically, one person's soul could be removed from their body and placed into another body without fundamentally altering the original soul. This ability to interchange body and soul renders the bearer's original body effectively obsolete. In this way, the body in Banks' universe is merely a vessel, a container, with no innate connections with the original soul that it contained — or any others — whatsoever. This procedure means that one is potentially protected from the consequences of the effects of fatal or life-altering violence, and even, effectively, from death itself. If someone in our world were to suffer, say, a blow to the head that caused actual death, or resulted in them being brain-dead, then life would obviously be unable to continue, as they would no longer be "alive." A backed-up individual from the Culture, though, would still have the possibility of life if their soul were to be retrieved, and Revented; all that they would lose would be memory of all that had happened between the time they last backed-up their soul, and the time of their Revention.

Despite the enormous benefits that Soulkeeper technology seems to offer, the character Yime from *Surface Detail* refuses to use it at all, stating that "that is not a life-choice I have chosen to make" (Banks 2010, 37). Yime debates the benefits of using a neural-lace with one of the Culture's Minds; the Mind argues that "neural-laces are just useful," especially in extreme circumstances, adding that "they let you back-up really easily" (Banks 2010, 37). Yime's response suggests that the soul-keeping properties of the lace are not infallible: "until they are corrupted, and possibly the person invested by the device as well" (Banks 2010, 37). Yime's comments raise questions about the way that such life-extending technologies affect the quality of life: for Yime, the possibility of her soul becoming corrupted outweighs the benefits of backing up, even if this would render her susceptible to a death from which she could never return.

Storage

The novels *Excession* and *Look to Windward* both feature another option for how Soulkeeper technology can be used to extend life after bodily death in the physical world: "Storage [...] where people went when they had reached a certain age, or if they had just grown tired of living [...] with whatever revival criterion they desired" (Banks 1996, 81). Storage can be seen as a kind of suspended animation, similar to the process of cryogenic freezing, where life processes are greatly slowed, but not enough to cause actual death or, to extend the Mind/Computer Analogy, where life is put on "pause." In *Excession*, it is the body and the soul together that can be placed into Storage and contained on a Culture spaceship. In *Look to Windward*, however, Storage can also apply to disembodied souls, such as the souls of long-dead warriors from the Chelgrian race, killed during a civil war, who are Stored in a computer substrate on their planet.

It is interesting to consider why an individual would choose Storage over Revention; this decision can reveal a great deal about the individual's attitudes towards extended life. Banks explains that many people go into Storage because they are inquisitive about the changing nature of society, wishing to compare the society they know now with one in the future when they leave Storage. Some chose to be awoken after one hundred years, to live "for a single day before returning to their undreaming, unageing slumbers" (Banks 1996, 83), as they are keen to exploit the unique potential for witnessing these changes that Storage offers, as, in Storage, many years can pass in what seems like moments for the individual. Others, however, especially those from the Culture, choose "to come back when something especially interesting was happening" (Banks 1996, 81). As this description implies, many people are simply bored in their current lives. For Culture denizens, life is already extended to between 300 and 400 years by genetic engineering and anti-ageing drugs, so it is perhaps not surprising that they might choose to "pause" their lives in this manner, after such a long time. This state of boredom reflects one of the most consistent criticisms aimed at utopian societies; as critic Johann Hari states: "After a while, wouldn't it be excruciatingly dull? When you live in the desert, a spring seems like paradise. But when you have had the spring for a thousand years, won't you be sick of it?" (Hari 2010, n.p.). If one can be Revented countless times into a utopia, then boredom is perhaps inevitable. It could be argued that, because of this, Culture citizens lead overly-protected, pampered and frivolous lives; for example, in this post-scarcity society, there is no need for anyone to have a job, or contribute to the greater good of society, which can potentially lead to a meaningless existence and a continuous state of *ennui*.

Co-Existing Souls

As well as raising and addressing existential issues, the concept of Storage is integral to the plot of *Look to Windward*; most notably for the way it enables the souls of two of the novel's protagonists, Quilan and Huyler, to co-exist in one body, and both function successfully and (mostly) independently. Both Major Quilan and Admiral-General Huyler were soldiers during a civil war that broke out among their people, the Chelgrians, as the result of a failed intervention by the Culture's division Special Circumstances. Due to the losses suffered by the Chelgrians during the war, many of Quilan's people still bear a long-standing hatred of the Culture, even though, at the time the novel is set, the two civilisations have established a generally peaceful relationship. Quilan survived this conflict, but Huyler and Quilan's wife, Worosei, also a soldier during this conflict, did not (they could not locate all of the deceased's Soulkeepers after the war). Quilan never fully recovered from his bereavement.

Many years after the war, Quilan becomes involved in a plot to attack the Culture, attempting to achieve political revenge on them for causing the civil war, and personal revenge on them for the death of his wife. The soul of long-dead Chelgrian General Huyler is revived from storage, where it has been for the eighty-three years since his bodily death, and implanted into Quilan's specially adapted Soulkeeper device, alongside his own soul. Huyler is chosen ostensibly for his advanced knowledge of the Culture, which will be invaluable for Quilan's successful completion of the mission. Quilan's knowledge of his exact mission brief is initially withheld from him as a security measure, in order to ensure that the Culture's Minds do not learn the real nature of his mission, as they can read thoughts.

Banks' exploration of the nature of co-existing souls in *Look to Windward* is complex, not just because of the various philosophical issues that it raises, but because of the formal intricacies necessary to clearly represent it in the text, and the ways in which it shapes the narrative itself. When Huyler's soul is initially transferred to Quilan's body, the pair establishes the parameters and rules of their relationship. Quilan, whose soul was originally attached to the now-shared physical body, is regarded as the primary consciousness of the two. Huyler on the other hand, exists in an entirely disembodied form as pure consciousness; essentially all he can do is share his thoughts with his partner and he seemingly has no direct control over the shared body. As Huyler describes it, Quilan is "*the one pulling all the strings here*," and Huyler himself is "*just [...] along for the ride*" (Banks 2000, 39; 41; author's emphasis). Quilan elaborates on Huyler's role, saying that "You [Huyler] would have access to all my senses and we would be able to communicate, though you would not be able to control my body unless I became deeply unconscious or suffered brain death" (Banks 2000, 40).

As this dialogue implies, the two co-existing souls are able to speak to one another in a manner they refer to as "communicating," though this dialogue can only occur within Quilan's head. For communicating, Quilan uses a kind of third "voice" that is differentiated from his speaking voice, and, crucially, from the "inner" voice that narrates his thoughts, which he assumes Huyler cannot hear. Huyler's voice is only audible inside Quilan's head. To clearly differentiate these conversations from Quilan's ordinary, external speech, Banks uses the wave dash symbol (~) prior to a line of dialogue to indicate that the speech is occurring inside Quilan's head; Huyler's dialogue is italicized and Quilan's is not. This raises the question: where exactly does Quilan's third voice emanate from? What kind of voice is it, if it is not his speech or his thoughts? The conclusion Banks forces us to draw is that it is a version of speech or thought that is enabled by the nature of Quilan's specially developed Soulkeeper, but this is deliberately not elaborated upon.

Probably the most important aspect of their relationship concerns the extent to which Huyler can hear Quilan's thoughts. Initially, Huyler raises this issue, asking: "*is it really true we can hear each other when we talk like this but not when we think? This seems like a damn fine distinction to me*" (Banks 2000, 45). This leads the pair to experiment with trying to read each other's mind, seemingly with no success:

~[...] *See if you can catch what I'm thinking.*
[...]
~*Well? Catch anything?*
~No, sir. Sir, I —
~*You don't know what you missed, Major. Okay, your turn. Go on. Think of something. Anything* [Banks 2000, 45].

Resulting from this discussion, they ascertain that they still have privacy and that, at certain times of the day, the pair will refrain from discussion, for moments of uninterrupted personal contemplation.

If, as Huyler observes, the distinction between Quilan's third Soulkeeper voice and his supposedly personal thoughts seems "damn fine," then that is because it is actually revealed later on to be non-existent. When Quilan's memories of his mission briefing return to him, they are simultaneously revealed to the reader, along with several plot twists along the way. When Quilan realizes that Huyler's knowledge of the Culture was in fact directly implanted into Huyler's consciousness from data reserves, and was not gleaned from the general's experiences at war, he (and *we*) realize that the real purpose of Huyler sharing Quilan's consciousness was to ensure that Quilan did not back out of his mission — to destroy an entire Culture habitat, killing millions of people — when he was allowed to remember it. In order to perform this duty effectively, Huyler has in fact been able to read Quilan's thoughts all along.

Virtual Afterlives

The nature of souls in Banks' fiction, as neurological processes captured as digital information, means that they are not constrained by the parameters of the Real, physical world, and, therefore, can exist in disembodied form in virtual environments. As Banks states: "The dozen or so civilizations which would eventually go on to form the Culture had, during their separate ages of scarcity, spent vast fortunes to make virtual reality as palpably real and dismissibly virtual as possible" (Banks 2000, 351).

In the Culture series, existing in Cyberspace is another option available for souls after bodily death, as with the processes of Storage and Revention. Banks' depictions of virtual environments allow him to blur the boundaries between reality and simulation, but also between the religious and secular: both *Surface Detail* and *Look to Windward* depict peculiarly postmodern varieties of afterlife.

In *Surface Detail*, the nature of Lededje's Revention is very unusual; the clandestine nature of the neural lace that captured Lededje's soul, and the eccentric, ostracized nature of the Mind who implanted it in her, meant that her automatic Revention had not been scheduled. For people who are *meant* to have neural laces, the device is registered, and therefore if anything happens to the person, the Minds will be notified and will begin the process of Revention automatically, according to the individual's previously requested specifications. As Lededje's is "unofficial," this has not occurred. Therefore, Lededje awakens to find that she has been placed into a kind of virtual limbo.

The *Encyclopaedia Britannica* describes limbo in Roman Catholic theology as "the border place between heaven and hell where dwell those souls who, though not condemned to punishment, are deprived of the joy of eternal existence with God in heaven. The word is of Teutonic origin, meaning 'border' or 'anything joined on'" (*Encyclopædia Britannica*, 2011). Lededje's gradual awakening after her "death" is described in dream-like terms: "From somewhere came the idea that there were many different levels of sleeping, of unconsciousness, and therefore of awakening" (Banks 2010, 58). These thoughts emerge "in the midst of [a ...] pleasant woozy calm — warm, pleasantly swaddled, self-huggingly curled up, a sort of ruddy darkness behind the eyelids" (Banks 2010, 58). At this stage, Lededje currently exists on the peripheries of consciousness, somewhere between the real world and the virtual. Eventually, Lededje awakens fully:

> She opened her eyes. She had the vague impression of a wide bed, pale sheets and a large, high-ceilinged room with tall open windows from which gauzy soft billowing white curtains waved out [....] She noticed that here was some sort of fuzzy glow at the foot of the bed. It swam into focus and spelled out the word SIMULATION [Banks 2010, 59].

A Culture Mind (in the form of a humanoid avatar) appears and speaks with her. Lededje learns that she is "presently, literally [...] in a computational substrate node of the General Systems Vehicle *Sense Amid Madness, Wit Amongst Folly*" (Banks 2010, 65); essentially, her soul-information is resting temporarily inside a spaceship's computer.

As Lededje explores her new simulated surroundings, she becomes aware that her environment is remarkably detailed on a sensory basis: "What she was looking at here — and feeling, and smelling — was effectively, uncannily flawless" (Banks 2010, 61). The environment of Lededje's virtual limbo is seemingly designed to be as comforting and reassuring as possible, partly to soften her inevitable initial disorientation, but also to help her deal with the traumatic memories of events leading up to, and including her physical death, which the Mind will slowly allow to re-emerge. As the Mind's avatar states: "I discovered that you've had a traumatic experience [...] which I've sort of held back, edited from your transferred memories, just for now, while you settle in" (Banks 2010, 67). This virtual limbo also serves as a neutral environment in which Lededje can choose what kind of body she is to be revented into subsequently: "I'll leave you with an image you can manipulate until you're happy with it, take a spec from that" (Banks 2010, 92).

From analysis of this scene, we can see that Lededje's limbo is more than a border place of deprivation and judgment: it is a liminal space, covering the threshold between consciousness and unconsciousness, and death and life. Comparing Banks' model of limbo with the religious definition makes it clear that there is little real resemblance between Banks' virtual limbo, a kind of post-death cyberspace waiting room for unassigned souls, and the religious model, with its emphasis on judgment and deprivation of pleasure. With its focus on the relationship between the conscious and the unconscious, the simulated Culture environment utilizes ideas associated with psychoanalysis, just as much as it does with those of religion. In religion, limbo means after death, and between heaven and hell, whereas, in Banks, it refers to the place between death and extended life, either in the virtual or the real.

Due to her ties with the Culture, Lededje was given the choice to return to the Real, choosing Revention into another physical body, effectively continuing to live on in the same manner as before; she chose this as it was necessary for her to achieve revenge. There are other options offered, however, some of which allow individuals to stay in virtual realms, which extend beyond limbo. In a manner much closer to theology, souls from both the Culture and other digital soul-supporting races live on in virtual afterlives, such as heavens, and while hells do exist in the universe that the Culture resides in, they do not advocate their use.

"Heavens"

In one sense, the utopian Culture is already a kind of heaven; by choosing to Revent into the Culture, Lededje does, in one sense, go to heaven. Another option available, aside from Revention and Storage, is emplacement into a virtual heaven, the defining feature of which is the ability to tweak the environment's parameters, effectively tailoring it to the individual's particular pleasure. As Banks explains: "Some Afterlives simply offered everlasting fun for the post-dead: infinite holiday resorts featuring boundless sex, adventure, sport, games, study, exploration, shopping, hunting or whatever other activities particularly tickled that species' fancy" (Banks 2010, 127–8).

Banks does not depict Culture heavens in great detail, nor does use them as an important narrative element. Instead, Banks uses them to satirize religious notions of heaven, focusing upon the subjective and arbitrary nature of the way in which they are imagined, highlighting the often hedonistic and futile pursuits that people chose to undertake. As Johann Hari states in his article "Heaven: a Fool's Paradise": "Heaven is constantly shifting shape because it is a history of subconscious human longings. Show me your heaven, and I'll show you what's lacking in your life" (Hari 2010, n.p.). Banks adopts an irreverent tone with the phrase "tickled that species' fancy," suggesting that he believes the heavens offered by many religions tend to be frivolous and morally suspect, such as numerous virgins promised to suicide bombers in religious extremism for example, and the ability to buy one's way into heaven in Catholicism. Hari's shares this view, but he is much less restrained, unleashing a vitriolic contempt for such a seemingly innocent notion:

> Its primary function for centuries was as a tool of control and intimidation. The Vatican, for example, declared it had a monopoly on St Peter's VIP list — and only those who obeyed their every command and paid them vast sums for Get-Out-of-Hell-Free cards would get them and their children onto it [Hari 2010].

Banks' portrayal of heaven is not all satirical. Other varieties of heaven that he describes are more focused around intellectual rather than just physical gratification, or "were of a more contemplative and philosophic nature" and therefore seem to offer a more genuinely fulfilling afterlife (Banks 2010, 128). It is not long before Banks returns to his satirical tone, offering further varieties of virtual heaven in *Excession*. While the idea of a virtual heaven may seem amazing in theory, and with its potential for individual manipulation and customization may be even greater even than a physical paradise (and those generic versions offered by various religions), there are of course drawbacks. For many people, endless immersion in supposedly idyllic surroundings of any nature, with little sense of conflict, change, or development does not necessarily produce eternal contentment or happiness. As Banks states: "those who had lived for a really long time in Afterlives were prone to becoming profoundly gravely bored, or going [...] mad" (Banks 2010, 82). Again, Hari argues Banks' implicit point perfectly: "Heaven is, in George Orwell's words, an attempt to 'produce a perfect society by an endless continuation of something that had only been valuable because it was temporary.' Take away the contrast, and heaven becomes hell" (Hari 2010, n.p.). In this way, no discussion of heaven — whether in cyberspace or elsewhere — would be complete without its antithesis: many of the various narrative threads of *Surface Detail* are concerned with the existence of virtual hells.

Virtual Hells

Surface Detail features Banks' most extended descriptions of Cyberspace in the Culture series to date. Lededje's quest for revenge is set against the background of war between the Culture and various other races over the existence of Cyber Hells. The Culture are Anti-Hell, others, such as the Chelgrians and the Pavuleans, are Pro-Hell. This war, originally confined to the safety of simulated space, has now bled over into the Real.

Hell in *Surface Detail* is not metaphorical, but is a simulation of an infernal realm where immoral souls are sent to suffer eternal damnation, as it is traditionally understood in many religions. Banks exploits the freedom that the nature of a virtual environment allows him, re-envisioning the vast interlinked networks of Gibson's Matrix, or *TRON*'s Grid: initially, the damned souls from each particular Pro-Hell race were sent to a specific space, but these were eventually linked together to form a vast network of interlinked infernal virtual realms. In this virtual space, the strict laws of physics concerning the body and its surrounding environment need not necessarily apply. In "the Thrice Flayed Footprint district of the Pavulean Hell" (Banks 2010, 58) the limb of one of hell's sufferers — first flayed, and then amputated — can be enlarged to such a scale that it constitutes part of the physical environment. The limb's amputation from the body, while physically disconnecting the two parts, does not necessarily disconnect nerves from their endings, and the sufferer's pain is eternally amplified whenever someone passes over the ridge that the flayed limb forms in the hell's landscape. Banks uses this network of hells to create an eternal network of fractal flesh that easily manipulates and defies the corporeal limits of the Real world. In other scenes, body parts are removed from their owners to constitute elements of the landscape, without freeing their owners from pain: fingernails decorate the roofs of buildings like tiles; bones form the structure of a mill wheel; and stretched skin lines the walls of the mill.

Banks' hells are rendered in all their gory details, recalling the famous visions of his literary and artistic predecessors, such as the vivid and imaginative realms of Dante or Milton, and the visceral and sadistic paintings of Bosch. But rather than merely revising previous depictions, Banks re-imagines the aesthetic of hell by juxtaposing imagery from various different historical eras. Archetypal infernal images such as vicious demons, rivers of blood, bleached bones, rotting corpses, and the emaciated, naked bodies of hells denizens, exist alongside more contemporary images, including *cheval de frise*, a "giant X of crossed spikes laden with impaled, half-decaying bodies" (Banks 2010, 48): a type of defensive obstacle used on the battlefields of World War One. When describing a demon, Banks also draws upon the simple technology of the Victorian era: "[t]he thing had a lantern head, like an enormous version of a four-paned, inward-sloping gas light from ancient history [...] At each of the four external corners of the lantern, a giant candle of tallow stood, each containing a hundred shrieking nervous systems intact and in burning agony within" (Banks 2010, 285). In this way, the overall effect is of an omnitemporal zone: a kind of morbid pastiche of infernal images.

Banks' extensive and complex descriptions of Cyber Hells in *Surface Detail* allow for an exploration of the theology behind the concept of hell. The Pro-Hell factions, such as the Pavulians, argue that hells give their existence an important moral purpose similar to the function of hells in Christianity: the souls of sinners will be cast into the virtual abyss to suffer eternally; the threat of unceasing damnation and punishment after death acting as a moral imperative for all to live a just and good life. For those opposed, such as those in Banks' liberal utopia, these cyber-hells are simply sites of unspeakable barbarism: "[t]he Culture took a particularly dim view of torture, either in the Real or in a Virtuality, and was quite prepared to damage its short-, and even—at least seemingly—long-term interests to stop it happening" (Banks 2010, 133).

Conclusion

Souls and the function of Soulkeeper technology, as depicted by Banks, form an integral component of the Culture universe, as they underpin the relationships between man and machine, reality and simulation, religion and secularism. Banks' depictions of souls in this way show the integration of Cyberpunk tropes into the fundamentally space opera framework of the Culture novels, combining science fiction sub-genres to create a unique hybrid form, reinvigorating the genre as a whole. Using elements such as Revention and co-existing souls, only possible in the science fiction genre, Banks not only highlights but recapitulates existing existential and philosophical dilemmas, causing the reader to contemplate age old ideas in a new light.

Banks' visions of Virtual Afterlives expand and reimagine the environments of Cyberspace from its origins in Gibson's *Neuromancer*, probably the definitive Cyberpunk text,[9] using them to comment upon theological as well as technological themes. By allowing for heaven and hell to be realized in a secular, tangible manner, Banks reveals that the morality at the heart of these ideas is dubious or even disturbing. Finally, the use of souls in the Culture series provides more than simply interesting, thought-provoking thematic content, but also drives and shapes the narratives themselves. As exemplified in novels such as *Surface Detail* and *Look to Windward*, Banks' use of Cyberpunk influenced elements, such as souls and related technology, allow him to explore unique and unprecedented forms of narrative, which attest to his status as an important writer of any genre, but especially within the genre(s) of science fiction.

Notes

1. See William Gibson's *Neuromancer* (1984), *Count Zero* (1986), and *Mona Lisa Overdrive* (1988).
2. See also *Ghost in the Shell 2: Innocence* (2004).
3. Andy and Larry Wachowski's *The Matrix* (1999), *The Matrix Reloaded* (2003), and *The Matrix Revolutions* (2003).
4. Stephen Lisberger, *TRON* (1982); *TRON: Legacy* (2010).
5. The original article for this reference is difficult to track down, presumably because as the magazine, Arena, has now folded. Several online sources reproduce Banks' original choices. Neuromancer is number 5 in Banks' list, available at the following link: http://www.i-dig.info/culture/culturefaq.html#RECOMMENDS (accessed 18/04/2010).
6. "Banks is a phenomenon: the wildly successful, fearlessly creative author of brilliant and disturbing non-genre novels, he's equally at home writing pure science fiction of a peculiarly gnarly energy and elegance" (Gibson qtd. Banks 1993, n.p.).
7. Some causes of death, however, such as explosions, may damage the lace irreparably, rendering the device useless.
8. It is difficult to ascertain who exactly first postulated the "Brain/Computer analogy." I have mainly drawn upon Karl Schroeder's blog article "Disembodied Art: Cartesian Dualism in Science Fiction" available on his website at http://www.kschroeder.com/archive/blog/1076527608/index_html.html (posted 11/02/2011; accessed 20/04/2011); and the article "Brain Computer Analogy" by Stephen A. Gisslasen, available at http://www.nutramed.com/Philosophy/computing.htm (posted 1995; accessed 20/04/2011).
9. Gibson himself coined the term Cyberspace in his 1982 story "Burning Chrome," well before it entered into common usage.

WORKS CITED

Banks, Iain M. 1993. *Against a Dark Background*. London: Orbit.
_____. 1996. *Excession*. London: Orbit.
_____. 2000. *Look to Windward*. London: Orbit.
_____. 2010. *Surface Detail*. London: Orbit.
Blackburn, Simon, ed. 2005. "Soul." *Oxford Dictionary of Philosophy*. Oxford: Oxford University Press.
Butler, Andrew M. 2003. "The British Boom: Whose Boom? What Boom? Thirteen Ways of Looking at the British Boom." *Science Fiction Studies,* no.9, November.
Descartes, Rene. 1998. "Letter to Princess Elizabeth (28 June 1643)." In *Philosophy Then and Now*. N. Scott Arnold, Theodore M. Benditt, and George Graham, eds. Oxford: Blackwell.
Encyclopædia Britannica. 2011. "Soul." *Encyclopædia Britannica Online Library Edition*. Web.
Guerrier, Simon. 1999. "Culture Theory: Iain M. Banks's 'Culture' as Utopia." *Foundation: The International Review of Science Fiction,* vol.28, no. 76 (Summer).
Hari, Johann. 2010. "Heaven: A Fool's Paradise." *The Independent.* 21 May 2010. http://www.independent.co.uk/opinion/faith/heaven-a-fools-paradise-1949399.html. Accessed 9 January 2011.
Jamneck, Lynne. 2011. "An Interview with Bestselling Science Fiction writer Iain M Banks." http://www.suite101.com/content/ian-m-banks-al14326. (accessed 22 April 2010).
Mendlesohn, Farah. 2005. "Iain M. Banks: *Excession*." In *A Companion to Science Fiction (Blackwell Companions to Literature and Culture)*. David Seed, ed. Oxford: Blackwell, 556–567.

"Hippies with mega nukes"
The Culture, Terror and the War Machine in Consider Phlebas *and* The Player of Games

WILLIAM STEPHENSON

Science fiction makes the world strange. It does this by projecting the author's and the reader's realities into outer space and/or an imagined future. Science fiction is "rooted in estrangement" but "validated by cognitive logic" (Suvin 1988, 37): the reader is continually alienated by the otherness of the science fiction world, but is nevertheless able to draw a series of parallels with his/her own environment, creating "a feedback oscillation between the two realities" (Suvin 1988, 37). Iain M. Banks' science fiction novels are populated by a plethora of estranging entities: sentient robots that turn different colors according to mood; supercomputers with mentational capacities a human cannot even imagine; evolved post-humans who live for hundreds of years, have their consciousness artificially backed up in case they die, change gender at will and carry drug glands in their bodies for pleasure, stimulation or the relief of pain; entire artificial worlds orbiting the huge computers that govern them; and so on. The milieu in which Banks situates these creations is the Culture, a non-hierarchical, loosely affiliated collective of humans, quasi-humans and machines (mostly sentient drones and super-powerful Minds) living in symbiosis. Banks has described the Culture as "hippies with mega nukes" (Banks 2007, n.p.), a paradoxical formulation that neatly encapsulates the Culture's utopian, nomadic pacifism and its capability to turn itself into a militaristic machine all the more deadly for being mobile and flexible. This machine is sometimes called "the Culture militant" (Banks 1989, 271). The Culture is secular but, when on a war footing, can take on the characteristics of a crusading or *jihadi* society. It is idealistic, but is not afraid to engage in all sorts of dirty tricks, especially with primitive cultures unaware of its existence, through the notorious Special Circumstances section: "the uncharacteristically coy name they employ for their combined intelligence, espionage and counter-espionage organization" (Banks 2000, 356). The Culture has its own high moral ground, and its equivalents of the received Western belief in democracy and equality, but also its own versions of aircraft carriers, cruise missiles, spy satellites and the coups and destabilizations arranged by the CIA. The Culture is a complex metaphor for a number of referents. It is, for instance, a future utopia, enabling humanity to "duplicate — through machine sentience — a process which evolution took billions of years to achieve," and is clearly held by Banks to be a broadly desirable goal for human evolution (Banks no date). At the same time, it can be read as the analogue of the contemporary West, with its refined expertise in violence and its rapacious desire to hold onto global dominance and material prosperity.

This essay will suggest how like its counterpoints in the real world, the Culture believes itself benign but is in fact a social formation that lends itself to militarism, and to aggression of the sort it despises as barbaric when perpetrated by its enemies. This gap between self-image and practice lends itself to analysis in terms of the distinction between the state and the war machine drawn by Gilles Delueze and Felix Guattari in *A Thousand Plateaus* (1988). The state is hierarchical and static (sedentary), whereas the war machine has the looser structure of a tribe or band, and is dynamic (nomadic). Deleuze and Guattari's first axiom is that the war machine exists *outside* the state apparatus (Deleuze and Guattari 1988, 351). However, they conclude that in fact the state can and does appropriate the war machine to its own ends. They address the late twentieth century in the light of this, in a passage that makes implicit reference to Korea, Vietnam and the Cold War. Read today, their text seems uncannily prophetic of the post–9/11 world of the War on Terror:

> [T]he present situation is highly discouraging. We have watched the war machine grow stronger and stronger, as in a science fiction story; we have seen it assign as its objective a peace still more terrifying than fascist death; we have seen it maintain or instigate the most terrible local wars as parts of itself; we have seen it set its sights on a new type of enemy, no longer another State, or even another regime, but the "unspecified enemy"; we have seen it put its counterguerrilla elements into place, so that it can be caught by surprise once, but not twice [Deleuze and Guattari 1988, 422].

The Culture does not share the paranoid sense of perpetual self-defense against a nameless enemy suggested in this account of the West. On the contrary, it perceives itself as the comfortably dominant galactic power, with most enemies known to it, and neutralized through diplomacy or assimilation. Terrorism is not a serious threat. In *Look to Windward*, when a terrorist suicide attack is planned against a Culture orbital, it turns out that one of the terrorists was a Special Circumstances agent all along, and the whole plan had been anticipated from the start (Banks 2000, 356). However, despite the Culture's self-satisfied sense of omnipotence, it does contain within it a massive military apparatus, which stands metonymically for the capacity of the whole Culture to become a war machine. This is perhaps best exemplified in *Excession* (1997), where the seemingly bare asteroid Pittance in fact conceals a huge fleet of stored warships, "sensory and weapon systems" guarded by "apocalyptically powerful devices," all ready for action at a moment's notice (Banks 1997, 145).

Excession is dated relatively late in Banks' Culture chronology, which lasts roughly 800 years, from the Idiran-Culture war to the present of *Look to Windward* (or 1300 to 2100 A.D., in Earth dating). This essay will focus on *Consider Phlebas* and *The Player of Games*, the first of Banks' Culture novels, which are set in earlier times in Culture history. They were published in 1987 and 1988 respectively, in the same Cold War context as *A Thousand Plateaus*. Just like Deleuze and Guattari's text, they address the problem of the state's appropriation of the war machine in terms just as relevant to the post–9/11 world. This essay will consider both novels in the light of Deleuze and Guattari's theory, as well as the work of Jean Baudrillard, in order to suggest that the Culture is a disturbingly complacent symbiosis of war machine and state that offers an estranged metaphor for the British and American regimes of the late twentieth and early twenty-first centuries.

The point of much of the violence perpetrated by the Culture is not to secure military victory but to demonstrate the Culture's strength and indeed assert its very existence to the enemy. Symbolic violence, where physical damage and casualties matter far less than what is *signified* by the violent act, is one of the terrains on which, in the real world, the battle is being fought between the contemporary West and the "unspecified enemy" of the War on Terror. Baudrillard discussed the 9/11 attacks in terms of a need to challenge the dominant power (the West) on the terrain of the symbolic (Baudrillard 2003, 25–26). According to this version of terrorism, the point of terrorist violence is not the actual damage inflicted on the enemy but the demonstration of an alternative world order of fatal struggle through dialectical opposition, interrogating the dominant power's claim of its own moral and material superiority. Terrorism thus challenges Francis Fukuyama's "pseudo–Hegelian idea" of the end of history (Žižek 2002, 132), "where pluralistic democracies and capitalist economies reign supreme" (Derrida 1994, viii).

It has become necessary to challenge this construction of terrorism, to "redefine and expand [terrorism's] terms so that it will also include (some) American and other Western powers' acts" (Žižek 2002, 51), so that

> subject to a polyphonic play of difference, the familiar word is displaced simultaneously onto so many different contexts that it loses its authority as a name for a specific phenomenon and is instead revealed as an instrument of rhetorical and political strategy [Spurr 1993, 190].

This essay will show how Banks' first two Culture novels sketch out a variety of science fiction landscapes (and spacescapes) in which terrorism is estranged and appropriated through such a process of play, from the exploding Orbitals and hyperspace raids of *Consider Phlebas* to the game boards and burning planets of *The Player of Games*. His novels understand that the powerful can be perpetrators of symbolic violence as well as the disenfranchised, and that the meaning of terrorism can vary widely according to one's social position, ideology and degree of freedom. Seeing terrorism as "the weapon of the weak" has been a "definitional device" intended to characterize terrorists as those who challenge "rightful authority" (Cooper 2004, 61). Banks shows how in fact it is often the so-called rightful authority that perpetrates terrorism, as an ideological instrument intended to disseminate an image of its own dominance. Towards the end of *Look to Windward*, for instance, an assassination is carried out by a sentient "Culture terror weapon" (Banks 2000, 170), whose main function is to kill the plotters against the Culture in such a grisly way as to deter others from attempting anything similar. The Culture is seen as a perpetrator of terrorist acts, and most importantly, as a master of the discourse of symbolic violence: the cognitive link to the U.S.A. and its European satellites is there for the reader to make.

Annihilation Made Into an Aesthetic Experience: Consider Phlebas

In *Consider Phlebas*, the shape-changing secret agent Horza Gobuchul works for the religious Idirans in their galactic war against the godless, technological Culture. He finds himself caught between the two sides in his mission to steal a valuable piece of Culture technology (a missing Mind, or sentient supercomputer) and the conflict eventually brings about his destruction. The first of Banks' Culture novels to be published, *Consider Phlebas* is especially important as a vehicle for background information about Banks' universe: although a gripping narrative, it takes on the function of "the always necessary element [in science fiction] of explicating the novum (the "lecture")" (Suvin 1988, 39). By situating his main novum (the Culture in opposition to the Idirans) Banks is able to demonstrate its secular, non-hierarchical, pacific but latently militant nature. Appendices give brief essays on the Idiran-Culture war. In a typical science fiction estranging device, the text is supposed to be in translation, and therefore gives dates local to the reader: the war officially began in 1327 A.D., when of course the actual Western world on Earth was in the Middle Ages (see Banks 1988, 459). The war goes well for the Idirans at first as although the Culture's General Contact Units are technologically superior to the Idiran navy they are not designed as war ships and they are much fewer in number than the opposition fleet. Gradually, though, the Culture puts itself on a war footing, a process which takes eight years. It now moves onto the offensive, and the Idirans find it frustratingly difficult to hit back, because

> [they were] attempting to inflict hoped-for body blows upon a foe which proved frustratingly elusive. The Culture was able to use almost the entire galaxy to hide in. Its whole existence was mobile in essence; even Orbitals could be shifted, or simply abandoned, populations moved. The Idirans were religiously committed to taking and holding all they could; to maintaining frontiers, to securing planets and moons; above all, to keeping Idir safe, at any price [Banks 1988, 461].

Eventual Culture victory is inevitable, although the Idirians do not see this and fight on. The basis of this victory is not merely technological: it lies in the different ideologies and military-political infrastructures of the two powers. The Culture is a mobile entity, based on a man-machine symbiosis and living mostly on constructed (and moveable) Orbitals or starships — indeed, the Culture's most precious resources, its Minds, usually *are* starships. In Deluze and Guattari's terms, the Culture is able rapidly to deterritorialize. It is not hampered by the fundamentally religious approach to space taken by the Idirans (where in the name of the Idiran God, their creator, the Idirans hold and preserve resources such as planets). The Idirian-Culture conflict is between the *polis* (state) and the *nomos* (nomadic trajectory):

> Even though the nomadic trajectory may follow trails or customary routes, it does not fulfil the function of the sedentary road, which is to *parcel out a closed space to people*, assigning each person a share and regulating the communication between shares. The nomadic trajectory does the opposite: it *distributes people (or animals) in an open space* [...] The *nomos* is the consistency of a fuzzy aggregate: it is in this sense that it stands in opposition to the law or the *polis*, as the backcountry, a mountainside, or the vague expanse around a city. [Deleuze and Guattari 1988, 380: authors' emphasis].

The Culture's nomadic space is an ideal vehicle for the eruption of the war machine. The Culture is a nominal state that is in fact a minimally organized, semi-anarchic alliance of Minds and attached humans (or near-humans). In this sense, the Culture is closer to a war machine than a state, or to a tribe than an empire, and this is how, as the novel suggests, the Idirans were defeated, as not only could they not match the Culture's war technology once it was fully deployed, but they could not *understand*, and therefore could not adequately damage, the Culture's mobile, deterritorialized power base.

This is the main irony of the novel's reference to the contemporary world. The Idirans are knowingly fighting a religious war, which the novel calls a *jihad* (Banks 1988, 455). However, they are doing so in the manner of a nineteenth-century imperialist state, seeking to invade, hold and colonize fixed resources: whereas the Culture militant, although secular, is much closer to the Crusading (or *jihad*-orientated) war machine conceptualized by Deleuze and Guattari: "when religion sets itself up as a war machine, it mobilizes and liberates a formidable charge of nomadism or absolute deterritorialization" (Deleuze and Guattari 1988, 384). It is the presence of the Idirans that releases the Culture's latent capacity to turn its nomadic population into a military society, armed and able to strike offensively with great rapidity, and because mobile and loosely defined, very difficult to conquer. Ironically, the godless Culture militant resembles, "early Islam, a society reduced to the military enterprise" which is what "the west invokes in order to justify its antipathy towards Islam" (Deleuze and Guattari 1988, 383). In *Consider Phlebas*, it turns out to be the secular side which is fighting the *jihad* in the sense of a deterritorialized, nomadic war. Banks' description of a raid by two of the Culture's new warships makes this plain:

> The two "Killer" class Rapid Offensive Units *Trade Surplus* and *Revisionist* raced through the hyperspace, flashing underneath the web of real space like slim and glittering fish in a deep, still pond. They wove past systems and stars, keeping deep beneath the empty spaces where they were least likely to be traced [Banks 1988, 281].

It is the Culture that fights with agility and speed, and the lumbering Idirans who pursue, but fail to find, the raiders. Significantly, the Culture's mobility emerges from its superior ability to negotiate the fluctuating boundary between real space and hyperspace, and distribute itself through the hyperreal.

The Culture's capacity for mobile, highly symbolic warfare is the estranged analogue of the capacity for symbolic violence (terror) which Baudrillard identifies as already present in the Western social formation before 9/11, connected to the hyperreality of its information systems:

> Our virtual reality, our systems of information and communication, have themselves too, and for a long time, been beyond the reality principle. As for terror, we know it is already present everywhere, in institutional violence, both mental and physical, in homeopathic doses. Terrorism merely crystallizes all the ingredients in suspension [Baudrillard 2003, 59].

The instances of Culture violence depicted in *Consider Phlebas* turn out to have a strong symbolic dimension: the raid undertaken by the two ships described above is in fact a simulation, a mission to explode mines and other ordnance in a specific area of space, intended to fool Horza and the Idirians into thinking an actual battle has taken place there. No damage is done: it is the spectacle and its misleading significance that matters. Similarly, the Culture announces its intention to destroy an entire orbital containing billions of sentient life forms, but gives a warning of when the destruction will occur, and provides a ship to evacuate the population. Again, the spectacle is more significant than the damage: the Culture is destroying the Vavatch orbital on principle, as the Idirans have refused the usual agreement not to leave it as neutral territory, but instead intend to claim it as their own, without occupying it. Significantly, the Idirans' occupation is intended as merely nominal, with "no military presence" (Banks 1988, 60). Nevertheless, and perhaps precisely for this reason, the Culture feels duty bound to annihilate the orbital. Horza understands how little the merely animal eye can appreciate the sight of the exploding artificial world, and in a bitter reference to the Culture's military technology, complains it is a "spectacle for the machines" (Banks 1988, 257). It is tempting to read this in the light of the current U.S. military's tactics of shock and awe: "annihilation made into an aesthetic experience. The arrogant grace of it" (Banks 1988, 265). The Culture has become run by artificial intelligences creating symbolic violence not only on principle but also to perpetuate an image of their own omnipotence.

With its central motif of a war between religious and secular powers, *Consider Phlebas* can be read in the context of Samuel P. Huntington's clash of civilizations thesis, in which the secular, democratic, capitalistic West is locked in ideological combat with a religious, autocratic, anti-capitalist Other, Islam. Huntington argues that Western culture is "challenged" by Islam and by internal groups including "immigrants from other civilizations who reject assimilation" (Huntington 2002, 304). Žižek argues that the continual conflict posited by Huntington is, in fact, far from being a war that must be won: instead, it is a perpetually necessary myth, ideologically vital to Western capitalism since the end of the Cold War. The alleged clash of civilizations is the Western order's "very mode of existence" (Žižek 2003, 133). As Jürgen Habermas has suggested, the clash of civilizations thesis "is often the veil masking the vital material interests of the West (accessible oilfields and a secured energy supply, for example)" (Habermas 2003, 36). Thus the West *depends* for its economic and structural integrity, and its sense of cultural superiority, on an ongoing conflict with an Other. Seen in this light, the Culture's deterritorialized militarism beneath a surface of enlightened benevolence becomes an ironic estranging device, showing the hypocrisy and elisions needed to sustain the theory of the West as simply civilized and Islam as simply a quasi-barbaric threat. It is the Idirans who have the religious ideology, but it is the Culture which is able to turn itself into a devastating, crusading war machine whose strength lies in the manipulation of the hyperreal. The names of the two raiding ships in the instance above can be read as more than merely a joke. *Trade Surplus* and *Revisionist* are the carriers of the Culture's rapid offensive, just as economics and image manipulation form the spearheads of the West's ongoing mythological battle for dominance over the Other, fuelled by the belief that the West alone is subject to symbolic violence, and can negate it through disseminating its own superior values: "[a]ll these institutions, all these social, economic, political and psychological mediations, are there so that no-one ever has the opportunity to issue this symbolic challenge, this challenge to the death" (Baudrillard 1993, 38).

The Culture's endless capacity for simulation, as in, for example the construction of Orbitals — entire artificial worlds — and the countless virtual reality applications enjoyed by its citizens, including its Minds, whose virtual reality is called "The Land of Infinite Fun" (Banks 1997, 140), can be linked to its atheism, as both are traits of the contemporary culture that Banks' science fiction alludes to

> the disappearance of God has left us facing reality and the ideal prospect of transforming this real world [....] What we see now, behind the eclipse of the "objective" real, is the rise of Integral Reality, of a Virtual Reality that rests on the deregulation of the very reality principle [Baudrillard 2005, 17].

The play of pleasurable images enjoyed by the Culture results from its secular evolution beyond the religious dogma of societies like the Idirans, but this evolution should not be seen as unproblematic progress, justifying the assumption of a superior degree of civilization. Instead, as *Consider Phlebas* demonstrates, a godless, hyperspatial society can show all the whirlwind belligerence of the most fanatical Crusade. This encourages the reader to make cognitive links to the West's capacity for warfare on a number of literal and symbolic levels: like the Culture, it has a mobile military machine which has become highly integrated with the state apparatus, and wages devastating wars, both literally and on the terrain of the hyperreal.

Terrible Energy Streaming Through Him: The Player of Games

This novel is where Banks addresses the relationship between violence and the symbolic at greatest length. The player of the title, Jernau Morat

Gurgeh, is blackmailed by Special Circumstances into undertaking a mission to the Empire of Azad, a less advanced civilization which is based on a game (also called Azad).[1] The winner of each tournament becomes Emperor of Azad. The final rounds of the game take place on the Fire Planet Echronedal that has its surface ravaged by an annual conflagration, a natural planet-wide fire whose progress can be monitored and predicted. Gurgeh ends up confronting the current Emperor, Nicosar, in the final game on Echronedal, just as the conflagration is about to erupt. The crucial discovery Gurgeh makes during the game is that Nicosar is playing as if the pieces on the board incarnate their two societies:

> The Emperor had set out to beat not just Gurgeh, but the whole Culture. There was no other way to describe his use of pieces, territory and cards; he had set up his whole side of the game as an Empire, the very image of Azad. Another revelation struck Gurgeh with a force almost as great; one reading — perhaps the best — of the way he'd always played was that he played as the Culture. He'd habitually set up something like the society itself when he constructed his positions and deployed his pieces; a net, a grid of forces and relationships, without any obvious hierarchy or entrenched leadership, and initially quite profoundly peaceful [Banks 1989, 269].

The shift in the balance of the game occurs when Gurgeh, having realized this, ceases his policy of relatively peaceful resistance to Nicosar and "remodelled his whole game-plan to reflect the ethos of the Culture militant" (Banks 1989, 271). Gurgeh engages in fierce deterritorializations, "trashing and abandoning whole areas of the board where the switch would not work" (Banks 1989, 271). From an anxious, thoughtful loser, he has become an inspired strategist "like a wire with some terrible energy streaming through him" (Banks 1989, 272).

In playing as the Culture militant, Gurgeh has become the war machine. Banks' image of the wire suggests dynamism, flow, a mentality of exerting energy in play rather than responding to his opponent in a dialectical, hierarchical scheme. Deleuze and Guattari distinguish between chess and Go, not in order to describe the two actual games but to offer a metaphor for the differences between the state apparatus (chess) and the war machine (Go): "Go is war without battle lines, with neither confrontation nor retreat, without battles even: pure strategy, whereas chess is a semiology" (Deleuze and Guattari 1988, 353). Gurgeh has rejected the chess-like semiology of the game so far imposed on him by Nicosar, in which Gurgeh had unwittingly accepted the image of the Culture as pacifist, and in which the pieces had become signs for Nicosar's understanding of their two societies. Now, becoming the vehicle for the expression of the Culture militant, he transforms his play in a way Nicosar cannot understand, and operates more like a Go master than a chess player:

chess codes and decodes space, whereas Go proceeds altogether differently, territorializing or deterritorializing it (make the outside a territory in space; consolidate that territory by the construction of a second, adjacent territory; deterritorialize the enemy by shattering his territory from within; deterritorialize oneself by renouncing, by going elsewhere ...) [Deleuze and Guattari 1988, 353].

Gurgeh's change of strategy does not end the game, though. Nicosar has, as he promised Gurgeh, "a surprise" in store (Banks 1989, 280). At the climax of the game, as the planet's regular conflagration is about to engulf the castle in which the tournament is played, Nicosar announces he has "made the game real" (Banks 1989, 289). He blows up the aqueduct system that protects the castle from the conflagration, and, on this signal, his guards begin massacring his own people. It turns out that Gurgeh's drone Flere-Imsaho (actually a Special Circumstances operative, rather than a library drone, as Gurgeh believes) has informed Nicosar that, although Gurgeh is ignorant of this, he is playing as the champion of the Culture, and should Nicosar lose, the Culture will move in and take over the whole Empire. As the drone points out, this may not have been true, but it was sufficient that Nicosar *believed* it to be so in order to provoke the fatal confrontation (Banks 1989, 295). Eventually, after the death of Nicosar, the Empire of Azad collapses of its own accord. The Special Circumstances conspiracy to destabilize Nicosar's Empire has worked: the game "had to be discredited. It was what had held the Empire together all these years — the linchpin; but that made it the most vulnerable point, too" (Banks 1989, 296).

Nicosar's unexpected shift from game warfare to actual shooting is a desperate invocation of the power of symbolic violence: afterwards, Flere-Imhaso dismisses it as the mere posturing of a "sore loser" (Banks 1989, 295), but it in fact forms the keystone of the novel's referential architecture. If the Culture is an estranged version of the modern West, and the flowing, aggressive energies unleashed by Gurgeh to defeat the uncomprehending Nicosar suggest the deterritorialized flow of contemporary capital (as well as the western war machine and propaganda apparatus in full flow), then a resort to physical violence by the beleaguered Emperor is an act of desperate resistance reminiscent of conventional descriptions of terrorism as the violence of those with no other option. Žižek described the 9/11 atrocities as an "irruption of the real," but only in the sense that the real is already an effect, both to image-based Western culture *and* to the terrorists:

> We can perceive the collapse of the WTC towers as the climactic conclusion of twentieth-century art's "Passion for the Real" — the "terrorists" themselves did not do it primarily to provoke real material damage, but *for the spectacular effect of it* [....] The authentic twentieth-century passion for penetrating the Real

Thing (ultimately, the destructive Void) through the cobweb of semblances which constitutes our reality thus culminates in the thrill of the Real as the ultimate "effect," sought after from digitalized special effects, through reality TV and amateur pornography, up to snuff movies [Žižek 2002, 11–12; author's emphasis].

Nicosar terminates the game through creating the spectacular effect of an actual attack, intended not to stop Gurgeh or the Culture (which he now realizes, cannot be done) but to assert his own values: as Baudrillard said of the 9/11 terrorists' view of the West: "everything still lies in the dual, personal relation with the opposing power. It is that power which humiliated you, so it too must be humiliated" (Baudrillard 2003, 25–26).

Nicosar, though, is still wedded to an outmoded conception of the political space around him and unable to map it cognitively. Banks' novel, through its defamiliarizing science fiction tropes, implies to the reader a cognitive map of a new political reality:

> The new political art (if it is possible at all) will have to hold to the truth of postmodernism, that is to say, to its fundamental object — the world space of multinational capital — at the same time at which it achieves a breakthrough to some as yet unimaginable new mode of representing this last, in which we may again begin to grasp our positioning as individual and collective subjects and regain a capacity to act and struggle which is at present neutralized by our spatial as well as our social confusion [Jameson 1988, 54].

Gurgeh, the unwitting agent of the state-cum-war machine, is as much a dupe as Nicosar: when he feels the war machine's energy running through him as if he is a wire, he is as much a tool of history as his opponent. The reader is offered a chance to construct their own subject position by finding their way out of this problem. By implying the inadequacy of the positions of Nicosar (master of an ordered imperialist state that is ceasing to exist), *and* of Gurgeh (the malleable component of the war machine, who understands its workings intuitively but has no capacity to change it or step outside it), *The Player of Games* offers the chance to "regain a capacity to act and struggle" in the face of contemporary capitalism's increasingly warlike deterritorialization: it thus begins, remarkably, to articulate that which Jameson had held to be "as yet unimaginable."

Conclusion: The Peace of Terror or Survival

The Culture is supposed to be utopian: and indeed, it offers its human citizens several hundred years of life, and all the material things they want.

The Culture is a utopia in the traditional sense of a society "organized on a more perfect principle than in the author's community" (Suvin 1988, 35). However, as my account of *The Player of Games* and *Consider Phlebas* has shown, the Culture is also based on some of the imperfect principles which have emerged as the West engages with the implications of 9/11 and the War on Terror and their impact on global capital and the culture of simulation. Neither of these novels offers a simple allegory for recent events (indeed, they were written too early to do so): instead, they produce complex metaphors which give the reader the opportunity to construct politicized interpretations. Suvin's discussion of metaphor in science fiction is too extensive to read in any detail here, but one particular passage is highly suggestive of Banks' early Culture novels:

> In other words, in any metaphoric series or system, textual coherence demands that the shifts in meaning implied by each single metaphor gradually produce also shifts in the "literal" meanings against which each succeeding metaphor of the series is being defined [Suvin 1988, 193].

Thus each new Culture story is a reworking of the basic metaphor of Culture-as-West, which demands cognitive changes in the reader's understanding of what the West is. By establishing in *Consider Phlebas* that the Culture has a nomadic, Crusading, militaristic potential latent within it, Banks successfully ironizes the West's current self-conception as the rational, civilized player in the game of world politics, whose violence is merely a regrettable defense of its own interests against the fanatical incursions of alien Others — in effect, of barbarians. *The Player of Games* refines this irony, by showing how although Gurgeh is about to win, he never actually does. This is because of the "irruption" of physical violence (which is at the same time highly symbolic) into the game's system of simulation. Gurgeh's eventual superiority in the game, after initial setbacks, emerges from his passive immersion in the energy of the war machine, until he seems like a blind force of nature: "a colossal wave tearing across the ocean towards the sleeping shore, a great pulse of molten energy from a planetary heart" (Banks 1989, 272). In dominating the game, he demonstrates his similarity to the belligerent, supposedly barbaric Azadian Emperor, and thus metonymically reveals the violent potential of his self-satisfied, avowedly peace-loving society. In each succeeding science fiction novel, Banks refines and reworks not only the detail of the world of the Culture by extending the "poetic surplus" of detail that makes science fiction rise above being merely a metaphor for the real world, but also enables shifts in the *meaning* of the referent (Delaney 1994, 174). Through Banks' estranging devices, the West is exposed as a conglomeration of states (effectively an empire), but one which has problematically appropriated a crusading war machine. This has been done in order to propagate what Deleuze and Guattari referred to as the second figure of the worldwide war machine, that follows fascism: "a war machine that takes peace as its object directly, as the peace of Terror or Survival" (Deleuze and Guattari 1988, 421). The two novels discussed were published in the late 1980s, and Banks' original readership, seeking parallels to the real world, will have looked towards the then contemporary Cold War and Balance of Terror. Today, as this essay has shown, in the context of the decentered, globalized War on Terror that has superseded the relatively simple East-West axis of the Balance, Banks' fictions of the Culture remain politically charged, and his complex, disturbing vision has lost none of its referential force.

NOTES

1. This is a territorially-based war simulation like a very complex version of chess, or of Civilization, Age of Empires or similar contemporary computer games.

WORKS CITED

Banks, Iain. 1988 [1987]. *Consider Phlebas*. London: Futura.
_____. 1989 [1988]. *The Player of Games*. London: Orbit.
_____. 1997 [1996]. *Excession*. London: Orbit.
_____. 2000. *Look to Windward*. London: Orbit.
_____. 2007. "Interview." homepages.compuserve.de/Mostral/interviews/sfx00.htm. Accessed 19 July 2007.
_____. n.d. "A Few Notes on the Culture." http://www.cs.bris.ac.uk/~stefan/culture.html. Accessed 20 July 2007.
Baudrillard, Jean. 1993. *Symbolic Exchange and Death*. Iain Hamilton Grant, trans. London: Sage.
_____. 2003. *The Spirit of Terrorism and Other Essays*. Chris Turner, trans. London: Verso.
_____. 2005. *The Intelligence of Evil or the Lucidity Pact*. Chris Turner, trans. Oxford: Berg.
Borradori, Giovanna. 2003. *Philosophy in a Time of Terror: Dialogues with Jürgen Habermas and Jacques Derrida*. Chicago: University of Chicago Press.
Cooper, H. H. A. 2004. "Terrorism: The Problem of Definition Revisited." In *The New Era of Terrorism: Selected Readings*. Gus Martin, ed. Thousand Oaks: Sage, 55–63.
Delany, Samuel R. 1994. *Silent Interviews: On Language, Race, Sex, Science Fiction and Some Comics*. Hanover, PA: Wesleyan University Press.
Deleuze, Gilles, and Felix Guattari. 1988. *A Thousand Plateaus: Capitalism and Schizophrenia*. Brian Massumi, trans. London: Athlone Press.
Derrida, Jacques. 1994. *Specters of Marx*. Trans. Peggy Kamuf. London: Routledge.
Fukuyama, Francis. 1992. *The End of History and the Last Man*. New York: Free Press.
Habermas, Jürgen. 2003. "Fundamentalism and Terror." In *Philosophy in a Time of Terror: Dialogues with Jürgen Habermas and Jacques Derrida*. Giovanna Borradori, ed. Luis Guzman, trans. Chicago: University of Chicago Press, 25–43.
Huntington, Samuel P. 2002. *The Clash of Civilizations and the Remaking of World Order*. London: Free Press.
Jameson, Fredric. 1988. *Postmodernism, or, the Cultural Logic of Late Capitalism*. London: Verso.

Roberts, Adam. 2006. *Science Fiction*. London: Routlege.
Spurr, David. 1993. *The Rhetoric of Empire: Colonial Discourse in Journalism, Travel Writing, and Imperial Administration*. Durham: Duke University Press.
Suvin, Darko. 1988. *Positions and Presuppositions in Science Fiction*. Kent, OH: Kent State University Press.
Žižek, Slavoj. 2002. *Welcome to the Desert of the Real! Five Essays on September 11 and Related Dates*. London: Verso.

Afterword

Katharine Cox

Banks has always been an author who has spoken candidly about his views and moral outlook. Espousing a love of whisky, fast cars, gadgets, music and for a period drugs (see the author's reflections on the writing of *Canal Dreams*), he genuinely seemed to be a writer having fun. Combine this with his popularity and his jibe that he does not really research (an assertion that this collection directly questions) it perhaps becomes apparent why academics have been slow to consider his work as worthy of serious study. This collection gives voice to academics who have become fans or indeed fans who have become academics. In doing so, we hope to demonstrate the complexities and richness of Banks' writing beyond the consideration of his early work (*The Wasp Factory*, *The Bridge*, *Use of Weapons*). Indeed, we had hoped that this collection might be considered as a moment on the journey of Banks' writing maturity, charting the development of his ideas and through examinations of both his mainstream and SF work to demonstrate his importance as a contemporary writer. As editors we were intrigued by Banks' anticipated change of pace to take a more 'weird' approach (as promised by the author). Sadly, just before publication it became apparent that Banks was very poorly indeed. In typical fashion he shared his terminal condition with his fans via the website on April 3, 2013, and died a couple of months later on June 9, 2013. Instead of gesturing to potential changes of direction in his writing we found ourselves considering his complete oeuvre.

Banks' impact stretched beyond his writing. Over the course of his career Iain Banks has cultivated a strong rapport with his fans. Although principally known as an author of fiction his non-fiction writing on whisky (*Raw Spirit* 2003), principled stands on political issues, his winning appearances captaining the Writers' team on University Challenge U.K. (2006) and Celebrity Mastermind U.K. (answering on whiskey in 2006) have endeared him to a larger audience. Taking a stand on the Iraq war he shredded his passport in an act of defiance, sending it to the then British Prime Minister Tony Blair, before remembering an upcoming publicity tour of Australia (see Ian Rankin's remembrance of this incident in *The Telegraph* qtd. Stock 2013).

The announcement of his terminal condition coincided with the end stages of writing his final novel, *The Quarry* (2013). When he heard of his prognosis Banks was already 90 percent through the book (Kennedy and Kelly 2013), which ironically and coincidentally has a character suffering from terminal cancer as one of the key elements of the novel. The novel is in the vein of his family saga novels (following such works as *The Crow Road*, *Whit* and *The Steep Approach to Garbadale*). Whilst reviewed sensitively, there is already a sense that the novel is not among his best though there are some interesting parallels to be drawn with *The Wasp Factory*. In a pre-emptive reflection on the work, Banks noted that he felt it a "relatively minor piece" (qtd. Kennedy and Kelly 2013) and that he felt the genre troubling *Transition* would have been a more fitting finale. However, there are some rich motifs to be explored there, such as the image of the teetering house as a metaphor for Guy's diseased body as well as the void of the quarry which is exposed within the core human relationships.

There is even a suggestion that some posthumous work might emerge perhaps in the form of some poetry that Banks has referred to (but this is likely to be a playful McGuffin in his part) or more likely a collaboration between his writer friends to realize one last Culture novel. Banks has repeatedly praised the intervention and advice of his friends in his writing and in reference to *Use of Weapons* modestly stated: "what may still be my best SF novel is largely the work of others." (qtd. Flood and Armitstead), so this seems feasible as a tribute.

This collection has laid the foundation for a critical re-evaluation of Banks' writing in the round. Such critical inquiry will no doubt establish Banks as one of the most intriguing, inventive and playful of our contemporary authors who is worthy of extended academic consideration. It has been a pleasure to work on this critical collection and to be part of Banks' journey, if only in a small way. Whilst the academics and critics will no doubt go on to argue the finer points of his writing and, in doing so, ensure the significance of his work for the future, Banks is "away the crow road" and we will miss him.

Works Cited

Flood, Alison and Armitstead, Claire. 2013. "Iain Banks Diagnosed with Gall Bladder Cancer." *The Guardian*, April 3

Kennedy, Maev, and Stuart Kelly. 2013. "Squeeze Any Tory, Blairite or Lib Dem…" *The Guardian*, June 15.

Stock, Jon. 2013. "Ian Rankin Pays Tribute to Iain Banks." *The Telegraph*, June 10.

Bibliography

This bibliography lists selected readings arranged according to the categories of this collection. This is not an exhaustive list, and this bibliography should be used in conjunction with the works cited that are given at the end of each of the chapters.

Iain Banks' UK Fiction

Banks, Iain. 1984. *The Wasp Factory*. London: Abacus.
_____. 1985. *Walking on Glass*. London: Abacus.
_____. 1986. *The Bridge*. London: Abacus.
_____. 1987. *Espedair Street*. London: Macmillan.
_____. 1989. *Canal Dreams*. London: Abacus.
_____. 1992. *The Crow Road*. London: Abacus.
_____. 1993. *Complicity*. London: Abacus.
_____. 1995. *Whit*. London: London: Abacus.
_____. 1997. *A Song of Stone*. London: Abacus.
_____. 1999. *The Business*. London: Abacus.
_____. 2002. *Dead Air*. London: Abacus.
_____. 2007. *The Steep Approach to Garbadale*. London: Little, Brown.
_____. 2009. *Transition*. London: Little, Brown [published in the U.S. with the authorial "M"].
_____. 2012. *Stonemouth*. London: Little, Brown.
_____. 2013. *The Quarry*. London: Little, Brown.

Iain M. Banks' UK Fiction

Banks, Iain M. 1987. *Consider Phlebas*. London: Orbit.
_____. 1988. *The Player of Games*. London: Orbit.
_____. 1990. *Use of Weapons*. London: Orbit.
_____. 1991. *The State of the Art*. London: Orbit [this is a selection of short stories. From the collection the stories "Road of Skulls," "A Gift from the Culture," "Odd Attachment," "Descendant," "Cleaning Up," "Piece," "Scratch" and "The State of the Art" had been previously published in magazines or in anthologies].
_____. 1993. *Against a Dark Background*. London: Orbit.
_____. 1994. *Feersum Endjinn*. London: Orbit.
_____. 1996. *Excession*. London: Orbit.
_____. 1998. *Inversions*. London: Orbit.

_____. 2000. *Look to Windward*. London: Orbit.
_____. 2004. *The Algebraist*. London: Orbit.
_____. 2008. *Matter*. London: Orbit.
_____. 2010. *Surface Detail*. London: Orbit.
_____. 2012. *The Hydrogen Sonata*. London: Orbit.

Iain M. Banks' U.S. Fiction

Banks, Iain M. 1987. *Consider Phlebas*. London: Orbit.
_____. 1988. *The Player of Games*. London: Orbit.
_____. 1990. *Use of Weapons*. London: Orbit.
_____. 1993. *Against a Dark Background*. London: Orbit.
_____. 2008. *Matter*. London: Orbit.
_____. 2009. *Transition*. London: Little, Brown [published in the UK without the authorial "M"].
_____. 2010. *Surface Detail*. London: Orbit.
_____. 2012. *Stonemouth*. New York and London: Pegasus [published without the M.]
_____. 2012. *The Hydrogen Sonata*. London: Orbit.
_____. 2013. *The Quarry*. London: Orbit [published without the M.]

Iain M. Banks' Culture Fiction

Banks, Iain M. 1987. *Consider Phlebas*. London: Orbit.
_____. 1988. *The Player of Games*. London: Orbit.
_____. 1990. *Use of Weapons*. London: Orbit.
_____. 1991. *The State of the Art*. London: Orbit [this is a selection of short stories. From the collection the stories "Road of Skulls," "A Gift from the Culture," "Odd Attachment," "Descendant," "Cleaning Up," "Piece," "Scratch" and "The State of the Art" had been previously published in magazines or in anthologies].
_____. 1996. *Excession*. London: Orbit.
_____. 1998. *Inversions*. London: Orbit.
_____. 2000. *Look to Windward*. London: Orbit.
_____. 2008. *Matter*. London: Orbit.
_____. 2010. *Surface Detail*. London: Orbit.
_____. 2012. *The Hydrogen Sonata*. London: Orbit.

Miscellaneous Short Stories and Non-Fiction

Banks, Iain. 1988. "Introduction." *Viriconium*. By M. John Harrison. London: Allen and Unwin, vii–xii.
_____. 1993. "Under Ice." *Granta*, vol. 43 [this short story is incorporated into Banks' later novel, *Complicity* 1993].
_____. 2003. *Raw Spirit*. London: Century.
Banks, Iain M. 1987. "A Gift from the Culture." *Interzone*, no. 20.
_____. 1987a. "Descendant." Roz Kaveney, ed. *Tales from the Forbidden Planet*. London: Titian.
_____. 1987b. "Cleaning Up." *NOVACON 17*. Birmingham: Birmingham Science Fiction Group.
_____. 1987c. "Scratch." *The Fiction Magazine*, vol. 6, no. 6.
_____. 1988. "Road of Skulls." Peter Straus, ed. *20 Under 35*. N.p.: Sceptre.
_____. 1989. "Odd Attachment." Alex Stewart, ed. *Arrows of Eros*. N.p.: NEL.
_____. 1989a. "Piece." *The Observer Magazine*. London: Observer.
_____. 1994. "A Few Notes on the Culture." www.rec.arts.sf.written.

Adaptations of Iain Banks' Novels

Millar. G. Dir. 1999. *Complicity*. Union Pictures/BBC Scotland.
———. Dir. 2002. *The Crow Road*. Talisman.

Part I. Scottish Context

Bell, Eleanor, and Gavin Miller, eds. 2004. *Scotland in Theory: Reflections on Culture and Literature*. Amsterdam: Rodopi.
Bell, Ian A., ed. 1995. *Peripheral Vision: Images of Nationhood in Contemporary British Fiction*. Cardiff: University of Wales Press.
Brewster, Scott. 2005. "Borderline Experience: Madness, Mimicry and the Scottish Gothic." *Gothic Studies*, vol. 7, no. 1, 79–86.
Carruthers, Gerard, David Goldie, and Alastair Renfrew, eds. 2004. "Re-Mapping Renaissance in Modern Scottish Literature." In *Beyond Scotland: New Contexts for Twentieth Century Scottish Literature*. Amsterdam: Rodopi.
Craig, Cairns. 1996. *Out of History: Narrative Paradigms in Scottish and British Culture*. Edinburgh: Polygon.
———. 1999. *The Modern Scottish Novel: Narrative and the National Imagination*. Edinburgh University Press: Edinburgh.
———. 2006. "Devolving the Scottish Novel." In *A Concise Guide to Contemporary British Fiction*. James F. English, ed. Oxford: Blackwell, 121–140.
Daiches, David. 1993. *New Companion to Scottish Culture*. Edinburgh: Polygon.
Devine, T.M., and R.J. Finlay, eds. 1996. *Scotland in the Twentieth Century*. Edinburgh: Edinburgh University Press.
Gifford, Douglas, Sarah Dunnigan, and Alan MacGillivray. 2002 *Scottish Literature*. Edinburgh: Edinburgh University Press.
Laing, L., and J. Laing. 2001. *The Picts and the Scots*. Stroud: Sutton.
Lynch, Michael. 1992. *Scotland: A New History*. London: Pimlico.
MacGillivray, Alan. 2002. *Scotnotes: Iain Banks' the Wasp Factory, the Crow Road and Whit*. Glasgow: Association of Scottish Literary Studies.
MacIlvanney, Liam. 2002. "The politics of narrative in the post-war Scottish novel." Zachary Leader, ed. *On Modern British Fiction*. Oxford: Oxford University Press, 181–208.
Manlove, Colin. 1994. *Scottish Fantasy Literature: A Critical Survey*. Edinburgh: Cannongate Academic.
March, Christie. 2002. *Rewriting Scotland: Welsh, McLean, Warner, Banks, Galloway and Kennedy*. Manchester: Manchester University Press.
Mitchell, James. "Scotland in the Union 1945–95." T.M. Devine and R.J. Finlay, eds. *Scotland in the 20th Century*. Edinburgh: Edinburgh University Press.
Nairn, Tom. 2004. "Break-Up: Twenty-Five Years On." Eleanor Bell and Gavin Miller, eds. *Scotland in Theory: Reflections on Culture and Literature*. Rodopi: Amsterdam.
Paterson, Anna. 2002. *Scotland's Landscape: Endangered Icon*. Edinburgh: Polygon.
Petrie, Duncan. 2004. *Contemporary Scottish Fiction: Film, Television and the Novel*. Edinburgh: Edinburgh University Press.
Punter, David. 1991. "Heartlands: Contemporary Scottish Gothic." *Gothic Studies*, vol. 1. 1, 101–118.
Riach, Alan. 1996. "Nobody's Children: Orphans and Their Ancestors in Popular Scottish Fiction After 1945." Susanne Hagemann, ed. *Studies in Scottish Fiction: 1945 to the Present*. Frankfurt am Main: Peter Lang GmbH, 51–84.
Stevenson, Randall. 2004. "A Postmodern Scotland." Gerard Carruthers, David Goldie and Alastair Renfrew, eds. *Beyond Scotland: New Contexts for Twentieth Century Scottish Literature*. Amsterdam: Rodopi, 209–228.

Wallace, Gavin, and Randall Stevenson, eds. 1993 *The Scottish Novel Since the Seventies: New Visions, Old Dreams*. Edinburgh: Edinburgh University Press.
Witschi, Beat. 1991. *Scottish Studies: Glasgow Urban Writing and Postmodernism*. Frankfurt: Peter Lang.
Wright, Angela. 2007. "Scottish Gothic." Catherine Spooner and Emma McEvoy, eds. *The Routledge Companion to the Gothic*. Abingdon: Routledge, 73–82.

Part II. Geographies

Barrell, John. 1982. "Geographies of Hardy's Wessex." *Journal of Historical Geography*, vol. 8, 347–61.
Brosseau, Marc. 1994. "Geography's Literature." *Progress in Human Geography*, vol. 18, 333–53.
Brown, Chris. 2001. "Special Circumstances: Intervention by a Liberal Utopia." *Millennium: Journal of International Studies*, vol. 30. 3, 625–633.
Gifford, Douglas. 1996. "Imagining Scotlands: The Return to Mythology in Modern Scottish Fiction." Susan Hagemann, ed. *Studies in Scottish Fiction: 1945 to the Present*. Frankfurt am Main: Peter Lang GmbH, 17–50.
Harvey, D. 1985. *The Urbanization of Capital*. Oxford: Blackwell.
_____. 2001. "The Cartographic Imagination: Balzac in Paris." V. Dharwadker, ed. *Cosmopolitan Geographies: New Locations in Literature and Culture*. New York: Routledge, 63–87.
Hones, Sheila. 2005. "Spectral Geography and Fictional Setting." Paper presented at the Royal Geographical Society/Institute of British Geographers Annual Conference, London.
Jackson, Peter. 1989. *Maps of Meaning: An Introduction to Cultural Geography*. London: Routledge.
Kneale, James. 2009. "Space." Mark Bould, Andrew Butler, Adam Roberts and Sherryl Vint, eds. *The Routledge Companion to Science Fiction*. London: Routledge, 423–432.
Massey, Doreen. 2005. *For Space*. London: Sage.
Mighall, Richard. 1993. *A Geography of Victorian Gothic Fiction: Mapping History's Nightmares*. Oxford: Oxford University Press.
Moretti, Franco. 1998. *Atlas of the European Novel 1800–1900*. London: Verso.
Morton, Oliver. 2002. *Mapping Mars: Science, Imagination and the Birth of a World*. London: Fourth Estate.
Parsons, Coleman O. 1964. *Witchcraft and Demonology in Scott's Fiction*. Edinburgh: Oliver and Boyd.
Paterson, Anna. 2002. *Scotland's Landscape: Endangered Icon*. Edinburgh: Polygon.
Vint, Sheryl. 2007. "Cultural Imperialism and the Ends of Empire: Iain M. Banks' *Look to Windward*." *Journal of the Fantastic in the Arts*, vol. 18. 1, 83–98.

Part II. Genre

Armitt, Lucie. 1996. *Theorising the Fantastic*. London: Hodder Arnold.
_____. 2001. "The Magical Realism of the Contemporary Gothic." David Punter, ed. *A Companion to the Gothic*. Oxford: Blackwell, 305–316.
Brewster, Scott. 2005. "Borderline Experience: Madness, Mimicry and the Scottish Gothic." *Gothic Studies*, vol. 7. 1, 79–86.
Chanady, Amaryll Beatrice. 1985. *Magic Realism and the Fantastic: Resolved Versus Unresolved Antinomy*. New York: Garland.
Cornwell, Neil. 1990. *The Literary Fantastic: From Gothic to Postmodernism*. Hertfordshire: Harvester Wheatsheaf.

Horner, Avril, and Sue Zloznik. 2005. *Gothic and the Comic Turn*. Hampshire: Palgrave Macmillan.
Hume, Kathryn. 1984. *Fantasy and Mimesis: Responses to Reality in Western Literature*. London: Methuen.
Manlove, Colin. 1994. *Scottish Fantasy Literature: A Critical Survey*. Edinburgh: Cannongate Academic.
McCracken, Scott. 1998. *Pulp: Reading Popular Fiction*. Manchester: Manchester University Press.
Nicholls, Stan. 1993. *Wordsmiths of Wonder: Fifty Interviews with Writers of the Fantastic*. London: Orbit.
Punter, David. 1996. *The Literature of Terror: A History of Gothic Fictions, Volume 2: The Modern Gothic*, 2d ed. Essex: Longman.
_____. 1999. "Heart Lands: Contemporary Scottish Gothic." *Gothic Studies*, vol. 1, no. 1, May 1999, 101–118.
Roberts, Adam. 2005. *Science Fiction: The New Critical Idiom*, 2d ed. New York: Routledge.
Sage, Victor, and Allan Lloyd-Smith, eds. 1996. *Modern Gothic: A Reader*. Manchester: Manchester University Press.
Suvin, Darko. 1979. *Metamorphoses of Science Fiction*. New Haven: Yale University Press.
Wolfreys, Julian. 2008. *Transgression: Identity, Space, Time*. Hampshire: Palgrave Macmillan.

Part IV. Gender, Games and Play

Cixous, Hélène, and Catherine Clément. 1986. *The Newly Born Woman*. Betsy Wing, trans. Manchester: Manchester University Press.
Frasca, Gonzalo. 1999. "Ludology Meets Narratology: Similitude and Differences Between (Video)Games and Narrative." *Ludology.Org: Videogame Theory*. http://www.ludology.org/articles/ludology.htm. Last accessed 17 August 2007.
Irigaray, Luce. 1985. *Speculum of the Other Woman*. Gillian C. Gill, trans. Ithaca: Cornell University Press.
Macdonald, Kirsty A. 2007. "Anti-Heroes and Androgynes: Gothic Masculinities in Contemporary Scottish Men's Fiction." *The Irish Journal of Gothic and Horror Studies*, no. 3, n.p. http://irishgothichorrorjournal.homestead.com/ScottishGothicMasculinities.html. Accessed 24 July 2008.
Schoene-Harwood, Berthold. 2000. "'Dams burst': Devolving Gender in the *The Wasp Factory*." *A Review of International English Literature*, 131–148.
_____. 2000a. *Writing Men: Literary Masculinities from Frankenstein to the New Man*. Edinburgh: Edinburgh University Press.

Additional Criticism on Banks

Alegre, Sara Martin. 2000. "Consider Banks: Iain M. Banks' *The Wasp Factory* and *Consider Phlebas*." *Revista Canaria de Estudios Ingleses (RCEI)*, vol. 41, 197–205.
Armitt, Lucie. 2002. "The Crow Road." *The Literary Encyclopedia*. 31 July. http://www.litencyc.com/php/sworks.php?rec=true&UID=1177. Accessed 22 November 2011.
Binns, Ronald. 1990. "Castles, Books, and Bridges: Mervyn Peake and Iain Banks." *Peake Studies*, vol. 2. 1, 5–12.
Bloom, Clive. 2002. "Bestsellers: Popular Fiction Since 1900." Basingstoke: Palgrave Macmillan.
Brewster, Scott. 2006. "Beating, Retreating: Violence and Withdrawal in Iain Banks and John Burnside." James McGonigal and Kirsten Stirling, eds. *Ethically Speaking: Voice and Values in Modern Scottish Writing*. Amsterdam: Rodopi, 179–198.

Brown, Carolyn. 1996. "Utopias and Heterotopias: The 'Culture' of Iain M. Banks." Derek Littlewood and Peter Stockwell, eds. *Impossibility Fiction: Alternativity, Extrapolation, Speculation.* Amsterdam: Rodopi, 57–74.

Brown, Chris. 2001. "Special Circumstances: Intervention by a Liberal Utopia." *Millennium: Journal of International Studies,* vol. 30. 3, 625–633.

Butler, Andrew M. 1999. "The Strange Case of Mr Banks: Doubles and *The Wasp Factory.*" *Foundation: The International Review of Science Fiction,* vol. 28. 76, 17–27.

Colebrook, Martyn. 2010. "'Journeys into Lands of Silence': *The Wasp Factory* and Mental Disorder." Ruth Bienstock Anolik, ed. *Demons of the Body and Mind: Essays on Disability in Gothic Literature.* Jefferson, NC: McFarland, 217–226.

Craig, Cairns. 2002. *Iain Banks' Complicity: A Reader's Guide.* Continuum: London.

____. 2005. "Player of Games: Iain M. Banks, Jean-François Lyotard and Sublime Terror." James Acheson and Sarah C.E. Ross, eds. *The Contemporary British Novel Since 1980.* New York: Palgrave Macmillan, 229–239.

De Coning, Alexis. n.d. "Sympathizing with a Monster: An Exploration of the Abject 'Human Monster' in Iain Banks' *The Wasp Factory.*" Google search "De Coning Sympathizing with a Monster."

Dodou, Katherina. 2006. "Evading the Dominant 'Reality': The Case of Iain Banks' *Walking on Glass.*" *Studio Neophilologica: A Journal of Germanic and Romance Languages and Literature,* vol. 78. 1, 28–38.

Duggan. Rob. 2007. "Iain M. Banks, Postmodernism and the Gulf War." *Extrapolation,* vol. 48. 3, 561–578.

Guerrier, Simon. 1999. "Culture Theory: Iain M. Banks' 'Culture as Utopia.'" *Foundation: The International Review of Science Fiction,* vol. 28. 76, 28–38.

Hardesty, William H. 1999. "Mercenaries and Special Circumstances: Iain M. Banks' Counter-Narrative of Utopia, *Use of Weapons.*" *Foundation: The International Review of Science Fiction,* vol. 28. 76, 39–47.

Hardesty, William. 2000. "Space Opera Without the Space: The Culture Novels of Iain M. Banks." Gary Westfahl, ed. *Space and Beyond: The Frontier Theme in Science Fiction* Westport, CT: Greenwood, 115–122.

Heilman, James, and Patrick Jackson. 2008. "Outside Context Problems: Liberalism and Other in the Work of Iain M. Banks." Donald M. Hassler and Clyde Wilcox, eds. *New Boundaries in Political Science Fiction.* Columbia: New Carolina Press, 235–258.

Hutchinson, Colin. 2008. *Reaganism, Thatcherism and the Social Novel.* Basingstoke: Palgrave Macmillan.

Jones, Stephen R. 2004. "Action at a Distance: Narrative Structure and Technique in Iain Banks' *Whit.*" *Studies in Scottish Literature,* vol. 33–34, 372–86.

Kulibicki, Michal. 2009. "Iain M. Banks, Ernest Bloch and Utopian Interventions." *Colloquy: Text, Theory and Critique,* vol. 17, 34–43.

Leishman, David. 2009. "Coalescence and the Fiction of Iain Banks." *Études Écossaises,* vol. 12, 215–230.

Lippens, Ronnie. 2002. "Imachinations of Peace: Scientifictions of Peace in Iain M. Banks' *The Player of Games.*" *Utopian Studies: Journal of the Society for Utopian Studies,* vol. 13, 135–47.

Lyall, Roderick. 1993. "Postmodernist Otherworld, Postcalvinist Purgatory: An Approach to *Lanark* and *The Bridge.*" *Études Écossaises,* vol. 2, 41–52.

MacGillivray, Alan. 1996. "The Worlds of Iain Banks." *Laverock,* vol. 2, 22–27.

McVeigh, Kevin P. 1997. "The Weaponry of Deceit: Speculations on Reality in *The Wasp Factory.*" *Vector,* vol. 191, 2–7.

Mendelsohn, Farah. 2005. "The Dialectic of Decadence and Utopia in Iain M. Banks' Culture Novels." *Foundation: The International Review of Science Fiction,* vol. 93, 116–24.

_____. 2005a. "Iain M. Banks: *Excession.*" David Seed, ed. *A Companion to Science Fiction (Blackwell Companions to Literature and Culture).* Oxford: Blackwell, 556–567.
Middleton, Tim. 1995. "Constructing the Contemporary Self: the Works of Iain Banks." Tracey Hill and William Hughes, eds. *Contemporary Fiction and National Identity.* Bath: Sulis Press.
_____. 1996. "The Works of Iain M. Banks: A Critical Introduction." *Foundation: The International Review of Science Fiction,* vol. 28. 76, 5–16.
Miller, Gavin. 2007. "Iain (M.) Banks: Utopia, Nationalism and the Posthuman." Berthold Schoene-Harwood, ed. *Edinburgh Companion to Scottish Literature.* Edinburgh: Edinburgh University Press, 202–209.
Nairn, Thom. 1993. "Iain Banks and the Fiction Factory." Gavin Wallace and Randall Stevenson, eds. *The Scottish Novel Since the Seventies: New Visions, Old Dreams.* Edinburgh: Edinburgh University Press, 127–135.
O'Connor, Edmund. 2006. "Mr. Iain and Mr. Iain (M.) (Banks)." *Chapman,* vol. 108, 119–125.
Palmer, Christopher. 1999. "Galactic Empires and the Contemporary Extravaganza: Dan Simmons and Iain M. Banks." *Science Fiction Studies,* vol. 26.1, 73–90.
Radin-Sabados, Mirna. 2005. "Beyond Crime and Punishment: Metaphors of Violence in Ian Banks' *Complicity.*" *English Language Overseas Perspectives and Enquiries,* no. 2, 155–64.
Robertson, James. Dec. 1989–Jan. 1990. "Bridging Styles: A Conversation with Iain Banks." *Radical Scotland,* vol. 42, 25–29.
Sage, Victor. 1996. "The Politics of Petrification: Culture, Religion, History in the Fiction of Iain Banks and John Banville." Victor Sage and Allan Lloyd-Smith, eds. *Modern Gothic: A Reader.* Manchester: Manchester University Press, 20–37.
Wilkinson, Gary. 1999. "Poetic Licence: Iain M. Banks's *Consider Phlebas* and T. S. Eliot's *The Waste Land.*" http://www.fearful-symmetry.co.uk/poeticl.htm. Accessed 17 August 2007.

Encyclopedia Entries

Kincaid, Paul. 1996. "Iain M. Banks." Jay P. Pedersen, ed. *The St. James Guide to Science Fiction Writers,* 4th ed. Detroit: Detroit University Press, 45–6.
Latham, Rob. 2002. "Iain M. Banks." Darren Harris-Fain, ed. *British Fantasy and Science-Fiction Writers Since 1960.* Detroit: Gale, 63–77.
Middleton, Tim. 1998. "Iain Banks." Merritt Moseley, ed. *British Novelists Since 1960: Second Series.* Detroit: Thomson Gale, 19–26.
_____. 2006. "Iain (Menzies) Banks." Dominic Head, ed. *The Cambridge Guide to Literature in English,* 3d ed. Cambridge: Cambridge University Press, 67.
Rennison, Nick. 2005. "Iain Banks." *Contemporary British Novelists.* Abingdon: Routledge, 21–22.

Selected Interviews (more comprehensive listings can be found on Iain Banks' webpage, www.iain-banks.net)

Amith, Aidan. 2009. "Interview: Iain Banks—A merger of two banks." *The Scotsman,* 13 September 2009. http://news.scotsman.com/interviews/Interview-Iain-Banks-A.5640948.jp.
Banks, Iain. 2009. "In Conversation with Tim Haigh." *Tim Haigh Reads Books.* http://timhaighreadsbooks.com/.
Brooks, Libby. 2002. "The Word Factory." *The Guardian.* 26 August. http://www.guardian.co.uk/books/2002/aug/26/fiction.iainbanks.

Garnett, David S. 1989. "Interview: Iain M. Banks." *Journal Wired* no. 1 (Winter), 51–69.
Howe, David. 1996. "An Interview with Iain Banks." *Starburst*, no. 151, 11–13.
Gifford, Douglas.1991. "Interview with Iain Banks." *Festival Times*, 23 August, 57.
Haddock, David. 2005a. "The Player of Games." *Banksoniain: An Iain Banks Fanzine*, v01.7, 4–5. http://www.banksoniain.netfirms.com/banksoniain_07.pdf. Accessed 17 August 2007.
Hedgecock, Andrew. 1998. "The Edge Interview: Iain Banks." http://www.theedge.abelgratis.co.uk/iainbanksiview.htm.
Jamneck, Lynne. 2011. "An Interview with Bestselling Science Fiction Writer Iain M Banks." http://www.suite101.com/content/ian-m-banks-a114326. Accessed 22 April 2010.
Kelly, Stuart. 2013. "Iain Banks: the final interview." *The Guardian*, 15 June 2013.
Kelman, Kate. 1998. "A Collision of Selves." *Cencrastus*, no. 60, 19–22.
Livingstone, Ken. 2009. "The Books Interview: Iain Banks." *The New Statesman*, 17 September 2009. http://www.newstatesman.com/books/2009/09/livingstone-interview-culture.
Lowe, Greg. 2008. "Iain Banks — Interview." *Spike Magazine*, March 24, 2008. http://www.spikemagazine.com/iain-banks-interview.php.
Metcalfe, Tim. 1989 "An Interview with Iain Banks." *GM Magazine*, no. 2. 3, 7–10.
Mitchell, Chris. 1996. "Iain Banks: *Whit* and *Excession*: Getting Used to Being God." *Spike Magazine*. http://www.spikemagazine.com/0996bank.php.
Moore, John. 2009. "Iain M. Banks: Nearly God." *Exposure Magazine*.
Mullan, John 2008. "Iain Banks on *The Wasp Factory*." 17 July. http://www.guardian.co.uk/books/audio/2008/jul/16/guardian.bookclub.podcast. Accessed 19 July 2008.
Murray, Isobel. 2002. "Iain Banks." Isobel Murray, ed. *Scottish Writers Talking 2: Iain Banks, Bernard MacLaverty, Naomi Mitchinson, Iain Crichton Smith, Alan Spence*. East Lothian: Tuckwell Press, 1–34.
Nicholls, Stan. 1994. "Cultural Difference." *Interzone*, no. 86, 22–23.
Orbit. 2002. "Interview with Iain M. Banks." SSFworld.com. http://www.sffworld.com/interview/2p0.html.
Ricketts, Ed. 1996. "Interview with Iain Banks." http://www.futurehi.net/phlebas/text/banksint15.html. Accessed 15 August 2007.
Robertson, James. December 1989/January 1990. "Bridging Styles: A Conversation with Iain Banks." *Radical Scotland*, no. 42, 26–27.
Rosser, Adam. 2000. "An Interview with Iain Banks." *Science Fiction World*, no. 3, 16–18.
Ryan, Nick. 2008. "The King of Culture." http://www.nickryan.net/articles/banks.html. Accessed 17 June 2010.
Williams, Owen. 2009. "Iain M Banks Talks Culture." *Empire*. 2 November 2009. http://www.empireonline.com/news/story.asp?NID=26180.
Wilson, Andrew. 1994. "Iain Banks Interview." *Textualities*. http://textualities.net/andrew-wilson/iain-banks-interview/.

Selected Book Reviews

Adair, Tom. 1989. "Doomsday in Panama." *The Scotland on Sunday*, 27 August, 32.
"Briefly." 1984. *The Daily Mail*, 16 February, 7.
Craig, Patricia. 1984. "Exterminating Agents." *The Times Literary Supplement*, 16 March, 287.
Edwards, Malcolm. 1992. "Review of *The Wasp Factory*." Stephen Jones and Kim Newman, eds. *Horror: 100 Best Books*, 2d ed. London: Hodder and Stoughton, 268.
Gifford, Douglas. 1992. "Raven's Way and Crow's Road." *Books in Scotland*, no. 43, 11–16.

Gimson, Andrew. 1984. "Hype the Good Hype." *The Sunday Times*, 16 February, 11.
Haddock, David. 2004. "Walking on Glass." *Banksoniain: An Iain M. Banks' Fanzine*, vol. 2, 3–6.
_____. 2004a. "*The Bridge*." *The Banksoniain: An Iain M. Banks' Fanzine*, vol. 3, 3–5.
Hastings, Selina. 1984. "Recent Fiction." *The Daily Telegraph*, 17 February, 17.
Lord, Graham. 1984. "Books." *Sunday Express*, 19 February, 6.
Marr, Andrew. 1984. "Mad, bad and dangerous to know." *The Weekend Scotsman*, 25 February, 5.
Murphy, Marese. 1984. "When History Became Fiction." *The Irish Times*, 10 March, 12.
Reynolds, Stanley. 1984. "A Stinging Tale." *Punch*, 29 February, 42.
Walther, Natasha. 1992. "Growing up in the Glens." *The Times Literary Supplement*, 17 April, 21.

Selected Magazine and Newspaper Articles

Hughes, Colin. 1999. "Doing the Business. Profile: Iain Banks." *The Guardian*, 7 August, 6.
Morton, Oliver. 1996. "A Cultured Man." *Wired*, 46–48.
Mullan, John. 2008. "Behind It All." *The Guardian*, 28 June, 6.
_____. 2008a. "Born Free." *The Guardian*, 5 July, 6.
_____. 2008b. "Out of This World." *The Guardian*, 12 July, 6.
_____. 2008c. "Shock Tactics." *The Guardian*, 19 July, 6.
"The Player of Games." 2005. *Banksoniain* 7 (August), 4–5. http://www.banksoniain.net firms.com/banksoniain_07.pdf. Accessed 17 August 2007.
Sutherland, J. 1993. "Binarisms." *London Review of Books*, 18 November, 24–25.

Doctoral Dissertations

Armstrong, David. 1999. *Gestures Towards a Better Place: Approaches to Contemporary British Fiction*. De Montforte University.
Colebrook, M. 2012. *Bridging Fantasies: A Critical Study of the Novels of Iain Banks*. University of Hull.
Ebdon, Melanie. 2004. *Remembering Identity After Postmodernity*. University of Wales, Bangor.
Macdonald, Kirsty A. 2005. *Spectral Ambiguities: The Tradition of Psychosomatic Supernaturalism in Scottish Fiction*. University of Glasgow.
Martingale, Moira. J. 2007. *Iain Banks: The Renovation of the Gothic*. University of Bristol.

About the Contributors

Martyn **Colebrook**, in 2012, completed his dissertation on the novels of Iain Banks and earned his Ph.D. from the University of Hull. He has published extensively on contemporary literature, including the work of J.G. Ballard, Paul Auster, Don DeLillo, H. P. Lovecraft and China Mieville. His research interests include contemporary American literature, transgression and contemporary culture and apocalypse fictions.

Katharine **Cox** is the head of the Department of Humanities at Cardiff Metropolitan University and a principal lecturer in English. Her research interests are primarily in contemporary literature and include a particular focus on mazes and labyrinths. She is also interested in literary tourism in Cardiff.

Sarah **Falcus** is a senior lecturer in English literature at the University of Huddersfield. Her research interests are in the field of contemporary writing and the study of aging and contemporary fiction, considering in particular the representation of Alzheimer's disease in both literary and nonliterary narratives.

Emily **Garside** is a Ph.D. student at Cardiff Metropolitan University researching representations of HIV and AIDS in theatre. She investigates identity in the contrasting theatrical landscapes of New York and London.

David **Haddock** is interested in Iain Banks' pre-publication works. He edits the Iain Banks fanzine *The Banksoniain*, available at http://efanzines.com/Banksoniain/index.htm, and also writes about Douglas Adams.

Bethan **Jones** is a lecturer at the University of Hull, specializing in modernism, contemporary literature and creative writing. She is the author of *The Last Poems of D.H. Lawrence* (Ashgate, 2010). She conducts researches and writes on a number of contemporary authors.

James **Kneale**'s research concerns the literary geographies of fantastic fiction. He edited with Rob Kitchin *Lost in Space* (Continuum, 2002), has written about William Gibson, H. P. Lovecraft, Kim Stanley Robinson and others, and helps run a website supporting collaboration in literary/geographical studies (http://literarygeographies.word press.com/). He is studying the historical geographies of alcohol.

Kirsty A. **Macdonald** is a lecturer in cultural studies with the University of the Highlands and Islands, based in Oban on the west coast of Scotland. Her research focuses on contemporary Scottish literature and film, the Gothic, and representations of the Highlands and Islands in literature and popular culture.

Tim **Middleton** is a professor and Vice Provost for Research and Postgraduate Affairs at Bath Spa University. His research explores the function of the literary in contemporary culture via studies of real and imagined locations in cultural heritage tourism.

Joseph **Norman** teaches literature and creative writing at Brunel University, London, where he is a postgraduate researcher examining the intersections of utopia and empire in Iain M. Banks' "Culture" series. He has published on H. P. Lovecraft and his other research interests include the relationships between music and literature, and science, slipstream, speculative and transgressive fiction.

David **Pattie** is a professor of drama at the University of Chester. He has published extensively in a wide number of areas: Scottish literature and drama, Samuel Beckett, contemporary theatre, theatre history, popular music, and popular culture.

Independent scholar Will **Slocombe** specializes in experimental literature and metafiction, with a particular interest on the impact of new media and technology upon literary studies. He has published on a variety of topics, including nihilism, deconstruction, postmodernism, and pedagogy, as well as poetry.

William **Stephenson** is a senior lecturer in English at the University of Chester. His latest book is *Gonzo Republic: Hunter S. Thompson's America* (Continuum, 2011). He has published articles on a number of contemporary novelists including J. G. Ballard, Bret Easton Ellis, Alex Garland and Irvine Welsh. His poetry collection *Rain Dancers in the Data Cloud* was published by Templar in 2012.

Index

Numbers in ***bold italics*** indicate pages with photographs.

Adams, Douglas 98*n*10
Against a Dark Background 3, 55, 61, 97*n*3, 164
Aldiss, Brian 28, 58, 61
The Algebraist 6, 16, 46–47, 51–52, 54, 58, 61, 98*n*10
American Psycho 120
Angenot, Marc 50, 61
Argyllshire 63, 65–66, 73–74, 111*n*7
Armitt, Lucie 66, 75, 102, 108–109, 110*n*2, 111; *see also* fantastic; fantasy; Jackson, Rosemary
Atlantic 67
Austen, Jane 112

Baldick, Chris 102, 111
barbarian 29, 33–34, 57, 78, 124, 133, 141–142, 176
Barrie, J.M.: *Farewell Miss Julie Logan* 111*n*3
Bataille, Georges 87–88, 99; *see also* Foucault, Michel; Jenks, Chris; "A Preface to Transgression"; transgression; Wolfreys, Julian
Baudrillard, Jean 167, 170, 172, 175, 177
Berlin Wall 63
The Big Man 13; *see also* MacIlvanney, William
bildungsroman 64, 89, 115
Blake, William 35
body politic 40
The Book of One Thousand and One Nights 136
borders 1, 15, 93, 106, 158–159
Bould, Mark 61*n*5, 62, 91
The Bridge 3, 6, 12, 16, 22, 26, 28–43, 43*n*1, 48, 61, 63–65, 76–86, 86*n*1, 89, 92–93, 98*n*12, 101, 137, 140–142, 147, 148*n*2, 149, 179; *see also* Forth Rail Bridge
bridges 16, 35, 48, 76, 79–80, 83, 140; *see also The Bridge*; Forth Rail/Road Bridge
Bridie, James 10
Brigadoon 111*n*3
Britain 9–10, 14, 78, 90, 111*n*3, 135
Brontë, Charlotte 112–113; *Jane Eyre* 113
Brontë, Emily 112
brother 13, 74, 82, 93, 95, 97*n*3, 104, 105, 107, 110, 117–118, 120, 133; *see also* family
Brown, Carolyn 141

Brown, George Douglas: *The House with the Green Shutters* 13
Brydon, Bill 10
Bukatman, Scott 59, 61, 152
Burgess, Anthony 25*n*3, 28, 43
The Business 2, 7, 8, 16, 22, 26, 65, 97*n*1, 101, 123, 125–132, 134*n*6; *see also* gender
Butcher's Broom 13
Butler, Andrew 62, 150, 164
Butler, Judith 119, 122, 134*n*3; *see also* gender

Caillois, Roger 137; *see also* games
Calvin, John 18
Canal Dreams 16, 93–94, 179
Capitalism 16, 20, 24, 36, 40–42, 50, 55, 62, 65, 125–127, 129, 132, 134*n*6, 150, 167, 171, 175, 177
Carswell, Catherine 10
Carter, Angela: *The Passion of New Eve* 113, 115
Cartesian dualism 152–153, 163*n*8
cartography 26, 46–47, 51, 54–55, 60, 62, 65–66, 75, 175
Cassini-Huygens spacecraft 58
castle 48, 66–73, 145–146, 174
Catch-22 5
Catholicism 52, 158, 160
Cauldhame, Frank/Frances 3, 14–15, 19, 89, 92–93, 97*n*1, 105–107, 111*n*6, 115–121, 121*n*3, 124–128, 131, 133–134; *see also* gender; identity; masculinities; *The Wasp Factory*
Celtic 73–73
Chanady, Amaryll Beatrice 110*n*1, 111
chess 145, 173–174, 177*n*1
chronotope 35, 41, 43, 61; *see also* Bakhtin, Mikhail Mikhailovich
civilization 4, 22, 53, 57, 139, 158, 171–173, 177*n*1
Cixous, Hélène 134
Clément, Catherine 134
cognitive estrangement 48, 92, 165; *see also* estrangement; Suvin, Darko
Cold War 166–167, 171, 177
Colebrook, Martyn 8*n*2, 111*n*6
coma 29, 35–36, 40–41, 76–77, 79–80, 83–85, 140–141, 147

complicity 16–18, 24–25, 142; *see also* Complicity
Complicity 7, 23–24, 26, 42, 43, 55, 61, 63–65, 93–94, 100, 111, 137, 138–140, 142, 148n3, 149; *see also* complicity
computer gaming 137, 140, 152, 177n1
Conservative party 11, 25n7, 150; *see also* Reganism; Thatcher, Margaret; Thatcherism
Consider Phlebas 3, 7, 48, 52, 56–57, 61n3, 90, 138, 140–142, 149n4, 165, 167–172, 176, 177
Cornwell, Neil 102, 110n2, 111
cousin 48, 95–96, 97n3, 103, 110, 117; *see also* family
Craig, Cairns 5, 8, 10–12, 16–17, 19–20, 22–24, 25n1, 25n9, 26, 29–31, 34, 42, 43, 64, 75n1, 101, 106, 111, 121n1, 124, 132–133, 134; heterocentricity 101
The Crow Road 6, 7, 12, 19, 26, 49, 61, 63–75, 100, 107–110, 180
Csicsery-Ronay, Istvan 50, 62
cultural geography 63–65, 75n1
The Culture 1–4, 7, 16–17, 20, 23, 26, 32, 43, 46–47, 52–54, 56–57, 61n3, 62, 90, 92, 94–97, 98n11, 98–99, 140–144, 149n5, 150–164, 165–177
Cyber Hell 151
Cyberpunk 4, 150–152, 158–159, 161, 163
Cyberspace 51, 53, 163, 163n9

Daiches, David 65–66, 74, 75
Dante, Alighieri 35, 94, 162
Dark Ages 66, 70–74
daughter 103, 109, 127–128; *see also* family
Dead Air 12
death 9, 20–24, 45n10, 29, 50, 53, 57, 81, 88, 95–96, 98n9, 98, 103, 107–109, 117–120, 124, 148, 149n4, 151–154, 156, 158–159, 162, 163n7, 166, 172, 174, 177; *see also* murder; suicide
de Coning, Alexis 117
Delaney, Samuel R. 91, 176
Deleuze, Gilles 7, 166–167, 169–170, 173–174, 177; *see also* war machine
Derrida, Jacques 167, 177
Descartes, René 152, 164
devolution 11, 24–25
A Disaffection 13; *see also How Late It Was, How Late*; Kelman, James
Docherty 13; *see also* MacIlvanney, William
doubleness 2, 6, 23, 59, 76–77, 79–85, 86n2, 94, 109, 140; author 2, 3–4, 6, 87–90, 97, 113, 140; *see also* games; identity
dream 78, 80–81, 83–86, 86n2, 92–94, 99, 101, 103, 131, 141, 143, 147, 155, 158
Dunadd 66, 70–71, 73–74
dystopia 29, 38, 93, 101, 151

Earth 4, 22, 55–56, 58–59, 145–146, 148n3, 167, 169
Edinburgh 14, 29, 31, 48, 76–77, 82, 103; *see also* Leith
education 6, 7, 10, 16, 112, 116; higher education 6, 112

Eliot, T.S.: *The Wasteland* 90, 141, 149n4
Ellis, Brett Easton 120
Elphinstone, Margaret 109, 111
Elsley, Brian 109
Empire 21, 52, 56–57, 138, 141, 144, 173–174, 177n1, 178
England 15, 74
Englishness 64
Espedair Street 65, 97n1
estrangement 39, 48, 59, 91–92, 165; *see also* cognitive estrangement
Europe 33, 62, 63, 73, 168
Excession 16, 52, 56–57, 61, 97n1, 99, 137, 143–144, 149n5, 151, 154–155, 160–161, 164, 167, 177

Falklands War 82, 121n1
The Fall of Kelvin Walker 16
family 14, 19, 45, 49, 52, 63–65, 73–74, 78, 92, 95–96, 97n3, 105–110, 111n5, 128, 141; *see also* brother; cousin; daughter; father; granddaughter; grandfather; grandmother; mother; sister; step-sister; uncle
fantastic 6, 29–40, 45, 48, 54–56, 58, 60, 61n5, 82, 89–92, 94, 97, 100–104, 108, 110, 110n1, 110n2, 111, 113–114, 119; *see also* fantasy; SF; Todorov, Tzvetan
fantasy 6, 15, 28, 30–31, 34, 40, 43, 55, 62, 81, 91–94, 99, 100–102, 110n2, 111, 113, 147; *see also* fantastic; SF
father 13, 19, 64, 73, 79–80, 92, 103, 107, 116–119, 124–128; *see also* family; mother
Fear and Loathing in Las Vegas 5
Feersum Endjinn 16, 48, 50, 53, 61, 142
femininities 7, 124, 126–130, 132–134; *see also* gender; masculinities
Forth Rail/Road Bridge 6, 48, 76, 79–80, 140, 141
Foucault, Michel 6, 87–88, 97n2, 98, 99; "Of Other Spaces" 97n2; "A Preface to Transgression" 6, 87–88, 98
Frankenstein: Or, The Modern Prometheus 6, 112–113, 115–121, 122; *see also* Shelley, Mary
free market 20, 24, 25n9; *see also* capitalism; Reganism; Thatcherism
Friel, George 10

Gaelic 32, 69, 74
Gallanach 49–50, 63, 66–**67**, 68–**71**, 73, 107, 111n7
Galloway, Janice 8, 10, 19, 43; *The Trick Is to Keep Breathing* 24
games 1, 3, 4, 7, 16–17, 19, 26, 52, 55–57, 61, 82, 86n2, 88, 90, 93, 95–97, 99, 101, 124, 132–134, 136–148, 148n1, 148n3, 149n4, 149n5, 149n6, 160, 165, 167–168, 172–177, 177n1; *see also* computer gaming; Go; *The Player of Games*
gender 1, 7, 16, 97n1, 106, 112, 115–119, 123–134, 134n3, 165; *see also* Butler, Judith; Schoene-Harwood, Berthold
genre 1–2, 6–8, 12, 28, 30–31, 33–35, 39, 53,

Index 195

60, 62, 64, 88–97, 98*n*7, 98*n*9, 99, 101–104, 111, 147, 150, 153, 163, 163*n*6; *see also* science fiction
geography 1, 5–6, 46–48, 50, 52, 54, 58–60, 61*n*6, 62, 63–65, 67, 75*n*2, 89, 106, 112, 126; *see also* geology; landscape
geology 37, 43*n*1, 77, 97*n*5, 141; *see also* geography
Ghost in the Shell 151, 163*n*2
Gibbon, Lewis Grassic: *Sunset Song* 13
Gibson, William 51, 55, 62, 112, 151, 161, 163, 163*n*1, 163*n*6, 163*n*9; *Neuromancer* 62, 151, 163, 161*n*1; *Sprawl* 151
Glasgow 5, 10, 14, 29, 31–32, 34, 40–42, 43*n*3, 44, 76–77, 103, 107, 127–128; *see also* Gray, Alasdair
globalization 51, 175
Go 145, 173–174
God 18, 36, 57, 88, 131, 148, 158, 169, 172; god-like 92
Gothic 27, 40, 43, 44, 52–54, 62, 106, 109, 110*n*2, 111, 113, 115, 127–128, 135
grand-daughter 103; *see also* family
grandfather 49, 104, 126; *see also* family
grandmother 19, 64, 107; *see also* family
Gray, Alasdair 1, 5, 9–23, 25, 25*n*3, 25*n*5, 26, 28–43, 75, 113; *The Fall of Kelvin Walker* 16; *Lanark: A Life in Four Books* 5, 9–19, 24, 26, 18–35, 37–39, 41–43, 75; *McGrotty and Ludmilla* 16; *1982 Janine* 12–14, 17–18, 24, 26; *Old Men in Love* 16, 22; *Poor Things* 12, 16–19, 22, 26; *Ten Tales Tall and True* 21, 26; *Unlikely Stories, Mostly* 16, 26
Guattari, Félix 7, 166–167, 169–170, 173–174, 177; *see also* war machine
Guerrier, Simon 32–33, 43, 150, 164
Gunn, Neil: *Butcher's Broom* 13; *Sun Circle* 13

handkerchief 78, 82–83, 141
Hardy, Thomas: Wessex 46–47, 61
Hari, Johann 155, 160–161, 165
Harrison, M. John 56, 62
Harvey, David 47, 55, 62; *see also* geography; Hones, Shelia; Kneale, James; Massey, Doreen; spatiality
heaven 22, 50, 94, 110, 158 161, 163–164
hell 29, 35, 40, 42, 43, 94, 158–163; *see also* Cyber Hell
heterogeneity 49–50; *see also* hybridity
hierarchy 19, 22, 29, 50, 52, 65, 74, 93, 130, 138, 165–166, 169, 173
Hogg, James: *The Private Memoirs and Confessions of a Justified Sinner* 25*n*8
Hones, Sheila 46–47, 62; *see also* geography; Harvey, David; Kneale, James; Massey, Doreen; spatiality
Hornby, Nick 112
The House with the Green Shutters 13
How Late It Was, How Late 31, 43; *see also A Disaffection*; Kelman, James
Hume, Kathryn 102, 110*n*2, 111

The Hungarian Lift-Jet 3–4
Hutchinson, Peter 137–139; *see also* games
hybridity 6, 49, 77, 103, 152, 163; *see also* heterogeneity

identity 14–16, 61, 64–65, 84, 87, 95, 99, 106, 117, 119, 124, 129, 131–134, 140–141, 148*n*2, 151; of author 90; *see also* doubleness; gender
ideology 20, 24–25, 29–30, 53, 62, 109, 130, 147, 168–169, 171–172
industrial Scotland 15, 29, 32, 39–40, 64; novel 34
Inversions 53, 61
Iraq War 20, 179
Irigaray, Luce 127, 134; *see also* gender
Ishiguro, Kazuo 91

Jackson, Peter 56, 64, 75*n*2
Jackson, Rosemary 62, 99, 102–103, 110*n*2, 111; *see also* Armitt, Lucie; fantastic; fantasy
Jameson, Fredric 51, 53, 59–60, 62, 175, 177
Jenkins, Robin 10
Jenks, Chris 88, 99
jihad 166, 170
Joyce, James: Dublin 46; *Ulysses* 10
Jupiter 48, 58
Jura 67

Kakfa, Franz 5
Kelman, James 13, 31, 43, 75, 113; *A Disaffection* 13; *How Late It Was, How Late* 31, 43
Kennedy, A.L. 8, 19
Kincaid, Paul 90
Kirk, Robert 108
Kneale, James 56, 61*n*2, 62; *see also* geography; Harvey, David; Hones, Shelia; Massey, Doreen; spatiality
Knight, Damon 91
Knights, Ben 112
Knox, John 18; *see also* education; Scotland
Korean War 166

Labour party 11
Lanark: A Life in Four Books 5, 9–19, 24, 26, 18–35, 37–39, 41–43, 75; *see also The Fall of Kelvin Walker*; Gray, Alasdair; *McGrotty and Ludmilla*; *1982 Janine*; *Old Men in Love*; *Poor Things*; *Ten Tales Tall and True*; *Unlikely Stories, Mostly*
landscape 6–7, 29, 35, 38, 45–46, 49, 60, 63–66, 73, 75, 93, 141, 161, 168; *see also* geography
language 5, 12, 17–19, 31, 36–37, 51, 84–86, 88, 119, 126, 141–143, 145–146, 177; English 5; incomprehensible 84–86, 142, 143; Scots 31, 36, 141
Lawrence, D.H.: *Sons and Lovers* 118
Leith 77, 82
Lem, Stanislaw 55–56, 58, 62; *Solaris* 55, 62
Levy, Andrea 112
Levy, Michael 89

Little Britain 111n3
Little, Brown Book Group 89, 114
Livingstone, Ken 90
loch 66–68, 71, 111n7
Lochhead, Liz 10
London 26, 30, 46, 48, 103, 125
Look to Windward 2, 16, 23, 26, 50, 56–57, 61, 90, 149, 151, 154–158, 163, 164, 167–168, 177; see also Quilan
Luckhurst, Roger 50–51, 62, 98n9

MacCaig, Norman 10
MacIlvanney, William 10, 13; *Docherty* 13; *The Big Man* 13
Mackintosh, Rennie 10
MacLean, Alistair 8n5
MacLean, Duncan 8, 75
MacLeod, Ken 5
Macmurray, John 19–23, 25n6, 26; see also utopia
magic 100–102, 108, 110; see also magical realism; supernatural
magical realism 101–102, 108–109, 110n1; see also magic; supernatural
mainstream 1–3, 5–7, 8n7, 30, 34, 46, 60n1, 87, 89–92, 94; 97n3, 100, 113, 123
Malmgren, Carl 54–56, 62
Manlove, Colin 107, 111
March, Christie 2, 5, 7n1, 8, 10, 12, 12n1, 129, 132, 134n1
masculinities 14, 99, 116, 119, 123–125, 128, 130, 132–133; see also femininities; gender
Massey, Doreen 49–50, 62; see also geography; Harvey, David; Hones, Shelia; Kneale, James; spatiality
The Matrix 151, 163n3
Matter 16, 22, 26, 56, 144, 147, 149
McGrath, Tom 10
McGrotty and Ludmilla 16
McGuffin 145, 149n6; see also games
McLuhan, Marshall 152
Mendlesohn, Farah 92, 150–151, 164
Menzies 90
"The Merry Men" 111n3; see also Stevenson, Robert Louis
Middleton, Tim 176
Miller, Gavin 114
Mills, Charles Wright 45, 62
Milton, John 162
Minds 16, 23, 57, 140, 142, 144, 152–154, 156 158–159, 165, 168–169, 172
Mitchell, David 91
Modernism 113
Morgan, Edwin 10, 75; "Sonnets from Scotland" 75
Morton, Oliver 58, 62
mother 19, 125–126, 128–133; absence of 126, 128–133; terrible 118; see also family; father
murder 23–24, 64, 92, 94, 96, 100, 105, 108, 117–120, 124, 139–142, 147, 153, 155, 157, 168; see also

myth 92, 106, 119, 126, 128, 131, 133, 141, 171–172

Nairn, Tom 2, 10, 14, 16, 43
Nasqueron 45–48, 51–52, 58–60; see also *The Algebraist*
neural lace 7, 152–154, 158
Neuromancer 62, 151, 163, 161n1; see also Gibson, William
9/11 7, 166–167, 170, 174–176
1982 Janine 12–14, 17–18, 24, 26; see also *The Fall of Kelvin Walker*; Gray, Alasdair; *Lanark: A Life in Four Books*; *McGrotty and Ludmilla*; *Old Men in Love*; *Poor Things*; *Ten Tales Tall and True*; *Unlikely Stories, Mostly*

O 3, 36
Oban 67–69, 111n7
Oedipal 127
"Of Other Spaces" 97n2; see also Foucault, Michel
Old Men in Love 16, 22
Orbitals 23, 54, 56, 61n3, 168–169, 172
Orlando 113
Orwell, George 98n8, 161
Oshii, Mamoro: *Ghost in the Shell* 151, 163n2
Other 19–23, 25n6, 56, 62, 97n2, 99, 110n3, 134, 155, 171–172, 176, 177
Outside Context Problem 143–144

Panama Canal 93–94
The Passion of New Eve 113, 115; see also Carter, Angela
Patterson, Anna 66, 75
Petrie, Duncan 2, 5, 8, 121n2, 133, 135
play 1, 6–7, 10, 13, 16–18, 22–23, 25, 35–36, 41, 48, 52, 56–57, 64, 67, 70, 76–77, 82, 87–88, 90, 92–95, 97, 98n9, 101, 102, 121, 124, 126–128, 131–134, 136–148, 149n5, 149n6, 168, 172–176; see also games; *The Player of Games*
The Player of Games 3, 4, 7, 16–17, 26, 52, 56–57, 61, 90, 134, 136, 138–140, 142, 146, 148n1, 149n5, 165, 167–168, 172, 175–177
politics 1, 4, 5, 7, 9–11, 14–15, 19–20, 24–25, 25n7, 26, 29–30, 32, 37–42, 59, 77, 93, 97n1, 97n2, 101–102, 110, 113, 121n1, 124, 130, 132, 135, 153, 156, 168, 169, 172, 175–177
Poor Things 12, 16–19, 22, 26
post-devolution 24–25; see also politics; Scotland (politics)
post-industrial Scotland 28, 31–32, 34–35, 38, 40, 42; novel 5, 34–35, 40, 42
postmodernism 5, 19–20, 26, 27, 30, 32–35, 39–40, 42, 43n2, 44, 51, 61, 62, 65, 75, 91, 101, 105, 110, 110n2, 111, 113, 136, 158, 175, 177
power 11–17, 19, 21–25, 32, 42, 50–52, 58, 65–68, 73–74, 79–80, 93, 95, 103–106, 108, 117–119, 124, 126–127, 130–132, 138, 143, 150–151, 165–171, 174–175

"A Preface to Transgression" 6, 87–88, 98; *see also* Foucault, Michel
The Prime of Miss Jean Brodie 13; *see also* Spark, Muriel
The Private Memoirs and Confessions of a Justified Sinner 25n8
Protestantism 18, 52
psychosomatic events 100–103, 109; *see also* magic; supernatural
Punter, David 15–17, 24, 27, 111

The Quarry 61, 90, 137, 180
Quilan 16, 23, 155–157; *see also* Look to Windward

Raw Spirit: In Search of the Perfect Dram 2, 67, 75, 179
realism 28, 31–32, 34, 39, 43, 100–103, 108, 110, 111n4; *see also* magical realism
Reganism 100; *see also* Thatcherism
rejection 32, 40–42, 46, 106–107, 116, 124, 130, 147, 161, 173; letter of 4, 8n6; *see also* mother
Reynolds, Alastair 92
Rhys, Jean: *Wide Sargasso Sea* 113
Roberts, Adam 91, 98n7, 178

Sage, Victor 124, 134n2, 135
Samuelson, David 47, 55–56, 62
Schoene-Harwood, Berthold 116, 123, 125–126, 128, 133, 134n3, 135
Scholes, Robert 91
science fantasy 91–92, 94; *see also* fantastic; fantasy
science fiction 1–7, 8n7, 16–17, 22, 29–30, 43n2, 46–48, 51–56, 58–60, 61n2, 61n5, 62, 87, 89–97, 97n3, 98n8, 98n9, 98n11, 99, 100, 102, 113, 122, 136, 150–151, 163, 163n6, 163n8, 164, 165–166, 168–169, 172, 175–176, 177, 178
Scotland 5, 8, 9–12, 15, 24–25, 25n2, 26, 27, 28, 31, 34–35, 41, 43, 63–66, 68, 73–76, 84, 103, 106, 108–111, 134; cities of 5, 10, 14, 29, 31–32, 34, 40–42, 43n3, 44, 48, 76–77, 82, 103, 107, 127–128; education in 7; Highlands of 13, 107, 109; identity of 14–16, 64–65, 84, 90; politics of 1, 5, 7, 9–11, 14–15, 20, 24–25, 25n7, 26, 30, 32, 37–42, 77, 101, 113, 124
Scott, Walter 110n3; *The Bride of Lammermoor*; *Waverley*
Scottish literature 5, 8n8, 9–10, 12–13, 16, 25, 25n8, 26–27, 30, 32, 36, 64, 75, 101, 112–114, 122, 134; *see also* Gray, Alasdair; Kelman, James; Spark, Muriel; Welsh, Irvine
Scottish National Party 25, 25n7
sexuality 97n2, 128–129, 133
SF 8, 47, 51, 54–56, 59–60, 62, 93, 150, 179–180
Shakespeare, William 112
Shelley, Mary 6, 112–113, 115–119, 121; *Frankenstein: Or, The Modern Prometheus* 6, 112–113, 115–121, 122

Shellworlds 17, 22, 144, 151
Shippey, Tom 98n8
sister 95, 120; *see also* family
Sma, Diziet 95–96, 142, 148n3; *see also* The State of the Art; Use of Weapons
Smethurst, Paul 29, 31–32, 34–35, 39–41, 43
socialism 9, 24, 25n5, 150
Solaris 55, 62; *see also* Lem, Stanislaw
A Song of Stone 25, 92, 97n3, 123, 134
"Sonnets from Scotland" 75; *see also* Morgan, Edwin
soul 7, 39, 138, 150–159, 161–164
space opera 4, 51, 53, 89, 91–92, 94, 98, 150, 163; *see also* fantasy; genre; science fiction; SF
Spark, Muriel 13, 19; *The Prime of Miss Jean Brodie* 13
spatiality 35, 40, 43, 45–47, 49–56, 58, 60–62, 64–65, 68, 82, 87, 89, 91–92, 97n2, 98, 99, 100, 144, 148, 150, 152, 158–159, 161, 163, 165, 168–171, 174–175; *see also* Cyberspace; geography; Harvey, David; Hones, Shelia; Kneale, James; landscape; Massey, Doreen
Special Circumstances 53, 56–57, 61, 147, 152, 156, 166–167, 173–174
speculative fiction 2, 29, 31, 33–34, 55–56; *see also* fantasy; genre; science fiction; SF
Spooner, Catherine 40, 43, 44
The State of the Art 3–4, 56–57, 61, 94, 142, 148n3, 149
The Steep Approach to Garbadale 12, 61n4, 65, 137–141, 144, 149, 180
step-sister 25n10, 97n3; *see also* family
Stevenson, Randall 9, 25n1, 27, 30, 43–44
Stevenson, Robert Louis 54, 62; 111n3: "The Merry Men" 111n3; *Treasure Island* 54, 62
Stonemouth 90
suicide 23, 39, 160, 167; *see also* death; murder
Sun Circle 13
supernatural 100–103, 106–110, 110n1, 153
Surface Detail 7, 98n15, 151, 153–154, 158, 161–163, 164
Suvin, Darko 47, 62, 91–92, 99, 165, 168, 176, 178; *see also* cognitive estrangement
Swift, Graham 112

The Tashkent Rambler 3–4
The Telegraph 180
Ten Tales Tall and True 21, 26
terror 26, 80, 118, 134, 165–168, 170, 174–177; *see also* War on Terror
Thatcher, Margaret 11; *see also* Reganism; Thatcherism
Thatcherism 24, 29, 78, 100, 121n1; *see also* Reganism; Thatcher, Margaret
The Tin Drum 5
Todorov, Tzvetan 91, 102–103, 111; *see also* fantastic
The Top of Poseidon 3
Torrington, Jeff 31, 44
trains 21, 78, 80, 83, 86

transgression 1, 6–7, 30, 34, 39, 87–89, 91, 93–97, 97*n*3, 97*n*4, 97*n*5, 98*n*9, 98*n*15, 101, 114
transition 39, 76
Transition 90, 92–93, 101, 121*n*4, 122, 180
Treasure Island 54, 62; *see also* Stevenson, Robert Louis
The Trick Is to Keep Breathing 24; *see also* Galloway, Janice
TRON 151, 161, 163

Ulysses 10; *see also* Joyce, James
uncanny 3, 52, 91, 97*n*2
uncle 49, 63–64, 70, 79, 107–108, 129; *see also* family
United Kingdom 89–91, 97*n*6, 179
United States 20, 29–30, 90, 97*n*6, 98*n*11, 121*n*6, 168, 171
Unlikely Stories, Mostly 16, 26
unreliable narrator 93, 106, 111*n*6, 113, 119–121, 121*n*3, 121*n*4
Use of Weapons 3, 5, 48, 61, 87, 94–95, 97*n*3, 139–143, 148*n*3, 149, 179, 180
utopia 2, 4–5, 20, 28–33, 38–39, 41–42, 50, 53, 57, 61, 62, 94, 101, 122, 141, 149, 150–151, 155, 160, 162, 164, 165–166, 175–176; *see also* Macmurray, John

Van Gogh, Vincent 96
Veidemanis, Gladys 121
Verne, Jules 50, 61
Vietnam War 166
violence 3, 8*n*3, 13, 23, 92, 105, 114, 116–118, 120, 123, 127, 133, 138, 153–154, 166–168, 170–172, 174, 176
virtual reality 151, 158, 170, 172

Walking on Glass 3, 6, 37, 43, 89, 92, 101, 136, 141, 145–147, 149
war machine 7, 165–167, 169–170, 172–177; *see also* Deleuze, Gilles; Guattari, Félix
War on Terror 166–167, 176–177; *see also* terror
Warner, Alan 10, 16, 68; *Morvern Callar* 68; *The Sopranos* 16
The Wasp Factory 3–4, 6–7, 8, 12–13, 15, 26, 61, 65, 89–90, 92, 97*n*1, 100–101, 105–107, 111*n*6, 112–123, 125–126, 128–131, 133–134, 135, 179, 180
The Wasteland 90, 141, 149*n*4
Welfare State 11, 20
Welsh, Irvine 10, 75, 113
Whit 6, 7, 16, 22, 26, 63, 65, 92, 97*n*3, 99, 100, 101, 103, 106–107, 123–125, 127–129, 131, 134*n*6, 180
Wilde, Oscar 112
Wilson, Andrew 2, 8*n*3, 8*n*5, 12, 93, 99
Wolfe, Gary 91
Wolfreys, Julian 88–89, 99; *see also* Bataille, Georges Foucault, Michel; Jenks, Chris; "A Preface to Transgression"; transgression
Woolf, Virginia 46, 113; *Orlando* 113

Zakalwe, Elethiomel/Cheradenine 95–96, 98*n*15, 140–141, 148–149*n*3; see also *Use of Weapons*, *Surface Detail*
Žižek, Slavoj 167–168, 171, 174–175, 178